FROM BRADSHAW TO WANDJINA

ABORIGINAL PAINTINGS OF THE KIMBERLEY REGION, WESTERN AUSTRALIA

David M. Welch

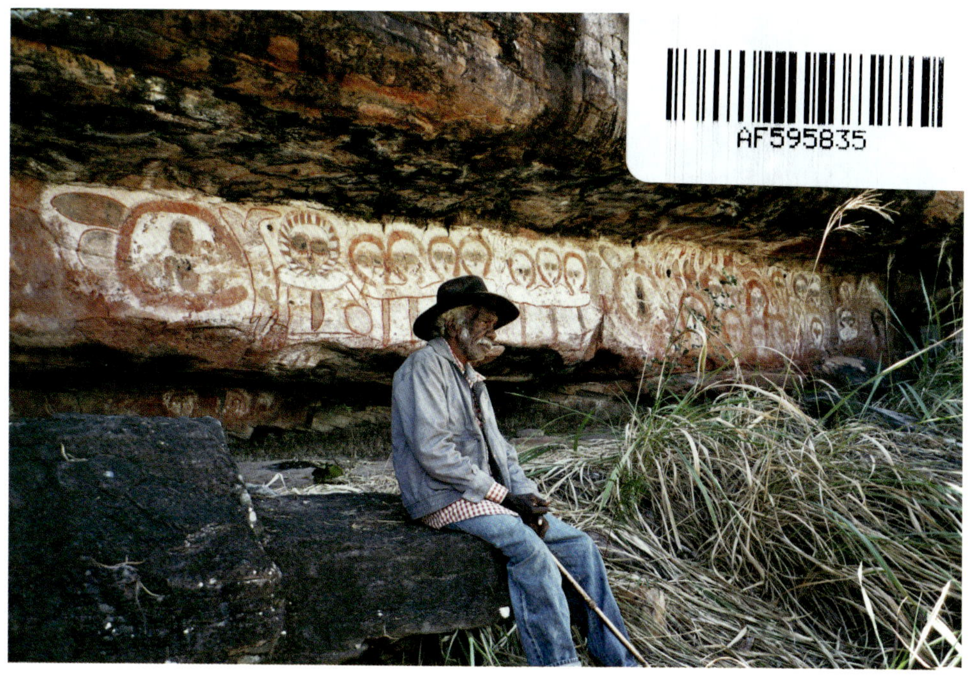

Published by David M. Welch

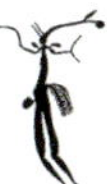

AUSTRALIAN ABORIGINAL CULTURE SERIES NO. 12

From Bradshaw to Wandjina: Aboriginal Paintings of the Kimberley Region, Western Australia

Australian Aboriginal Culture Series No. 12

Published by David M. Welch
P. O. Box 503, Coolalinga, Northern Territory 0839, Australia.
Fax. (61) (8) 8983 1145
www.aboriginalculture.com.au

National Library of Australia Cataloguing-in-Publication entry:
Creator: Welch, David M. (Maxwell), 1955- author

Title: From Bradshaw to Wandjina: Aboriginal Paintings of the Kimberley Region, Western Australia

ISBN: 978-0-9871389-9-6

Series: Australian Aboriginal Culture Series; No. 12
Subjects: Rock paintings – Western Australia – Kimberley Region – History.
Painting, Aboriginal Australian – Western Australia – Kimberley Region – History.
Artists, Aboriginal Australian – Western Australia – Kimberley Region.
Rock paintings in art.
Kimberley Region (W.A.)

Dewey Number: 709.0113

Designed and typeset by Bruce Welch in 12pt Adobe Garamond Pro.

Printed on 105 gsm Sun matt artpaper, section sewn.

Printed by Everbest Printing, China.

Photographs, maps and drawings by David M. Welch unless indicated otherwise.

Cover photograph: Bent Knee Figures wearing long headdresses, strings and feather bunches, carrying boomerangs and feather bunches, Roe River Valley. Wandjina paintings from Kandalngari, central Kimberley.

Title page photograph: Aboriginal custodian Reggie Tataya at Pandagurnya, central Kimberley. (Photograph by Michael Rainsbury.)

Back cover photograph: A Wandjina face painted with white clay, yellow ochre and black charcoal pigments.

CONTENTS

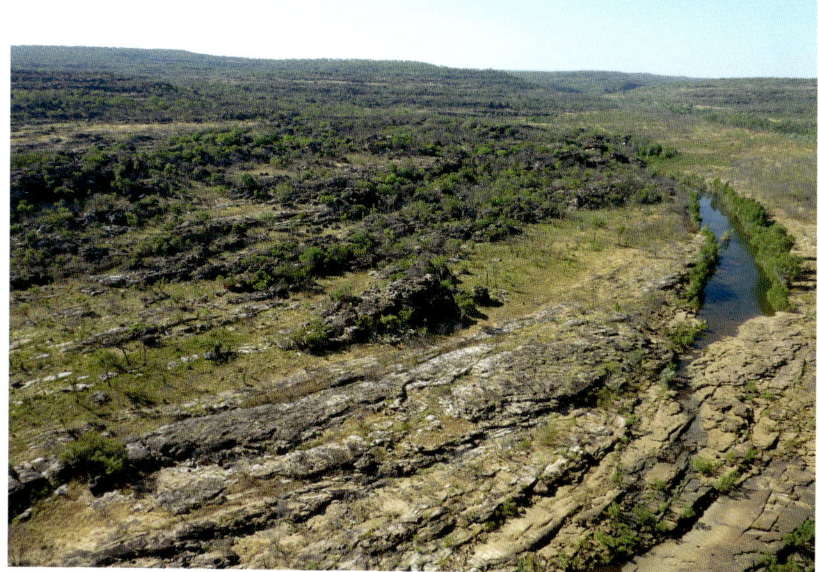

Low rocks containing shelters with paintings, beside the lower Mitchell River, northern Kimberley.

FOREWORD

The study of Australia's rock shelter paintings reveals that many changes have taken place throughout the 50,000-year history of Aboriginal occupation. The Kimberley region of north Western Australia, in particular, holds a significant record of how early Australians lived, thought and celebrated their beliefs.

Ancient paintings surviving in rock shelters reveal a progression of ceremonial costumes and customs from former times to the present. Religious beliefs evolve when images of *Rainbow Serpents, Yam Men* and *Plant People* flourish mid-way through the rock art sequence, later dominated by the enigmatic *Wandjina* beings (pronounced *won-jean-a*) with their bright white faces peering out from rock shelters across the region

Bradshaw Figures – early Kimberley human figures – have been described as being too refined and too ornate to have been painted by Aboriginal people. Such views reflect a lack of knowledge of traditional Aboriginal ceremonies and capabilities, a consequence of much of the ceremonial regalia and paraphernalia being secret-sacred within Aboriginal culture, and hidden from the outside world.

As a medical practitioner in Darwin in the Northern Territory since 1979, I have had opportunities to work with Aboriginal people and learn about their culture. Separate from my medical work, I have regularly explored remote areas and visited Aboriginal communities across Australia, discovering new rock art sites and seeking a deeper understanding of Aboriginal culture.

Following extensive field work in the Kimberley, exploring bushland and examining 700 rock art sites, I formulated a chronological sequence for the rock paintings of that region in 1992. By consulting with Aboriginal people, researching archival photographs and movies housed in our museums and state libraries, and attending Aboriginal ceremonies, I was able to match the ceremonial dress and body positions of the Bradshaw Figures with the regalia and postures used in traditional Aboriginal dance. The academic papers I produced aimed to illustrate these correlations and provide an understanding of the Bradshaw paintings.

We are fortunate that great masterpieces from early Australian artists have survived the elements and the ravages of time. *From Bradshaw to Wandjina: Aboriginal Paintings of the Kimberley Region, Western Australia* illustrates the art and demonstrates its significance as part of Australia's rich cultural heritage.

Dr. David M. Welch
Darwin, Northern Territory of Australia, 2016

THE CHRONOLOGICAL SEQUENCE OF KIMBERLEY ROCK ART

(Based on the 1992 chronology proposed by Dr David M. Welch)

1. ARCHAIC PERIOD

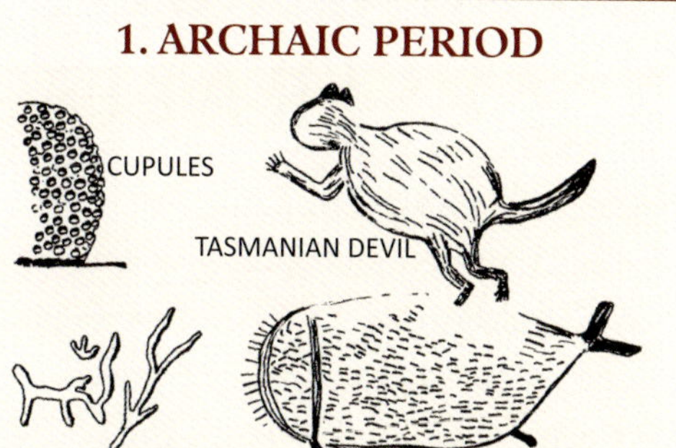

2. TASSELLED FIGURE PERIOD

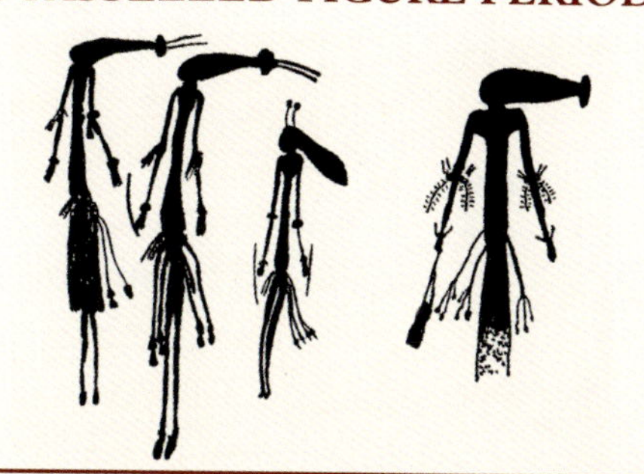

3. BENT KNEE FIGURE PERIOD

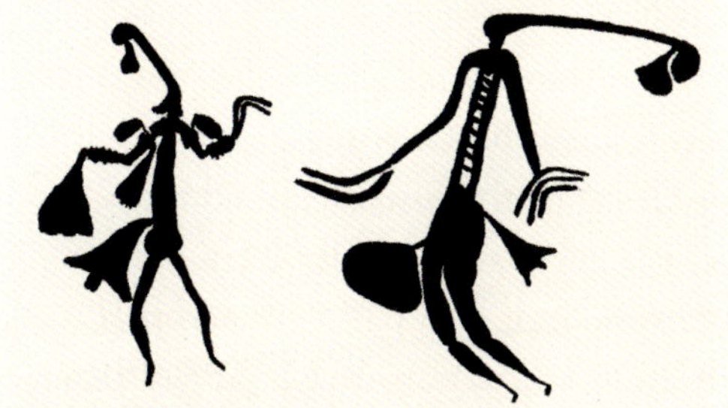

4. KIMBERLEY DYNAMIC FIGURE PERIOD

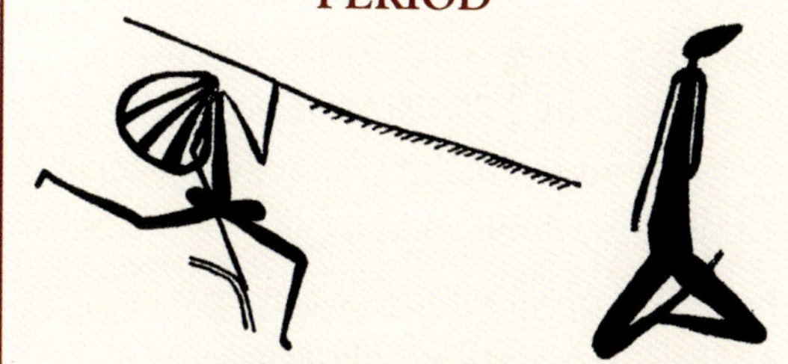

5. STRAIGHT PART FIGURE PERIOD

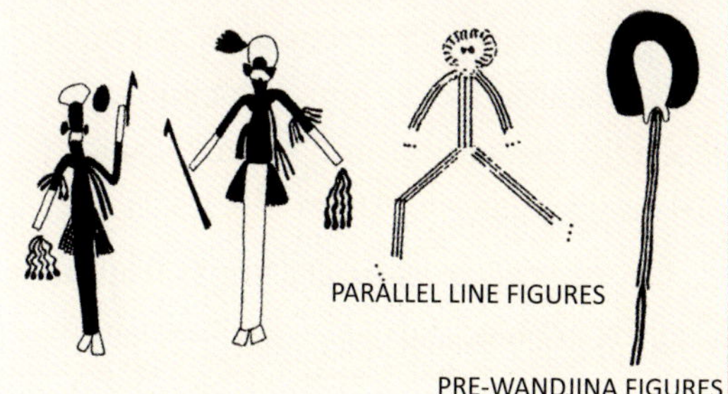

6. PAINTED HAND PERIOD

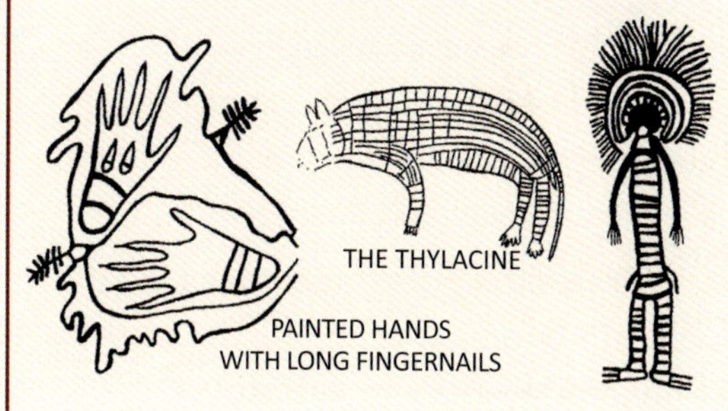

7. WANDJINA PERIOD

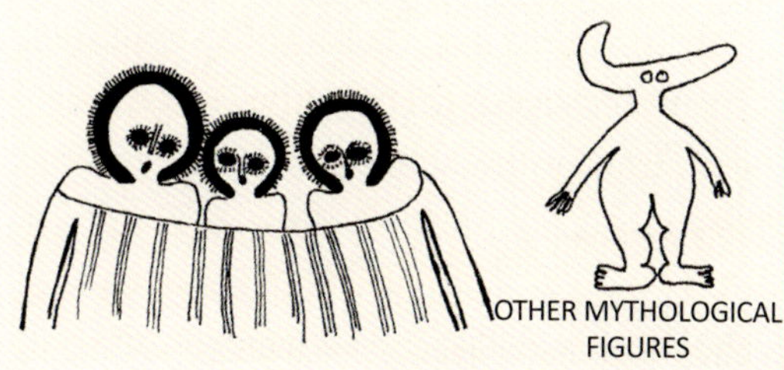

8. CONTACT PERIOD

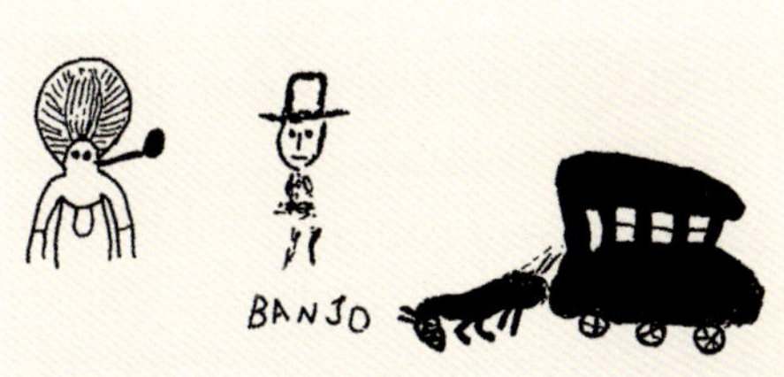

BRADSHAW PAINTINGS OF NORTH WESTERN AUSTRALIA

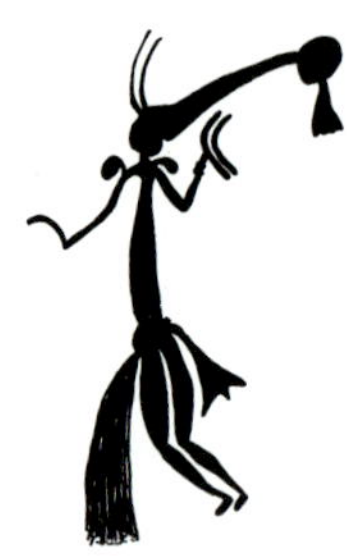

Kimberley rock paintings are dominated by two broad types: The more recent *Wandjina paintings*, characterised by large human-like figures, colourfully painted with bold reds, whites and yellows, and the early *Bradshaw paintings*, characterised by a range of smaller human figures surviving in reddish, brownish and purplish pigments.

Wandjina paintings are regarded by local Aboriginal people as self-images, originally painted by the legendary Wandjina when they arrived at their rock shelters. Wandjina are revered as *rain gods* or *rain spirits* who are responsible for producing each wet season's rains. Without Wandjina there would be no rain.

Bradshaw paintings are regarded by local Aboriginal people as the works of mythical spirits and ancestors. Folklore varies across the region. In the north, one version of events is that the small red figures are the works of *djimi*, bush spirits who painted images of themselves. Another northern legend is that the old red paintings are self-portraits of *giro giro*, tiny people who lived in the area in the past. When the author made inquiries in the 1980s and early 1990s, northern paintings were described as being created by *Kiera kiro*, a mythical bird that rubbed its wing or elbow on the rocks to make it bleed, and then used the blood to paint the pictures. (The term *kiera kiro* is a variant of *giro giro*. This is also spoken as *girri girri* with a trill on the *rr*.)

In the central Kimberley, the author was told by Ngarinyin elders that a mythical bird, *Guyon*, rubbed its beak on the rocks to make it bleed, and then used the blood to paint the red pictures. In 2000 a new narrative emerged from a group of Ngarinyin men living to the west, describing the early paintings as *gwion gwion* (a variation of *guyon*, also recorded as *kuyon*), the children of Djilinya (a mythical female), who painted images of themselves.

Bradshaw Paintings, the European term for these early figures, has arisen in memory of Joseph Bradshaw, who was the first white man to bring their existence to the attention of the outside world. Bradshaw, a pastoralist-explorer, stumbled upon them while travelling overland on horseback in 1891, and described his findings thus:

> Some of the human figures were life-size, the bodies and limbs very attenuated, and represented as having numerous tassel-shaped

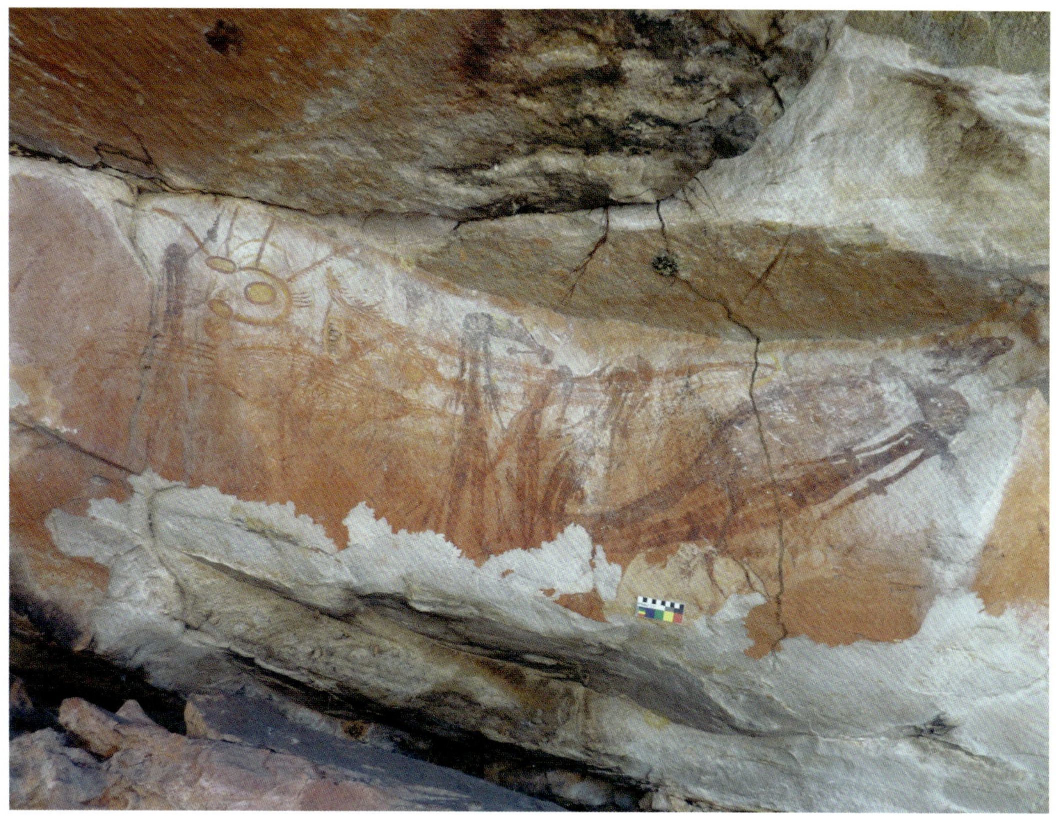

The panel of Tasselled Figures discovered by Joseph Bradshaw in 1891.

adornments appended to the hair, neck, waist, arms, and legs: but the most remarkable fact in connection with these drawings is that wherever a profile face is shown the features are of a most pronounced aquiline type, quite different from those of any natives we encountered. Indeed, looking at some of the groups, one might almost think himself viewing the painted walls of an Egyptian temple. These sketches seemed to be of great age, but over the surface of some of them were drawn in fresher colors smaller and more recent scenes, and rude forms of animals, such as the kangaroo, wallaby, porcupine, crocodile etc. (Bradshaw 1892: 100.)

Sketches of "terracotta" figures were made by G. Hill in 1910 and published by Charles Mountford in 1937. Then, in 1938, a team of visiting German anthropologists recorded paintings they considered similar to those described by Bradshaw, and coined the term "Bradshaw paintings" (Schulz 1956: 45). In his 1968 book, *The Art of the Wandjina*, Ian Crawford used the term "Bradshaw Figure" to describe "small red paintings which show people busy dancing and hunting" (Crawford 1968: 81). He later introduced the notion of a "classic form" to indicate "human figures in which body features such as muscles and shoulders, stomachs, sometimes facial profiles are very clearly and carefully depicted with curvaceous delineation" (Crawford 1977: 357).

These *classic Bradshaws* belong to the groups later described as *Tasselled Figures* and *Bent Knee Figures*.

Pigments

Aboriginal artists traditionally paint using a range of naturally-occurring pigments mixed with water. The basic colours are black charcoal (carbon), white clay (kaolin), red ochre (iron oxide) and yellow ochre (iron hydroxide).

Many more colours are obtained because red ochre varies from orange-reds to dark brownish colours. Pinks can be obtained by mixing red and white. Greys can be obtained by mixing black with white. In certain light, grey can appear bluish, but the author is unaware of the use of a truly blue pigment in Kimberley rock art. (Modern-day Reckitt's Blue was used in some recent paintings in the Kakadu / western Arnhem Land region, but not in the Kimberley.) The brilliant white pigment on some Wandjina paintings, sometimes mistaken for modern-day paint, is the mineral huntite (magnesium calcium carbonate).

Brushes are made by chewing and teasing out the fibres from small pieces of stringy bark *(Eucalyptus tetrodonta)*, stems of *Cyperus* grass, and other fibrous plants. Artists painting Wandjina figures

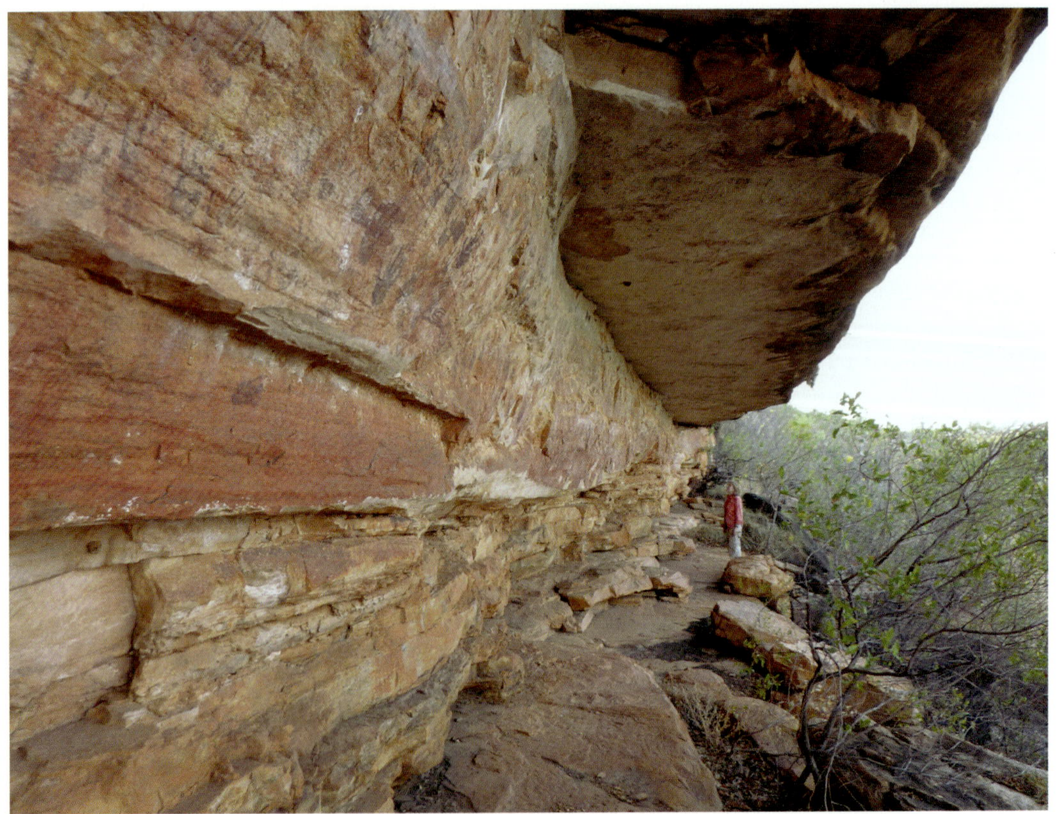

Ancient paintings adorn this cliff wall protected only by a jutting overhang in the central Kimberley.

sprayed a white background from their mouths, and then used broad bark brushes to paint their thick lines. In contrast, artists painting Bradshaw Figures used the finest brushes to produce their works.

Loss and change of pigment from weathering

Across northern Australia, the oldest paintings tend to survive in shades of red, brownish-red (maroon) and blackish-red. Here, painted art sites consist of shallow caves and recesses in eroded quartzite blocks, outliers and cliffs, where the paintings are partially exposed to sunlight and weather. Over the course of thousands of years, wind-blown sprays of mist from wet season storms have entered the shallow shelters and gradually removed surface pigments. Charcoal is the least stable, followed by white and yellow, and these gradually disappear from the paintings, leaving only reds. Red ochres, ground on flat rocks and mixed with water, have the finest grains which soak into the rock and bond with its surface. When early paintings were originally executed in multiple colours, only their red survives, leaving gaps where whites and yellows have weathered away.

This situation is very different from the famous European art sites such as Lascaux, Altamira, Pech Merle, and Chauvet. The early European art is contained in deep subterranean limestone caves, protected from sunlight and rain, and paintings survive with a range of pigments unaltered by weathering effects. Charcoal paintings are able to be carbon-dated, and the earliest are 32,000 years old, from the Chauvet cave in France.

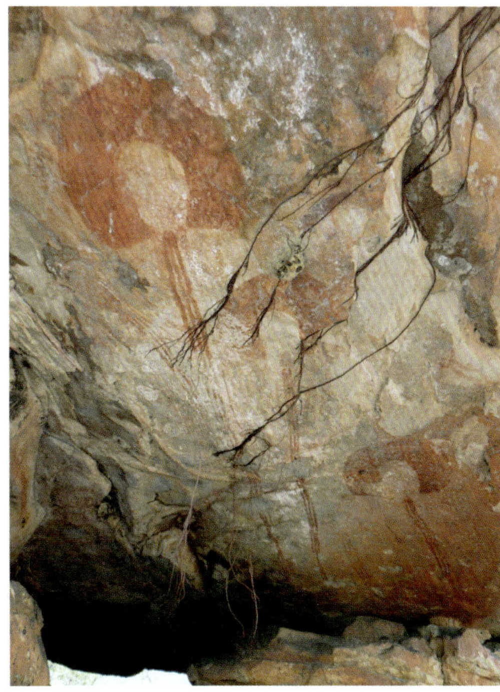

Pre-Wandjina Figures with only red pigment remaining. White originally filled their facial areas.

Where there is white and off-white mineral flow over the rock surface, some dark red-brown paintings develop a deep purplish or mulberry hue. There is a naturally-occurring mineral, jarosite (iron sulphide), that also accounts for the purplish colour on some Bradshaw Figures, but some may have altered from what was originally a deep red-brown. The following example illustrates this point.

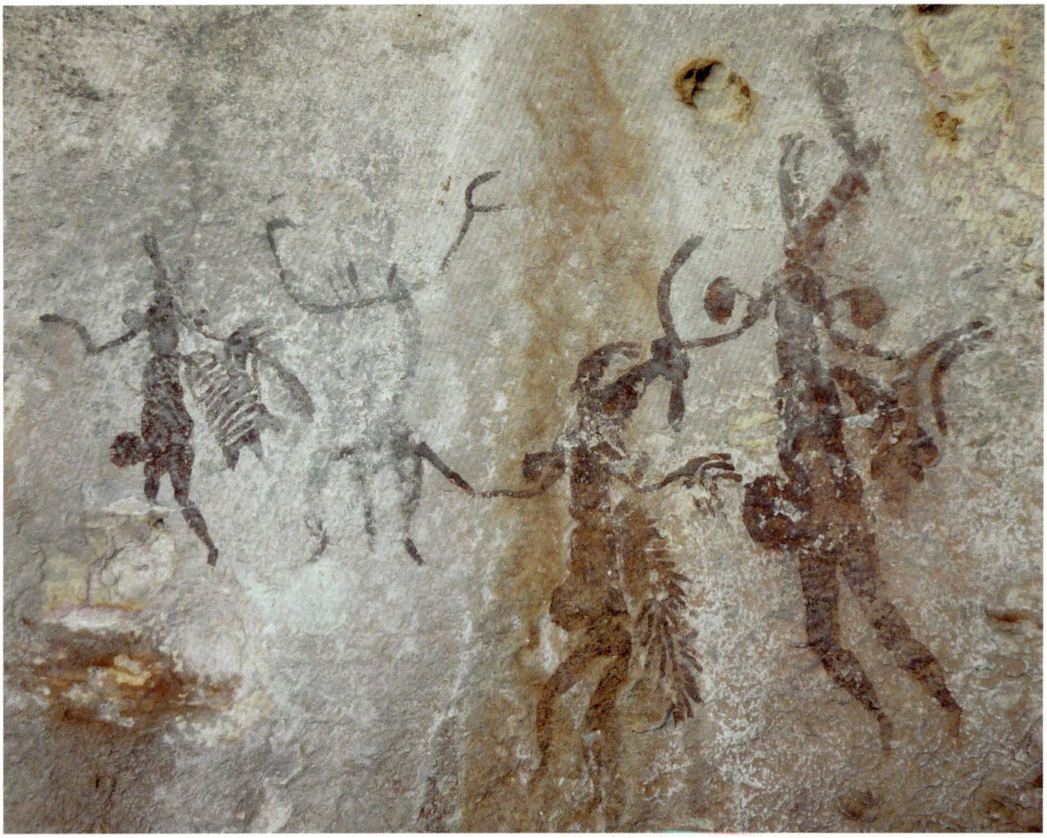

The central Bent Knee Figure on this vertical wall retains its original red-brown colour. However, where an off-white mineral flow occurs over the surface to each side, the paintings have developed a purplish appearance. Height of right-hand figure 36 cm. Drysdale River National Park.

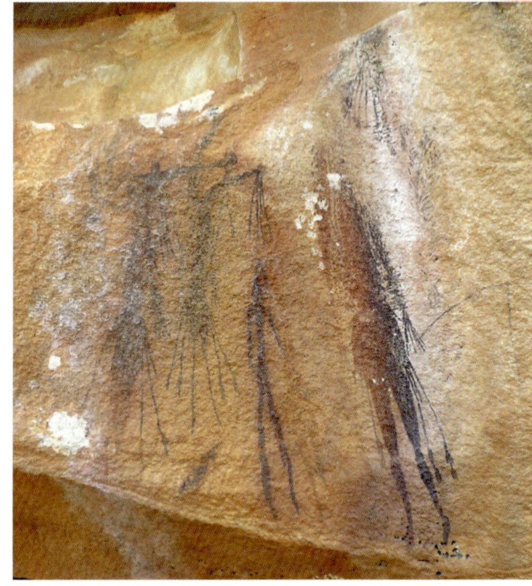

Differential weathering across the right-hand Tasselled Figure. Its left half retains the original red colour, while the right half, being more exposed to moisture, has become blackish. Central Kimberley. Height of figure 60 cm.

Another chemical and colour change occurs on the most ancient red pigments, generally with paintings from the Archaic Period and Tasselled Figure Period. Over thousands of years, exposure to light and moisture converts some reds into a blackish pigment. This is most evident when it occurs on only a portion of a painting. In the example here, the left side of an ancient Tasselled Figure is more protected from the weather and retains its original red pigment. The right side, however, is more exposed to moisture and has become blackish.

The Archaic Period

Bradshaw paintings are not the oldest of Kimberley rock art. An *Archaic Period* prior to their development features unadorned human figures and a range of animals painted in outlines with infills of *irregularly*-placed dots, dashes and angular patterns. These infills are in contrast to the much later Wandjina Period art, characterised by infills consisting of *regular* rows of dots and dashes.

During the Archaic Period, the first petroglyphs (rock engravings) and many enigmatic rock markings were also produced. These rock markings include *pits*, *cupules*, *pounding hollows (grinding hollows)* and *abraded grooves*, and some forms continued being made into more recent periods. These markings have resulted from repeated rubbing and pounding associated with increase rituals.

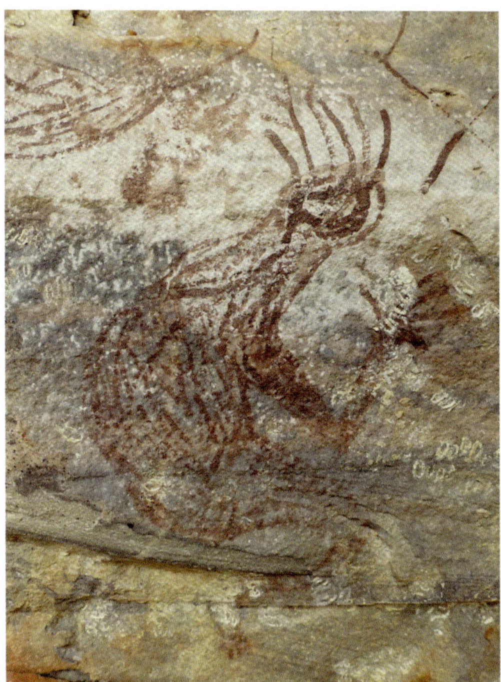

An unadorned human figure from the Archaic Period.

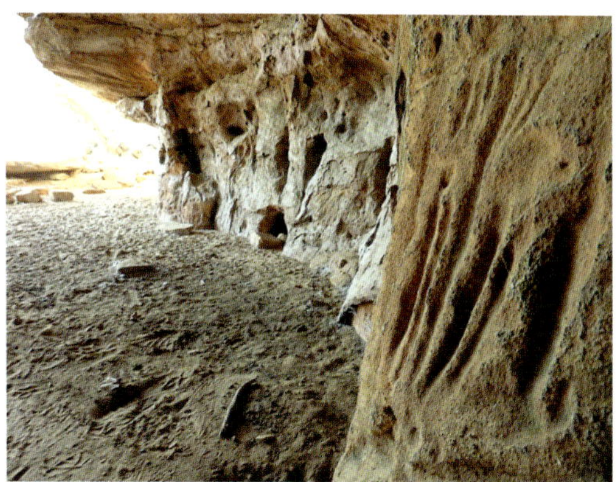

Man-made abraded grooves in the side walls of a low rock shelter. Northern Kimberley.

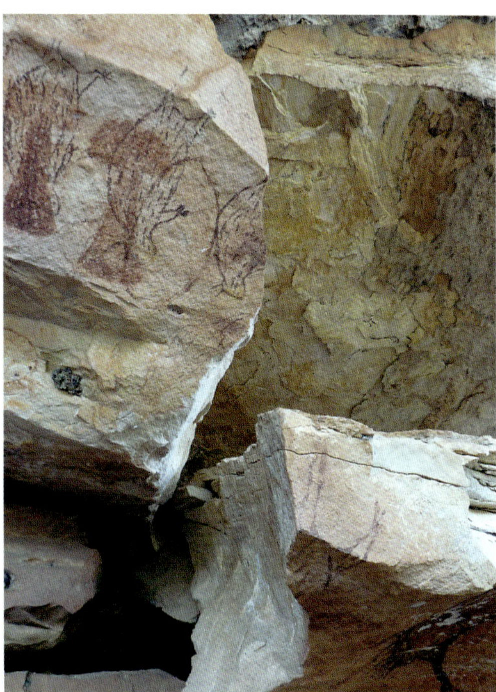

Weathering and disintegration of rocks is an ongoing process. Here, a section of panel with a row of Archaic Period flying foxes has split and fallen. The legs (facing upwards) of the flying fox above are on the fallen section below.

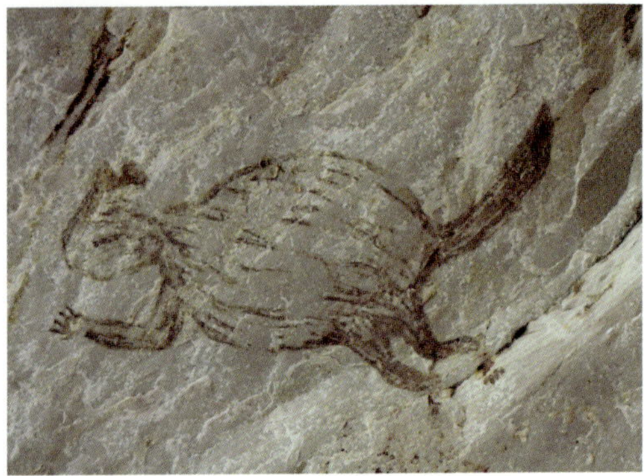

A Tasmanian devil *(Sarcophilus harrisii)*, extinct on mainland Australia for some 3,000 years, painted during the Archaic Period. Length approx. 60 cm.

Different styles of Bradshaw Figures

The most exquisite types of Bradshaw paintings, those referred to as ***Classic Bradshaws***, consist of two main types; *Tasselled Figures* and *Bent Knee Figures*.

Tasselled Figures wear a range of tassels hanging from their headdresses and bodies, and are occasionally painted in the horizontal position, even upside down, seemingly floating across the rock shelter walls. Such visions result in explanations that people must be reclining, floating during dreams and trances, or that deities are floating through the air.

Bent Knee Figures are characterised by having legs bent at the knees, lack tassels, and wear a range of waist adornments, particularly triangular shapes representing bunches of emu feathers and bunches of leaves. With their feet hanging down and arms outstretched, they also appear to float across the rock surface.

Other Bradshaw paintings include ancient forms of stick-like human figures, a style referred to as *Kimberley Dynamic Figures*, and a later style referred to as *Straight Part Figures*. Following these refined styles, artists progressed to more abstract, bold styles, creating paintings that stood out from the others. By now, they had entered the *Painted Hand Period* and this marks the end of the paintings that non-Aboriginal people might regard as Bradshaw art. For

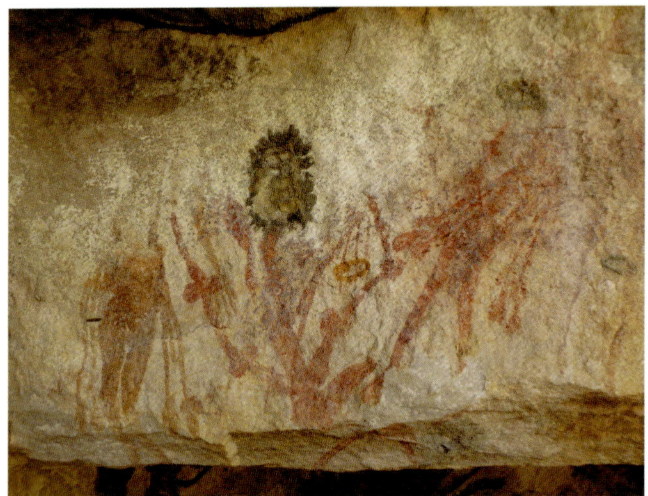

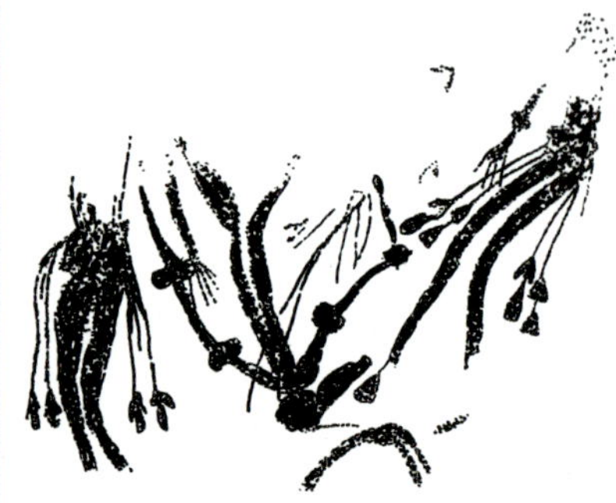

A heavily-weathered inverted Tasselled Figure at Munurru (pronounced *Moon-oo-roo*).

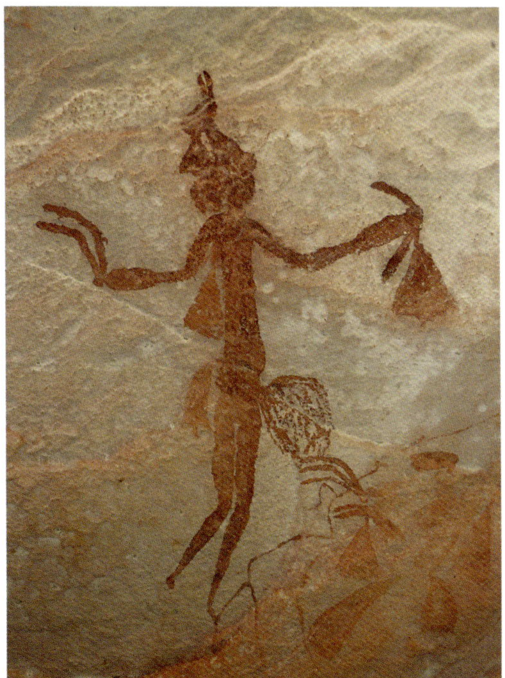

A Bent Knee Figure wearing a headdress, forearm bands, a suspended feather-bunch from the shoulder, and rounded and triangular waist appendages. It carries boomerangs and a ceremonial leaf or feather bunch. Height approx. 70 cm. Northern Kimberley.

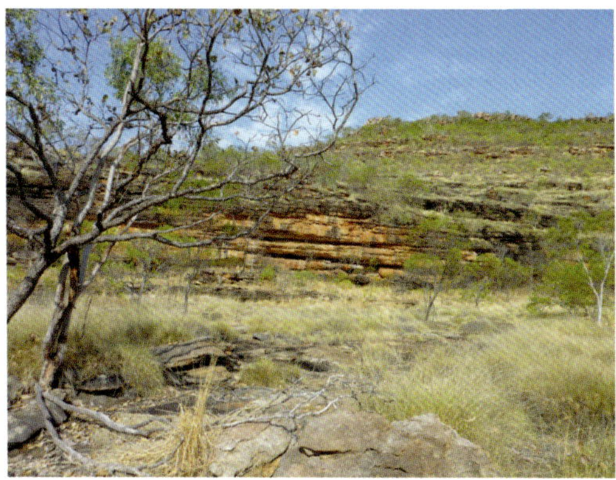

Long panels of simple and stick-like human figures are painted in deep recesses along this cliff wall in the Central Kimberley.

Aboriginal people, however, paintings from the Painted Hand Period are also considered the works of *djimi*, *kiera kiro*, and other creators of the early paintings.

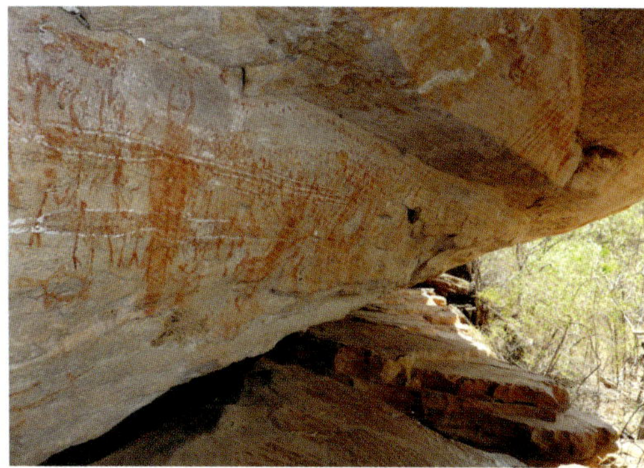

A gallery of simple and stick-like human figures within the recesses.

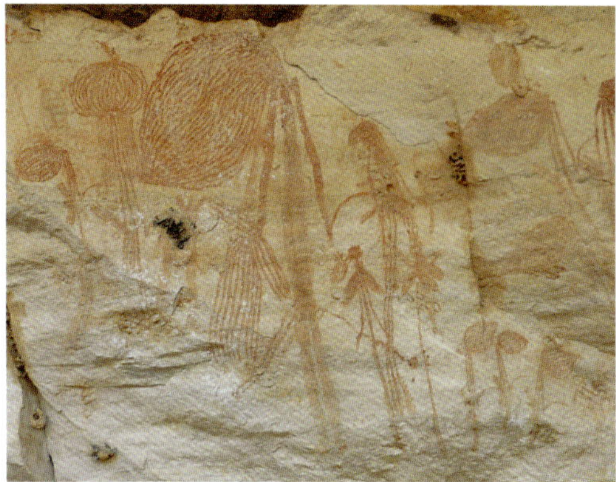

Early simple and stick-like human figures wearing large headdresses and carrying boomerangs and hanging strings. Central Kimberley.

The mystery of Bradshaw paintings

A number of reasons have led people to believe that Bradshaw paintings were painted by a mysterious pre-Aboriginal race:

- Local Aborigines regard the paintings as the works of mythical beings and spirits, not of their human ancestors.
- Tassels and some other accoutrements worn by Bradshaw Figures are not part of present-day Kimberley Aboriginal culture.
- The artists display a higher level of draughtsmanship in relation to their

depiction of human figures than is commonly seen on other Australian Aboriginal art.

- It is argued that Bradshaw Figures suddenly appear on the scene in their fully-developed form, as if representing the art of an intrusive foreign culture.
- People tend to regard the evolution of art styles as a progression from child-like to more sophisticated forms, and the presence of highly developed art in ancient times does not conform with this assumption.
- The notion of a mysterious pre-Aboriginal race was heavily promoted by rock art researcher Grahame Walsh, who produced two stunning books on Bradshaw paintings in 1994 and 2000. Grahame proposed that there were long gaps in time, when no art was produced, suggesting the original people vacated the Kimberley region and were replaced by later occupants. He grouped the art into three phases or "epochs", each separated by a "period of disconformity" or "apparent discontinuity". The earliest rock markings and paintings were assigned to an "Archaic Epoch". Bradshaw Figures were assigned to an "Erudite Epoch", and the later art was assigned to an "Aborigine Epoch" (Walsh 1994: 32 and 2000: viii).

Distancing Bradshaw art from Australian Aboriginal culture, Grahame referred to the tall conical *ngadari* headdress worn by some Bradshaw Figures as a "Dunce Cap Headdress" and the *mudara* style with the hair tied back as a "simple Dunce Cap". The *ngumuru* or bucket-style headdress, with leaves and other decoration hung from its sides, was described as a "Busby Headdress", referring to the tall fur hat with a cloth flap hanging to one side sometimes worn by the military. Figures with their hair spread out were described as having a "sweptback Watusi Headdress" (Walsh 2000: 151), and one style of human figure was named after old-fashioned clothes pegs.

Grahame's ideas and exotic descriptions of the human figures and their accoutrements captured people's imaginations. Lacking the knowledge that Aboriginal people often wore triangular-shaped bunches of emu feathers (called *maltara* by the Dieri tribe of inland Australia) hanging from thick hair belts tied around their waists, Grahame described the hair belt on Bradshaw Figures as a "Cummerbund Waistband" and the hanging bunches as "sashes", comparing the latter with ancient Mayan culture, and implying they were made from finely-woven material, unlike any known item of Aboriginal culture (Walsh 2000: 289). Hanging leafy branches tied to the chest and waist (called *tjintilli* amongst central Australian tribes) were described on Bradshaw Figures as "long plumes".

Grahame also reinforced the Bradshaw mystery – that the paintings were too advanced for Australian Aboriginal people – by comparing the

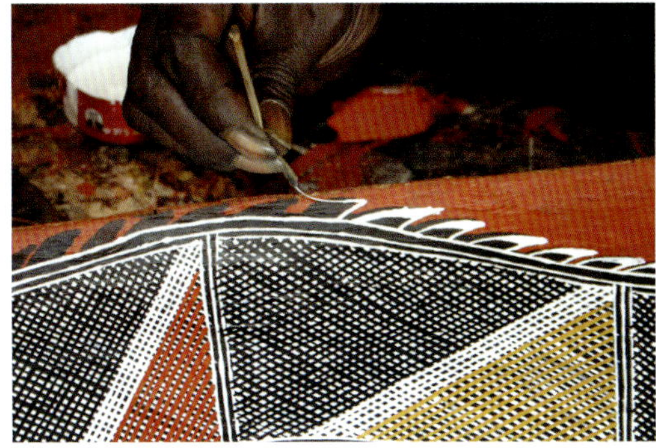

An extremely thin brush used for the finest line-work on Australian Aboriginal paintings, made traditionally by chewing the end of a grass stalk and teasing out the fibres. Grahame Badari at work, western Arnhem Land.

brushwork on the paintings with Chinese calligraphy, rather than researching the fact that Aboriginal people sometimes used fine brushes in their artwork.

The mystery of Bradshaw paintings has been maintained by others. In *Lost World of the Kimberley* (2006) Ian Wilson described a panel of figures which he and others interpreted as deer with antlers painted at "Reindeer Rock". To some, the figures look like deer: They are quadruped animals walking in a line across the landscape, and radiating lines from the head of each animal resemble antlers. What a great mystery!

Believing the paintings might represent deer, Archaeologists excavated part of the large shelter beside Reindeer Rock in 2010. Aboriginal people living in the region were informed by one archaeologist that deer must have occupied the area at some time in the past.

If the paintings represent deer, one might speculate whether (a) deer have been present in northern Australia at some time in the past, and have been recorded by an Aboriginal artist, (b) an Australian Aborigine visited parts of Indonesia or Malaysia and observed deer, then returned to record his vision, or (c) a foreigner visited our northern shores and painted the images of deer from his own lands. What could be the answer? You will have to wait!

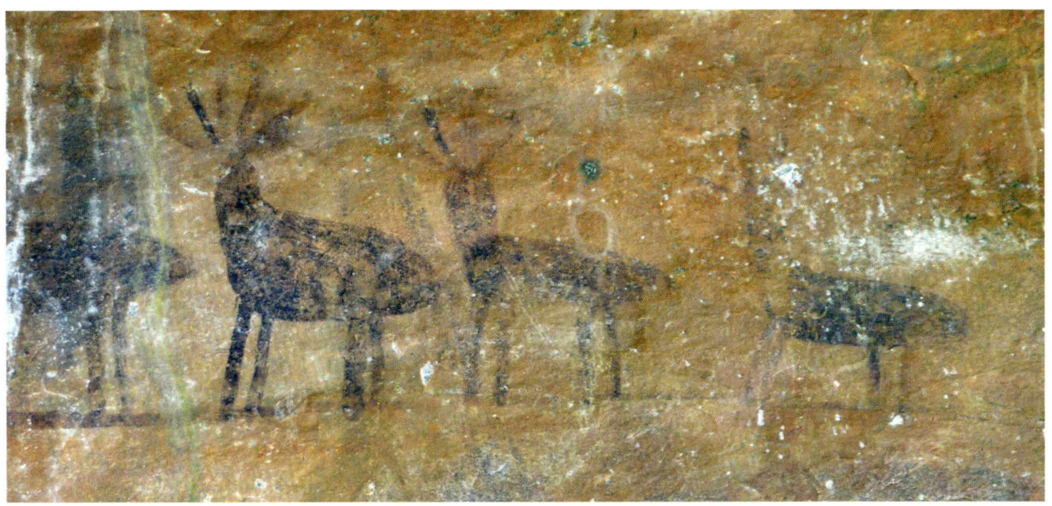

Another Bradshaw mystery: four-legged creatures with projections from their heads, painted over a horizontal line representing the ground. Are these deer with antlers painted in the northern Kimberley?

The significance of Bradshaw paintings

Achaeologists, "specialists"and others making pronouncements regarding the early paintings sometimes have little knowledge of Aboriginal cultural heritage and ceremonial practices, and this leads to fanciful conclusions.

By analysing the details on each figure, discussing them with Aboriginal people from communities across the Kimberley and northern Australia, and by studying the artefacts and old photographs in our museums and state libraries, the author was able to decode Bradshaw Figures in terms of who they represented and what activities were being portrayed. Some of these findings were published in the Australian Rock Art Research Association journals in the 1990s, but failed to become widely known.

Many of the ***accoutrements worn*** by the human figures in the paintings, while not present in current Kimberley Aboriginal culture, were worn during Aboriginal ceremonies held in other parts of Australia. These included feather tasselled belts, tasselled armbands, hair pendants, hanging strings, ceremonial bags hanging from the shoulders, decorated upper arm bands, large and small arm bands, bird wing and feather attachments, dancing skirts and aprons, triangular waist attachments made from bunches of emu feathers and bunches of leaves, and branches hanging from the waist.

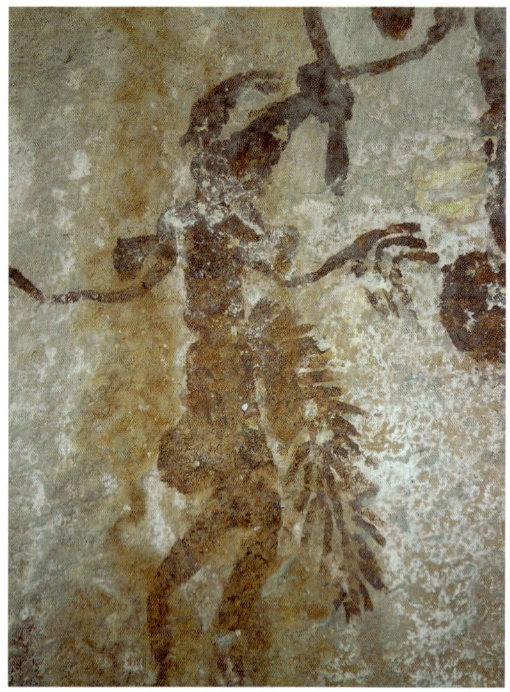

A Bent Knee Figure wearing a hanging branch tucked into its belt. Drysdale River National Park.

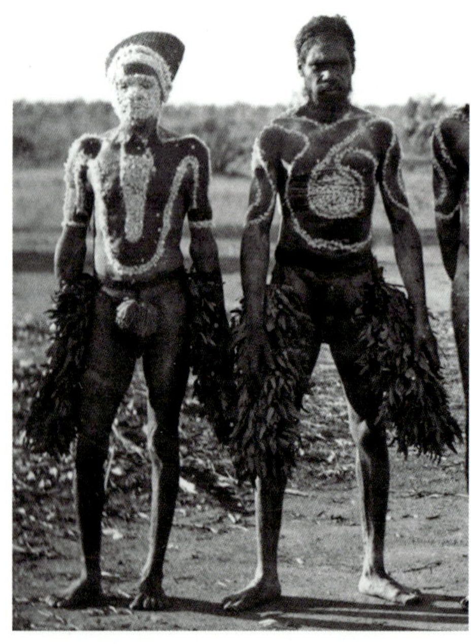

Central Australian men decorated with body paint and down, wearing *tjintilli*, leafy branches, hanging from their belts. The chest decoration on the left-hand man is similar to the *rangu* on some Wandjina paintings. Tennant Creek, 1906. (Photograph courtesy of the Northern Territory Library, Bradshaw Collection, PH0756/49.)

BRADSHAW HEADDRESS STYLES

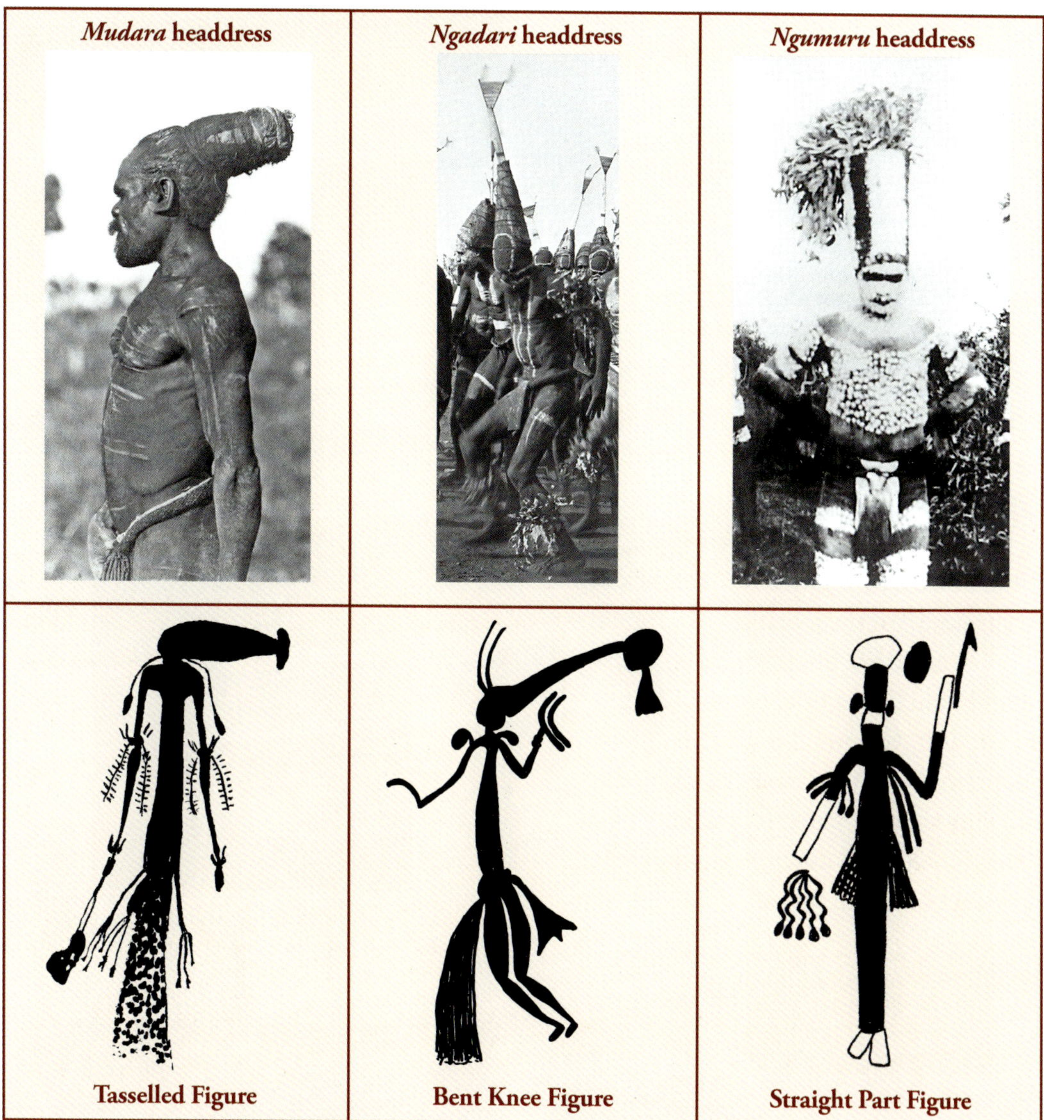

The major ***headdress styles*** appearing on the three main groups of Bradshaw Figures were still being worn by Kimberley men on ceremonial occasions up until the 1960s and 1970s. These were identified with their Kimberley Aboriginal names: Tasselled Figures predominantly wore their hair tied behind in the *mudara* style, Bent Knee Figures mostly wore tall conical headdresses, known as *ngadari*, made from rolled up paperbark (*Melaleuca* species), and Straight Part Figures frequently wore a barrel-like headdress, known as *ngumuru*, with feather or plant attachments.

Many of the ***items carried*** by the human figures in the early paintings were still being carried by Aborigines when performing their ceremonies in the 1980s. These included boomerangs, spears, spearthrowers, wands or dancing sticks, ceremonial poles, bunches of leaves and feathers, ceremonial bags, fly whisks, and hand-held ceremonial strings. Most of the triangular-shaped objects carried and worn by Bradshaw figures represent leaf and feather bunches, rather than bags.

Patterns of body painting on some Bradshaw Figures can be matched to similar patterns worn by Aboriginal people in the twentieth century. These include the use of dots and banding decoration. Coloured pigments, plant down, and feather down are applied to the skin to form patterns and motifs. Traditionally, the down is glued to the skin using human blood.

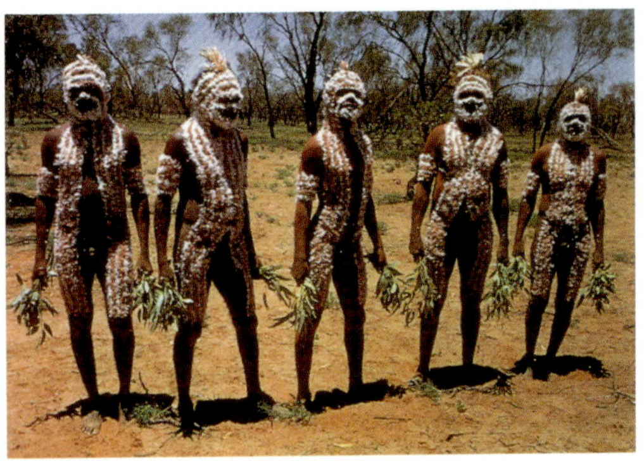

Aranda men from Central Australia wearing ochre and down body decoration, carrying bunches of leaves. (Photograph by Ted Strehlow, circa. 1949.)

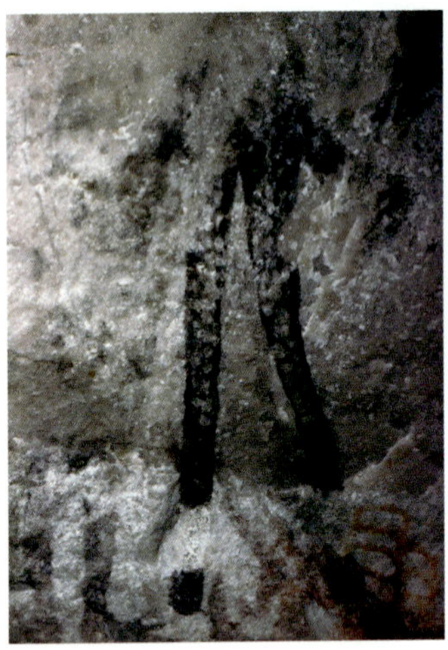

Small dots, originally painted with white pigment, are visible on the legs of this early human figure. Roe River Valley, central Kimberley.

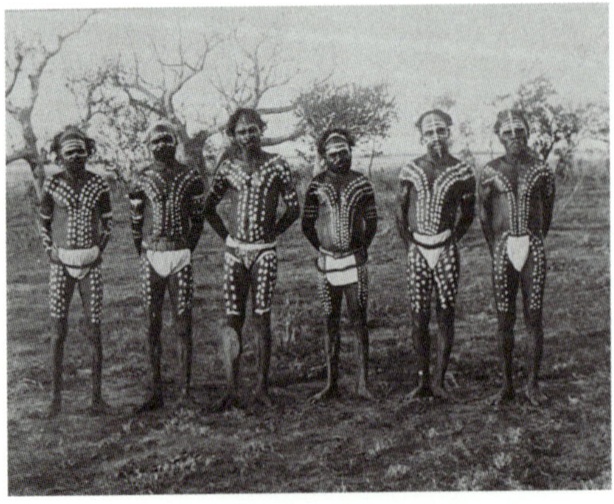

Dotted body paint on Kimberley Aboriginal performers. Derby, Western Australia, 1890s. (Photograph courtesy of the Battye Library, State Library of Western Australia, 26,315P.)

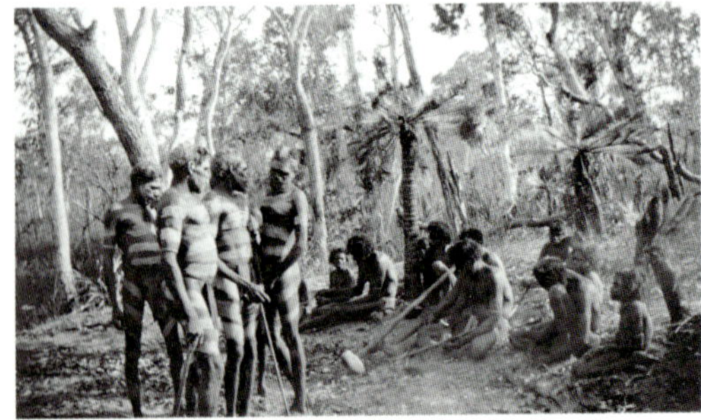

Banded decoration painted over the bodies of Aboriginal performers on Groote Eylandt in eastern Arnhem Land, Northern Territory, circa 1933. (Photograph from the Collection of the Caledon Bay Peace Mission, Courtesy of the Northern Territory Library, PH0731/40.)

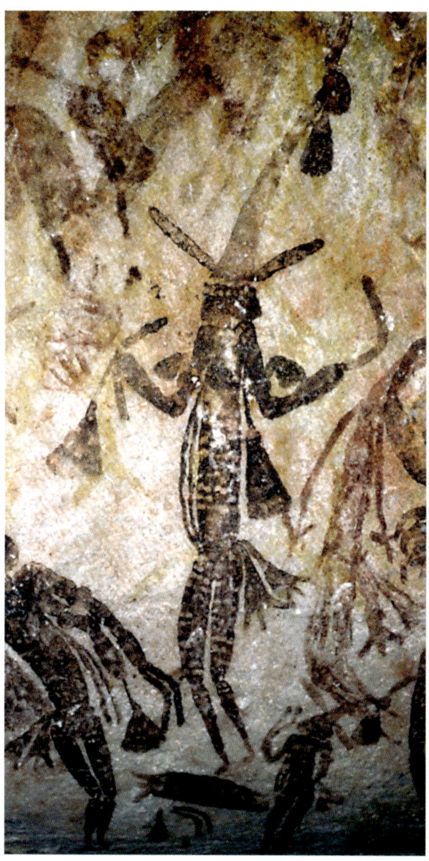

Banded decoration worn by an ornate Bent Knee Figure. Height 55 cm, Mitchell River.

Furthermore, several ***postures*** depicted amongst Bradshaw Figures were compared with traditional Aboriginal dance positions. The paintings often consist of groups of figures similarly aligned, and these reflect choreographed, synchronised dance positions or ritual movements. They include:

- Figures with arms held outstretched widely to the sides.
- Figures with both arms held forward together.
- Figures with both arms raised high above the head.
- Figures with both knees bent and held together.
- Figures facing each other.
- Figures with sway-back bodies depicting writhing sinuous body movement.
- Unequivocal dance positions include the "go-go" style and "the bump" style.

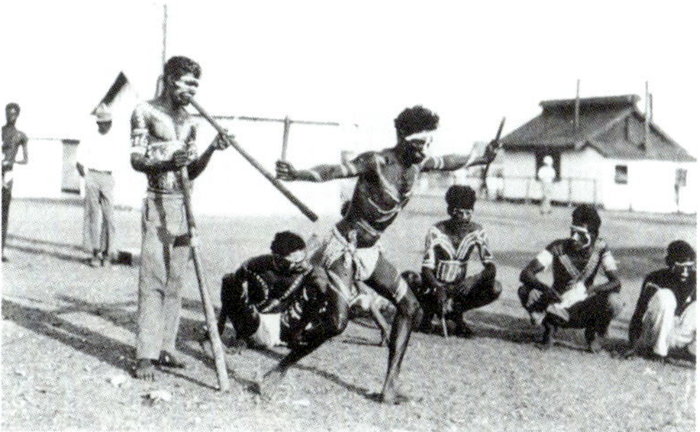

An Aboriginal man with outstretched arms holding dancing sticks. Darwin, Northern Territory, circa 1930s. (Photograph courtesy of the Northern Territory Library, Miscellaneous Collection, PH0280/5.)

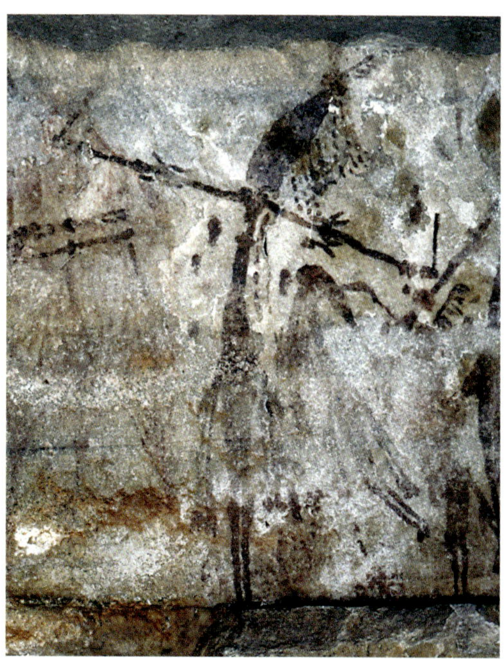

A Tasselled Figure with outstretched arms holding dancing sticks. Drysdale River National Park.

In summary, Bradshaw Figures are not wearing the everyday dress of a mysterious lost race of people. Rather, they are wearing the ceremonial dress of Aboriginal people, revealing the complexity of the culture some ten to twenty thousand years ago. Aboriginal culture has evolved locally, and items that once belonged to Kimberley people are now scattered amongst the people of other Australian tribes. Tassels survive in eastern Arnhem Land. The tall conical headdress, *ngadari*, made from rolled-up paper bark (*Melaleuca* species), is found across northern and central Australia, and was worn in Kimberley ceremonies until recently. The bucket headdress, *ngumuru*, still survives in the Kimberley and across parts of the Northern Territory.

Over the course of thousands of years, countless generations of Kimberley Aborigines have interpreted and reinterpreted the art of their ancestors, and the original meaning of Bradshaw Paintings became lost. Like many unexplained phenomena, the paintings entered into the spiritual and religious realm, and Aborigines came to believe they were the work of mythical beings and spirits. Similar views about early rock paintings are held by Aboriginal people in the Kakadu region and Arnhem Land to the east, where the early art is attributed to mythical *mimi* spirits, who live amongst the rocks and are rarely seen.

Regarding the concept that Bradshaw Figures suddenly appear on the scene in their fully-developed form, as if the artists have arrived bearing a new culture: In traditional Aboriginal societies, the production of artwork connected with ceremonial occasions, such as the Bradshaw paintings, is restricted to the domain of initiated males. Artists first practice on non-sacred objects. In the past, local artists would have practised on trees, pieces of bark, and flat rock surfaces as they developed their skills. Only then would they have produced permanent works on protected walls below rock overhangs and within rock shelters. In fact, some Tasselled Figures and Bent Knee Figures are clumsily portrayed, indicating some artists were less skilled than others.

Progression and continuity of Kimberley art styles from Bradshaw to Wandjina paintings

Regarding the theory that long gaps exist between art styles which are disconnected from each other through time, the author's initial Kimberley research, published in 1990, suggested the opposite, with a gradual progression of art from one style into the next. For example, the arcuate or horseshoe-shaped headdresses on Wandjina figures have their origins amongst some of the early Tasselled Figures. The headdress becomes common at a time when Straight Part Figures (one style of Bradshaw Figure) are painted, and continues through the Painted Hand Period.

PROGRESSION OF ARCUATE HEADDRESSES FROM BRADSHAW TO WANDJINA PAINTINGS

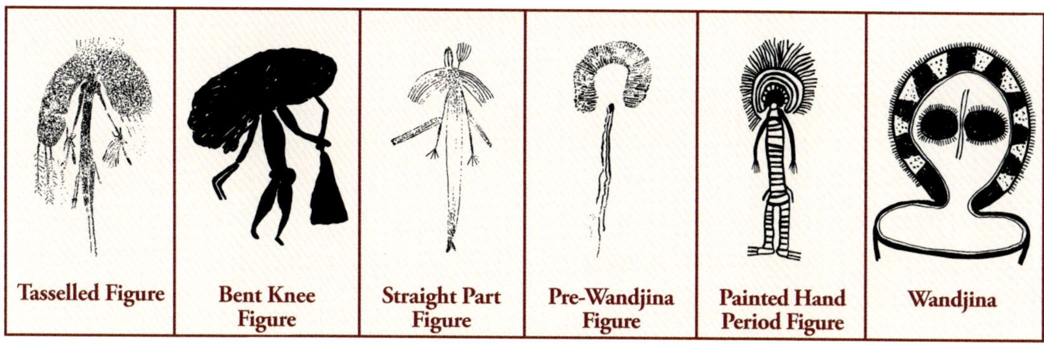

Tasselled Figure	Bent Knee Figure	Straight Part Figure	Pre-Wandjina Figure	Painted Hand Period Figure	Wandjina

The **style of infill** applied to the paintings is a significant marker when examining the progression from Bradshaw to Wandjina paintings. Infills are important to artists because they define the solid nature of their subjects. In the Kimberley they appear to follow a logical progression from the time before the appearance of Bradshaw paintings, through the major Bradshaw styles, to the most recent Wandjina paintings. (See chart on page 21.)

While the *outline and form* of human, plant and animal depictions evolved through the periods described in the Kimberley chronological sequence, the *infill styles* employed by those artists appear to have evolved at a slightly delayed pace, resulting in overlap from one period into the next. Thus, there appears to be continuity between each succeeding art style, from the Archaic Period to the Wandjina Period.

During the Archaic Period, the earliest artists painted their human and animal figures in outline and then filled the interior of the designs with roughly-placed dashes, wavy lines, dots and angular patterns. (In the field, I use the terms *irregular dash infill* and *irregular dot infill* to describe these, and this gave rise to Grahame Walsh's term *Irregular Infill Animal Period.*)

Later artists (of Bradshaw figures) painted their human figures with *solid infills*, but sometimes retained the use of irregularly-placed dashes and wavy lines on their largest animal figures, in order to conserve paint. These large animal paintings have bodies with irregular dashes and wavy lines as infills, but their heads, tails, and limb girdles are filled with solid pigment. (This can be described as a *peripheral solid infill* or *peripheral infill.*) Some of these large animals are associated with Bent Knee Figures, and thus there is continuity between the artistic styles of the early Archaic Period and the later Bradshaw Figures.

Next, there was experimentation with the use of solid infills, as artists moved from using single colours to *blocks of different colours*. This occurred during the time of the Straight Part Figures. The oldest Straight Part Figures have solid infills with single colours, but the majority were painted when artists had progressed to using blocks of different colours, particularly using white pigment on the forearms, lower legs and parts of the head and face of human figures.

Infills with blocks of colour continued into the next major art phase, the Painted Hand Period. During this phase, artists reverted to painting their subjects in outline, but differed from the earlier Archaic Period style by employing thick bold lines, choosing bright orange-red pigments, and painting in less naturalistic styles. Few paintings from this period survive with blocks of colour, and the majority have simple infills consisting of *connecting lines* or *transverse lines* joining one side of the motif to the opposite side, producing a segmented appearance.

Infills of connecting lines, conveying the solid nature of the subject, evolved during the Wandjina Period to become rows of finely and evenly-placed dots and dashes, placed across the painting. The Wandjina Period also saw an expansion in the use of spraying paint from the mouth of the artist, normally limited to the production of hand and other stencils. Sprayed white pigment now provided the background and solid infill for many subjects, with their outline and details painted over this.

Remarkably, while the outline or shape of subjects evolved from naturalistic (realistic) to stylised (often crude or basic) forms, the infill or internal decoration on the paintings evolved in the opposite direction, from rough, irregularly-placed dots, dashes and wavy lines to neat rows of carefully-placed dots and dashes.

These progressions evident in Kimberley rock art also appear across northern Australia, particularly in the art of the Kakadu and Arnhem Land regions. Paintings from those regions evolved from naturalistic to crude stylised forms, while their infills evolved from crude irregular dashes to finely-placed rows of parallel lines set at angles to each other, known as *rarrk*.

Despite the similarities (and there are many) between Kimberley and Arnhem Land rock art, two northern Australian rock art researchers promoted completely opposing views regarding the artists and its continuity. George Chaloupka developed Eric Brandl's 1973 Arnhem Land rock art sequence and promoted the notion of *continuity*, with *Journey in Time: The World's Longest Continuing Art Tradition* in 1993. Grahame Walsh, on the other hand, developed my 1992 Kimberley rock art sequence and promoted the notion of *discontinuity* and a pre-Aboriginal "Erudite Epoch" with *Bradshaws: Ancient Rock Paintings of North-West Australia* in 1994.

THE PROGRESSION OF INFILL STYLES IN KIMBERLEY ROCK ART

PERIOD	INFILL STYLE	HUMAN FIGURES	ANIMALS
ARCHAIC PERIOD	Irregular dash infill. Irregular dot infill. Irregular pattern infill.	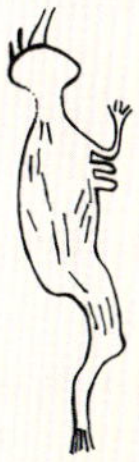	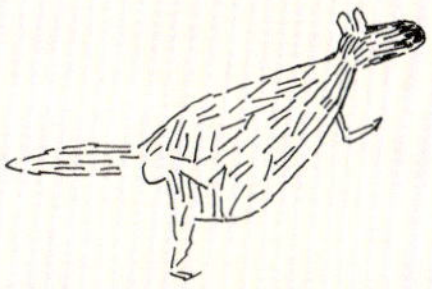
BENT KNEE FIGURE PERIOD	Solid infill on human figures. Irregular dash infill with peripheral solid infill on large animals.	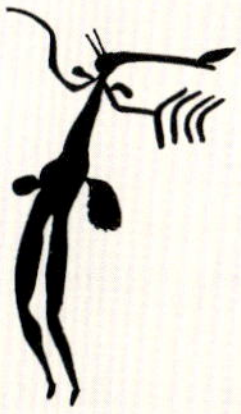	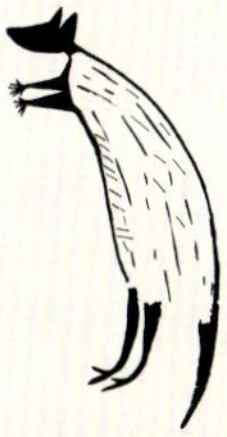
STRAIGHT PART FIGURE PERIOD	Solid infill in blocks of different colours.	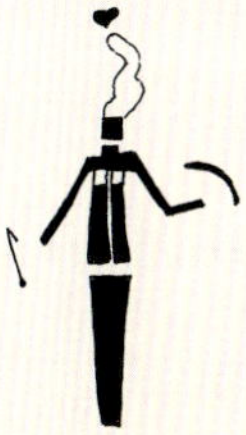	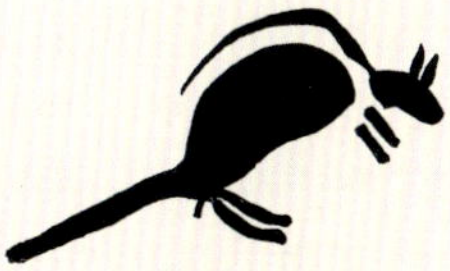
PAINTED HAND PERIOD	Transverse lines and grid patterns. Solid infill blocks on some figures.	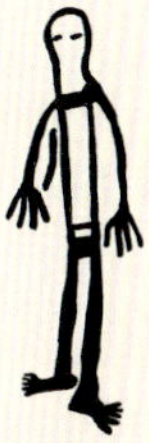	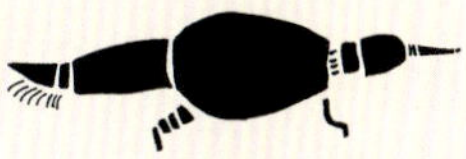
WANDJINA PERIOD	Sprayed infill. Transverse lines with regular rows of dots and dashes. Parallel lines.	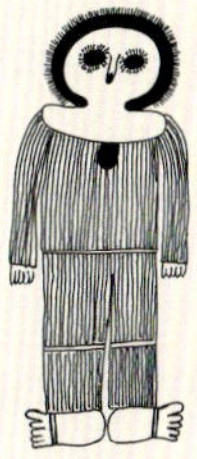	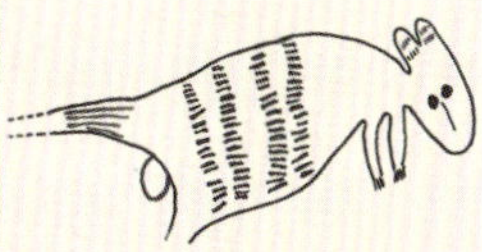

(Dr David M. Welch)

Oh dear! .... No deer!

And what about those deer painted at Reindeer Rock on page 13? I'm sorry to say they are not deer. In fact, they are representations of Aboriginal people performing their dances and ceremonies when mimicking the actions of four-legged animals. The "antlers" are their headdresses. It should be noted that:

- Although the overall shape of each motif is similar to four-legged animals, there are no details of paws, hooves, hands or feet, to suggest any particular animal.
- None of the figures have a tail. (Only humans on all-fours have no tail!)
- The radiating lines leaving the head of each motif differ considerably from deer antlers, which angle backwards and join at one point on either side of the head.
- One of the figures has a distinct gap at the waist, originally painted in less stable pigment such as white. This is a common feature on Straight Part Figures, and represents a hair belt worn around a person's waist.

The "deer" panel is three metres long and painted 2.5 metres above the present ground level. Twenty four figures are visible. Two other sites in the same river valley depict people on all-fours wearing different headdresses. An art panel one hundred kilometres south depicts thirty people on all-fours wearing tall straight headdresses, and similarities with the "deer" panel suggest they may have been painted by the same artist.

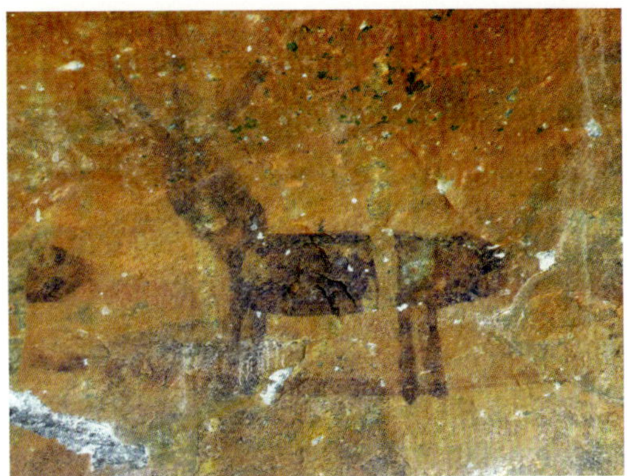

A gap at the waist on one of the "deer" where a belt, originally painted in less stable white pigment, was shown. Height 14 cm.

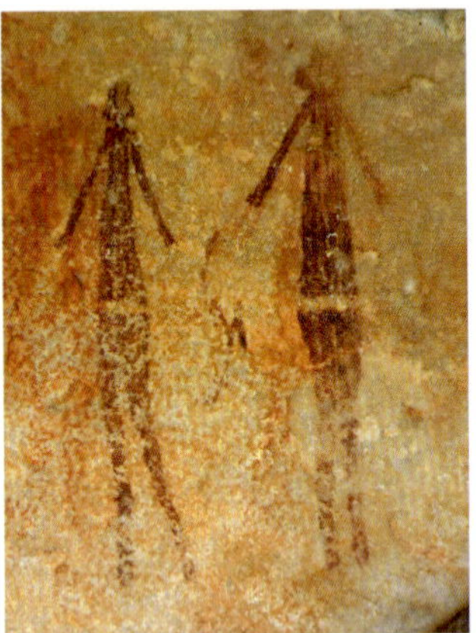

Two Straight Part Figures with gaps at their waists where belts were originally painted in white pigment.

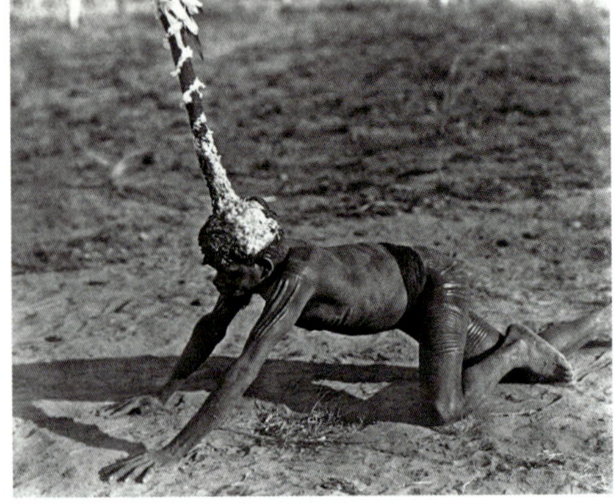

A Kimberley man wearing a *ngadari* headdress, hair belt around the waist, and performing on all-fours, photographed by Herbert Basedow in 1916. (Photograph courtesy of the Mitchell Library, State Library of New South Wales.)

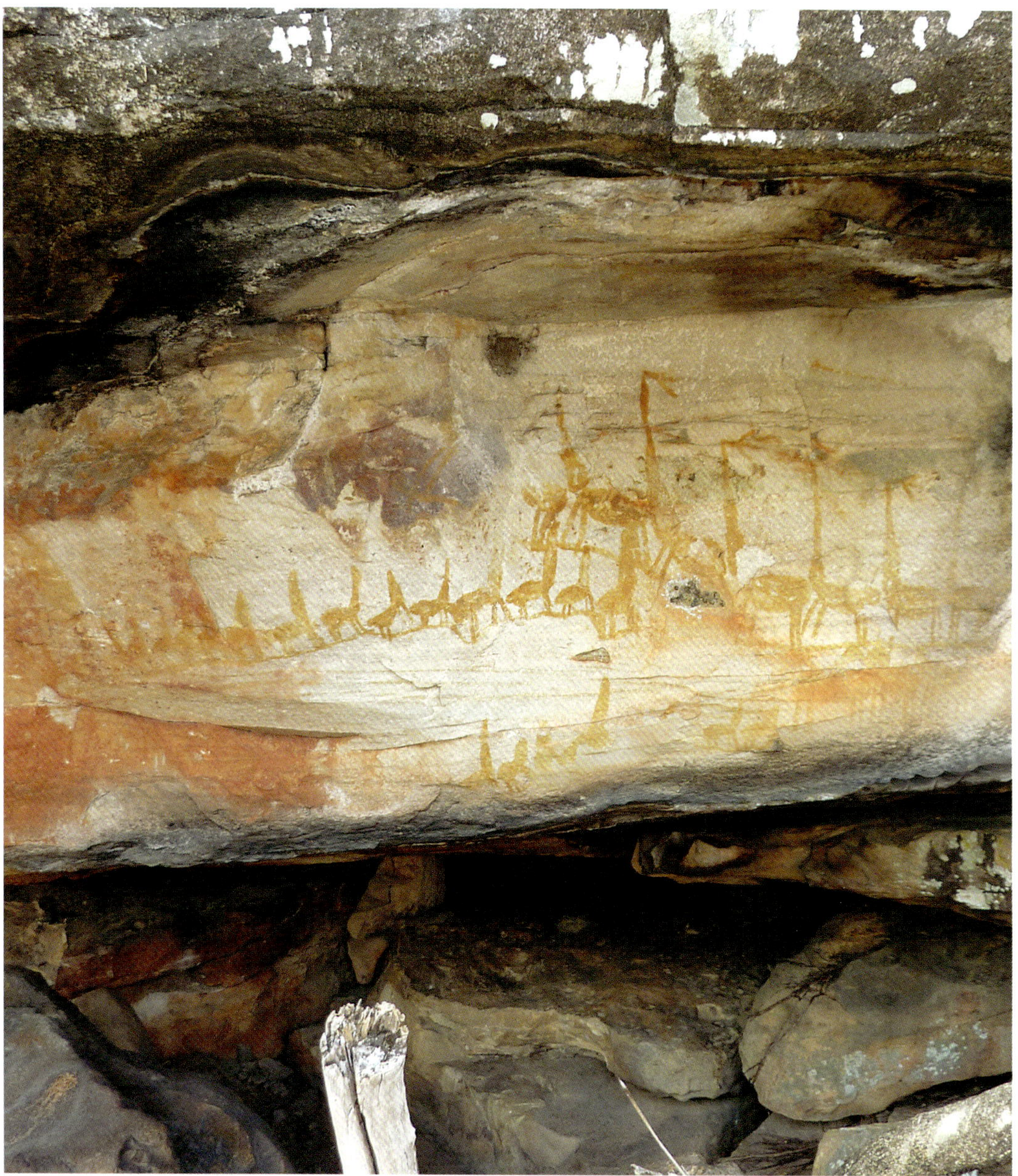

Rows of people performing on all-fours, wearing tall headdresses, and with horizontal lines representing the ground. Heights of the figures range from 10 to 26 cm. Central Kimberley.

TASSELLED FIGURES

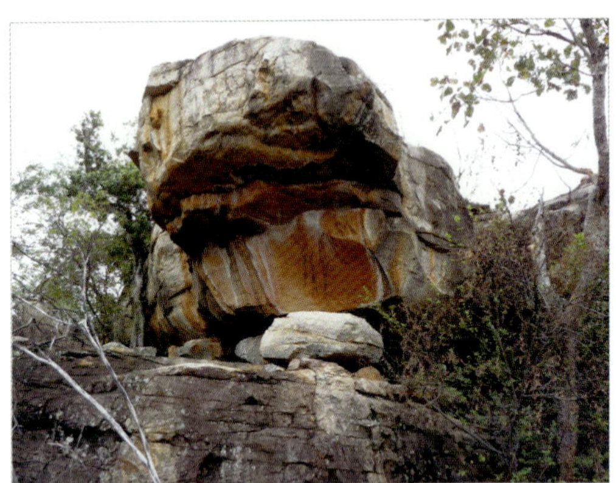

A quartzite block on a hillside slope containing a panel of early Tasselled Figures. Central Kimberley.

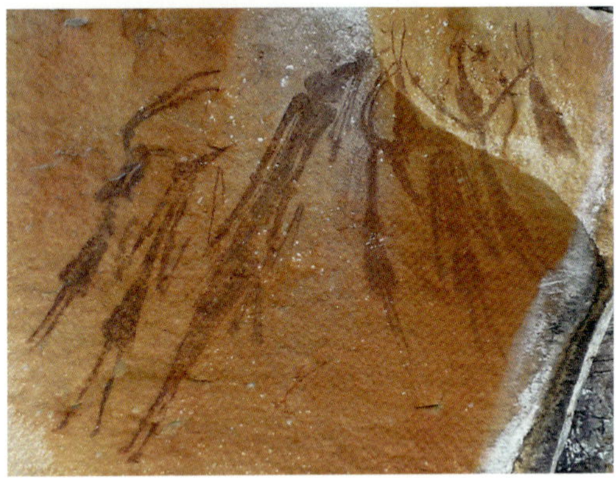

An exquisite panel of Tasselled Figures wearing tall conical headdresses, dancing skirts, arm bands, wrist bands, and hanging tassels. They carry a variety of dancing sticks (or *wands*) and bag-like ceremonial objects.

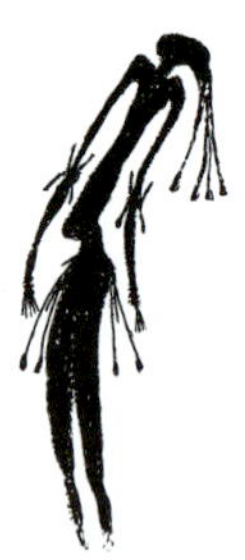

Tasselled Figures were the first large group of human figures to be painted across the Kimberley region, and follow on from the earlier Archaic Period. The paintings originally described by Joseph Bradshaw in 1892 were of this type, and the most elegant examples are referred to as *Classic Bradshaw Figures.*

Tasselled Figures have the following general characteristics:

- ✻ Human figures wear tassels hanging from the waist, headdress, arms and shoulders.
- ✻ Various headdresses are worn, the most common being the male *mudara* style, where the long hair is tied at the back and hangs down. Upper arm bands and single wrist bands are common.
- ✻ Some figures wear tassels and long full skirts, while others wear skirts and lack tassels.
- ✻ Carried items include boomerangs, ceremonial strings, ceremonial bags, and dancing sticks (wands) of various lengths. Long dancing sticks with a small string hanging from the end are interpreted as spears by some observers. Spearthrowers are absent. Carried items are often depicted beside, rather than in, the hands.
- ✻ Small animals, similar in shape to bandicoots, possums, and marsupial rats and mice, are occasionally painted over the shoulder or arm of Tasselled Figures. These are absent on the later Bent Knee Figures.
- ✻ The human body is stylised with slim elongated trunks and limbs, shown in graceful poses. Emphasis is placed on limb musculature, with exaggerated

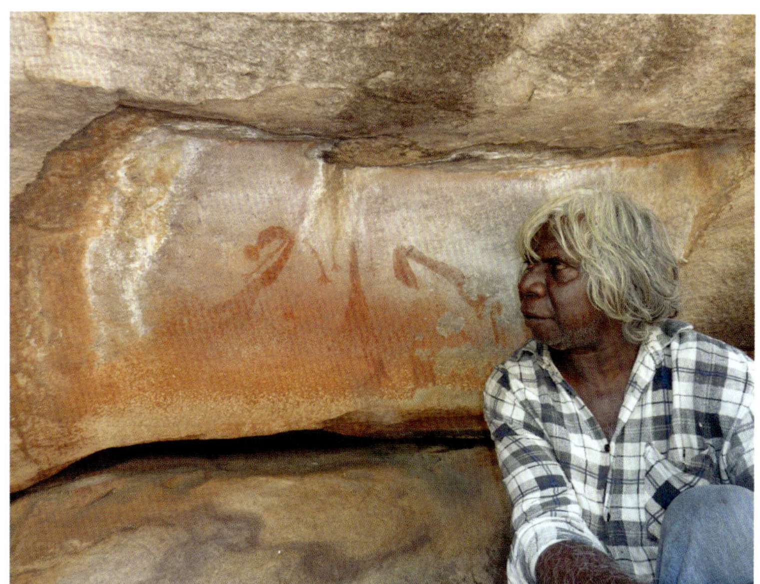

Gwini elder, Kevin Waina, beside Tasselled Figures near Kalumburu in the northern Kimberley.

calf muscles, pectoral regions, and shoulders. Shoulders and pectorals are emphasised even on some simple and stick-like forms. A prominent paunch, signifying a person of seniority, is common.

- Figures are portrayed using a *combined perspective* – combining a *profile* view of the head, paunch, leg musculature and feet with a *frontal* view of the limb girdles (the shoulder and groin regions).
- The majority survive as monochromatic (single colour) paintings in various shades of red to brownish-red pigment bonded to the rock. Weathered dotted and banded body decoration is present on some examples, revealing the use of more than one colour on the original paintings. Their great age is marked by the presence of weathering, exfoliation of the rock below, mineral coating over the art, and overpainting by later artists.
- Female Tasselled Figures are rare and are identified by the presence of breasts and lack of headdress and accoutrements. All Tasselled Figures wearing long headdresses, tassels and other elaborate body decoration represent males, unless breasts are shown.

Tasselled Figures appear to have been painted by many different artists with varying degrees of expertise, over a long period of time. Occasionally one group of Tasselled Figures are painted over the top of an earlier group. Stylistically, Tasselled Figures range from elaborate, full-bodied forms to simple and stick-like forms. In length, most are between thirty and seventy centimetres, with the smallest around seventeen centimetres and the tallest 233 centimetres. Generally, they are painted in groups, though occasionally a single Tasselled Figure is seen.

Tasselled Figures are predominantly painted in a vertical position with the head uppermost, and sometimes the

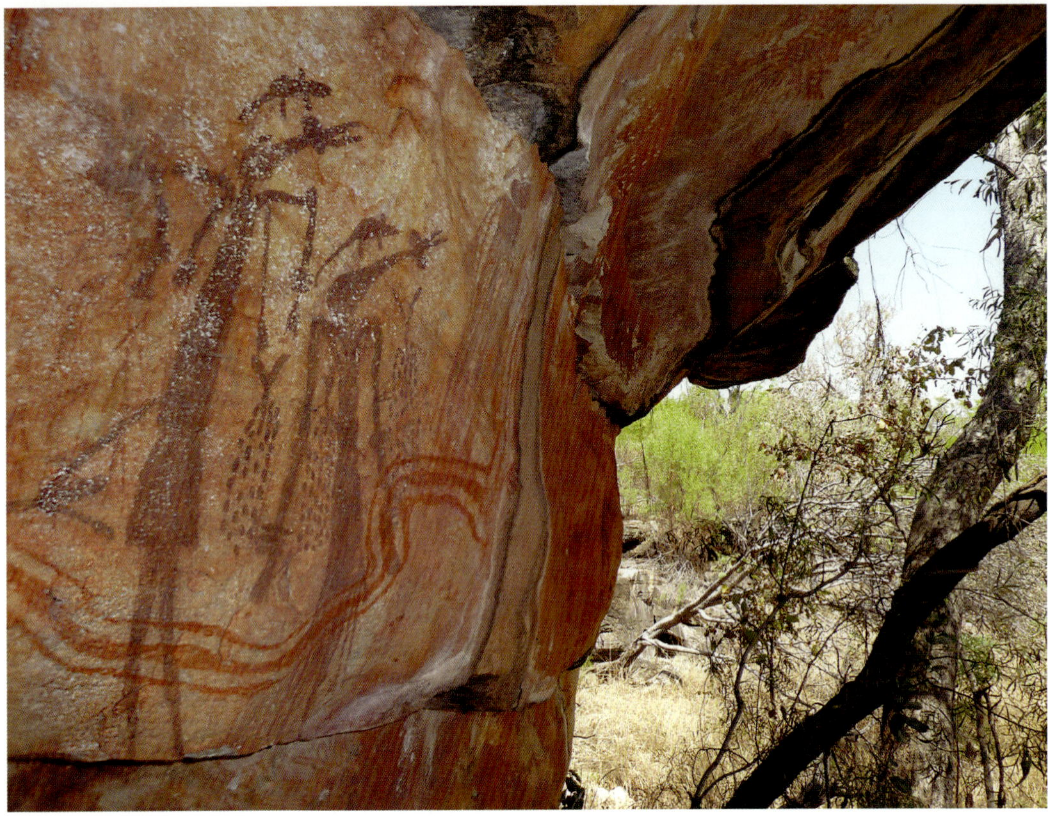

Tasselled Figures wearing skirts, with small animals placed over their headdresses. The orange-red lines painted over the figures are from the later Painted Hand Period. Central Kimberley.

legs continue below an overhanging rock ledge, giving the paintings a three-dimensional quality. Occasionally, they are painted sideways or in an inverted position with the head lowermost, as with the example on page 10. These portrayals have led to theories that the artists must have been depicting people in trance states, floating through the air, similar to *shamanism*, when people reached altered states of consciousness in order to contact the spirit world.

In fact, shamanism and entering trance states are not part of Australia's Aboriginal culture, though people do describe events which they believe occur when they dream.

The placing together of human figures in both upright and upside-down positions is not uncommon in Australian rock art. This device denotes altered perspectives, used by artists to portray people facing each other, dancing around each other, and interacting when performing their dances on the corroboree ground. Sometimes animals and plant-people are similarly placed, with upright and inverted figures together.

Another reason why some human

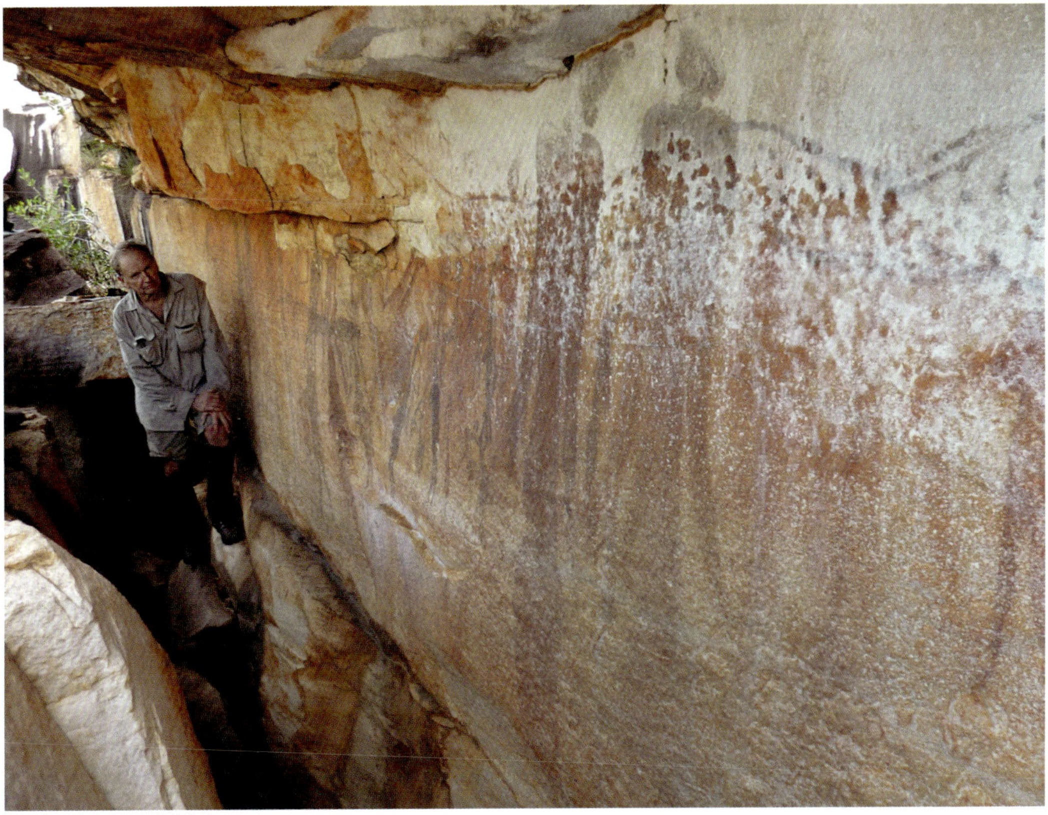

These are the tallest Tasselled Figures known, with their discoverer, Barrie Voorwinden. The tallest central figure measures 233 cm long. Located in the Lawley River Valley, northern Kimberley.

figures are inverted is that much of the art was intended to be viewed while a person lay on the ground below, resting in the shelters. A human figure that appears upside down or sideways when viewed from the standing position might look the right way up if the viewer is lying on their back and looking up at the painting.

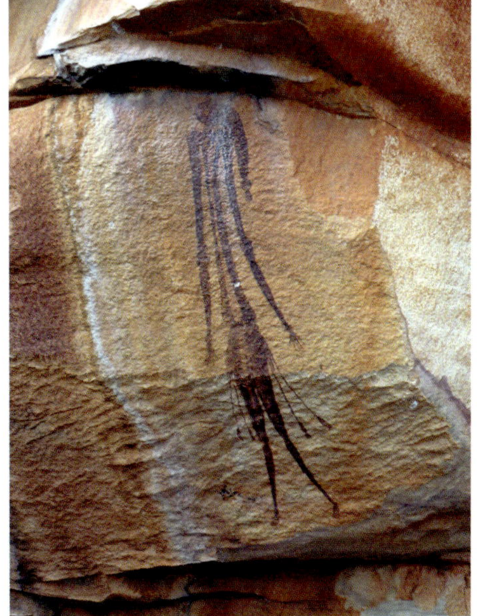

A Tasselled Figure placed over a protruding section of rock giving it a three-dimensional quality. Central Kimberley. Height 88 cm.

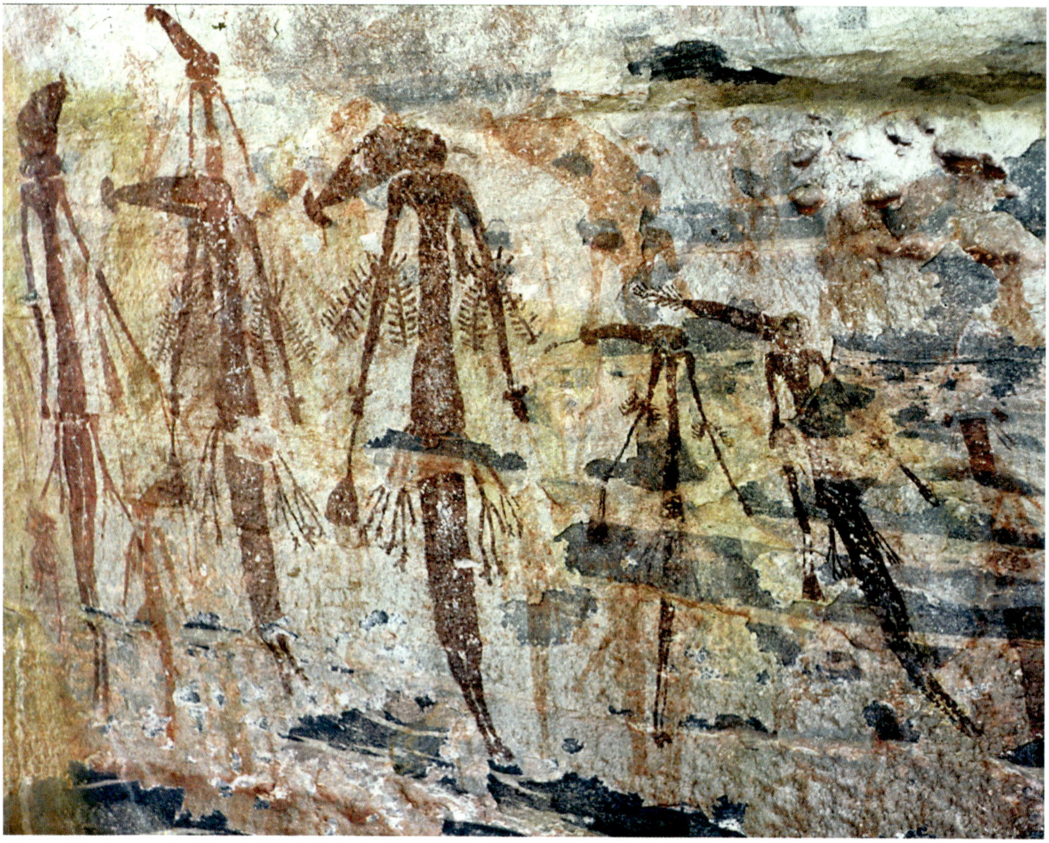

Dark brown-red Tasselled Figures painted over earlier pale red Tasselled Figures. King George River, northern Kimberley.

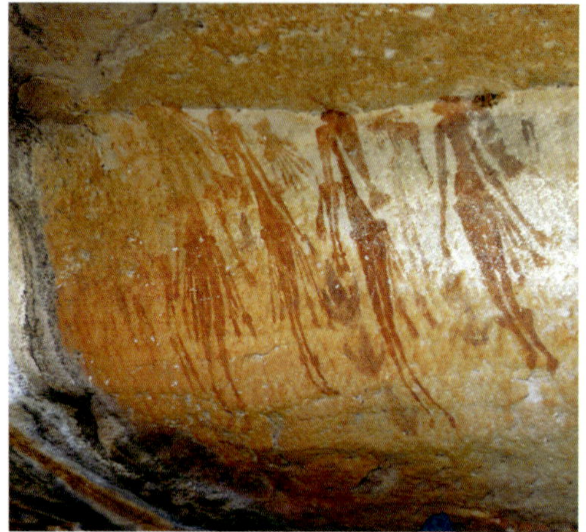

This artist painted his Tasselled Figures with their legs bent around the ceiling step, giving his painting a three-dimensional quality. Height of tallest figure 51cm. Roe River Valley, central Kimberley.

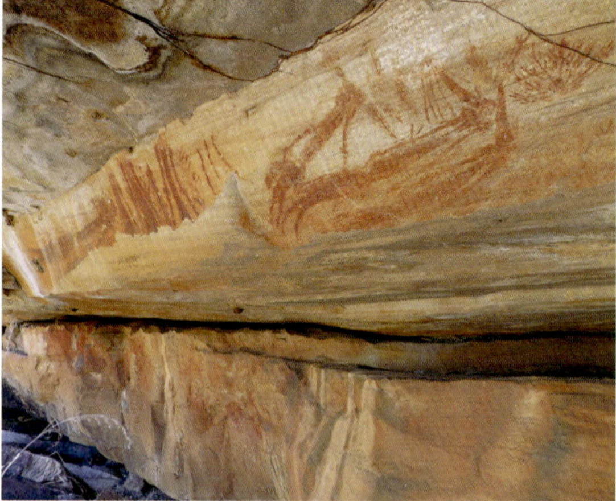

Tasselled Figures placed in both vertical and horizontal positions. Exfoliation of the rock surface has removed the lower portions of the art. Central Kimberley.

Artists often chose the steps along the back walls and ceilings of shelters for their paintings. In some instances, these included long Tasselled Figures placed in the horizontal position to allow for maximum size. With the example on the previous page, part of the rock surface has exfoliated, taking with it the lower portions of the vertical figures, but leaving the horizontal figure intact.

Insights into the culture behind the creation of Tasselled Figures can be gained by studying the culture of Arnhem Land Aborigines in the Northern Territory, one thousand kilometres to the east. There, many of the features appearing in these Kimberley paintings can be seen, including the wearing of tassels, the carrying of hanging strings and ceremonial bags, and the presence of dancing wands with a string hanging from the upper end.

Links between these cultural artefacts present in early Kimberley rock art and the people of Arnhem Land to the east have arisen through trade. Trade was not restricted to objects, and large gatherings of people on ceremonial occasions allowed ideas, stories, songs and dances to be spread from one Aboriginal group to another across the country.

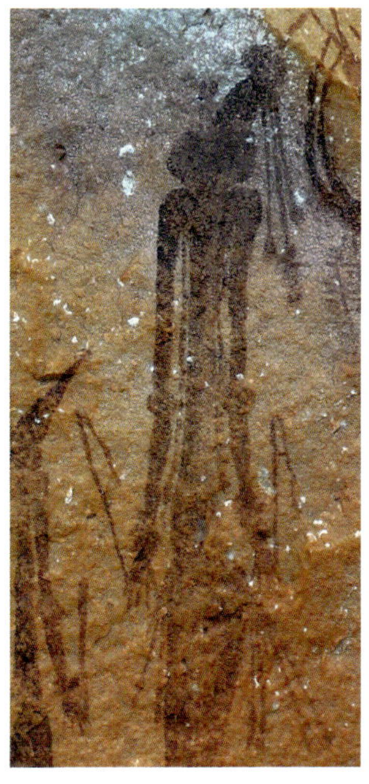

A Tasselled Figure carries dancing sticks with strings hanging from their ends.

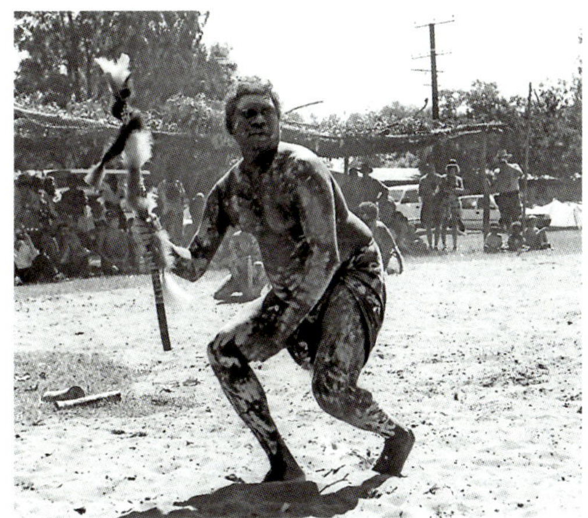

An Elcho Island dancer (from Arnhem Land in the Northern Territory) carries a dancing stick with feather tassels hanging from its end. (Photograph by the author at the Barunga Festival, 1995.)

Female Tasselled Figures

In modern Australian culture, we recognise females by how they dress, how they wear their hair, its length, and by their anatomical features – the presence of breasts and broad hips with a narrow waist. Many Tasselled Figures wear long hair and are painted with slender muscular bodies, leading observers to conclude that the most elegant of these – particularly if they have long flowing hair – represent females. However, these interpretations are based on the application of modern Western values to an ancient Australian culture.

The majority of Tasselled Figures and other Bradshaw Figures are painted without male genitalia or female breasts because their elaborate ceremonial dress and headdresses clearly denote that they are males. In Aboriginal culture, females are not permitted to wear the *mudara*, *ngadari* or *ngumuru* headdresses.

Female subjects are defined by the presence of breasts, and generally wear no headdress, little ornamentation, appear smaller than their male counterparts, have fuller (fatter) bodies, and do not carry boomerangs or other items. Exceptions occur, and when they do, female gender is expressed by the presence of breasts in order to distinguish the subject from the predominantly male figures.

Traditionally, Aboriginal women often wore short cropped hair because it was cut and spun to manufacture hair string belts for the men. The women of some tribes also cut off their hair as a sign of mourning following the death of a clan member. Bradshaw artists depicted this spectacle with their depictions of women with bald heads and spiky hair.

Female Bradshaw Figures are uncommon, and female Tasselled Figures are particularly rare, with only three of the latter identified in nearly 2,000 Kimberley rock art sites recorded by the author.

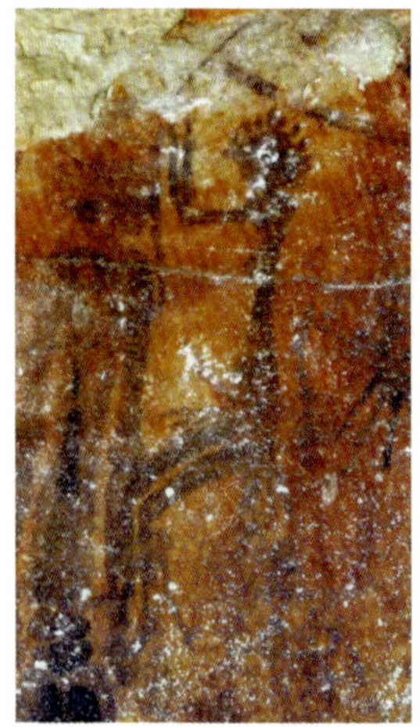

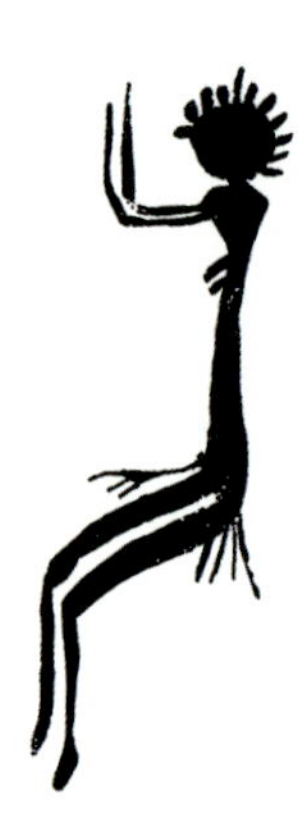

A rare female Tasselled Figure with spiky hair, raised arms, small breasts (two short lines from the chest), and lacking an elaborate costume. Lines to the left of the waist represent a small pubic apron. Height 35 cm.

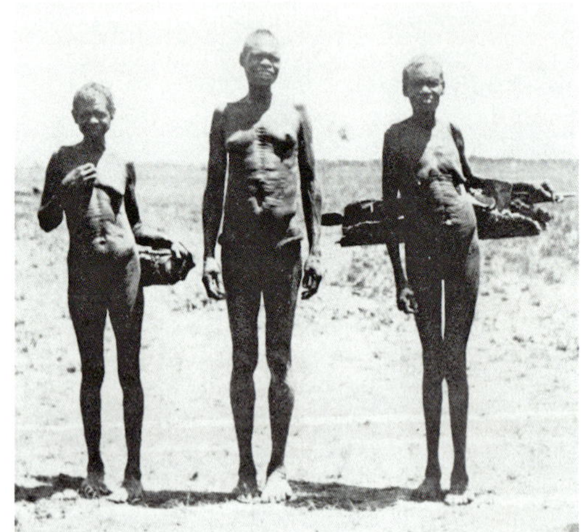

Northern Kimberley women with short spiky hair, holding bark carryalls. Circa 1916. (Photograph courtesy of the Battye Library, State Library of Western Australia, 65085P.)

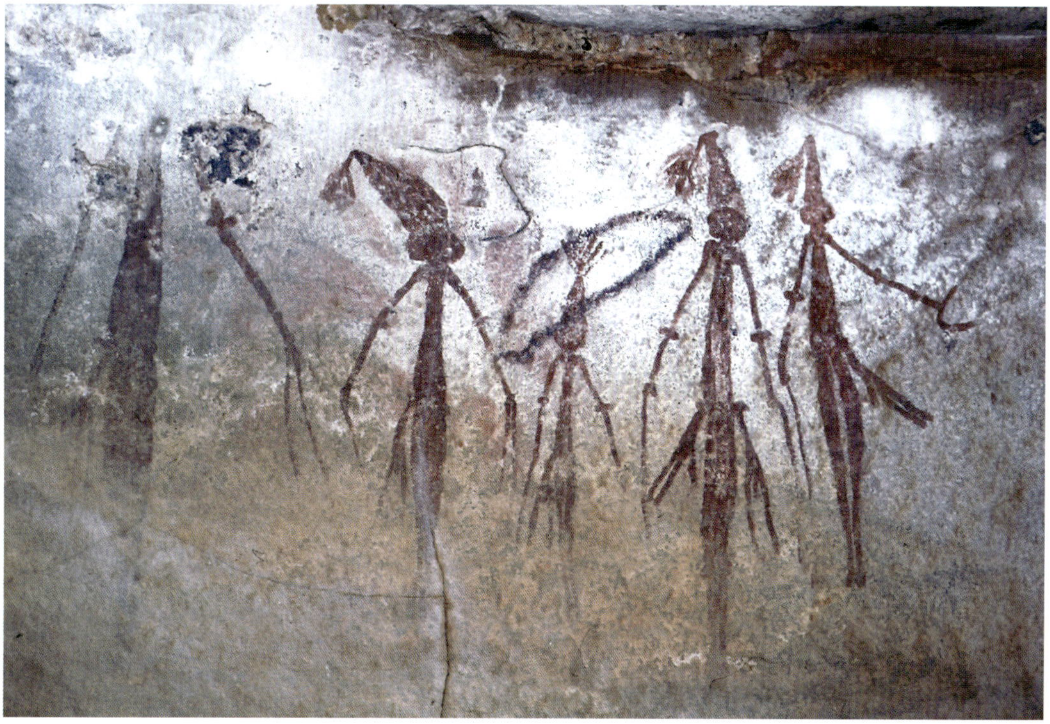

Tasselled Figures painted with a simple style wearing conical headdresses, simple armbands, and tassels from the waist. They carry lengths of string and the figure at right carries a small boomerang. Height of figure second from right 46 cm. Northern Kimberley.

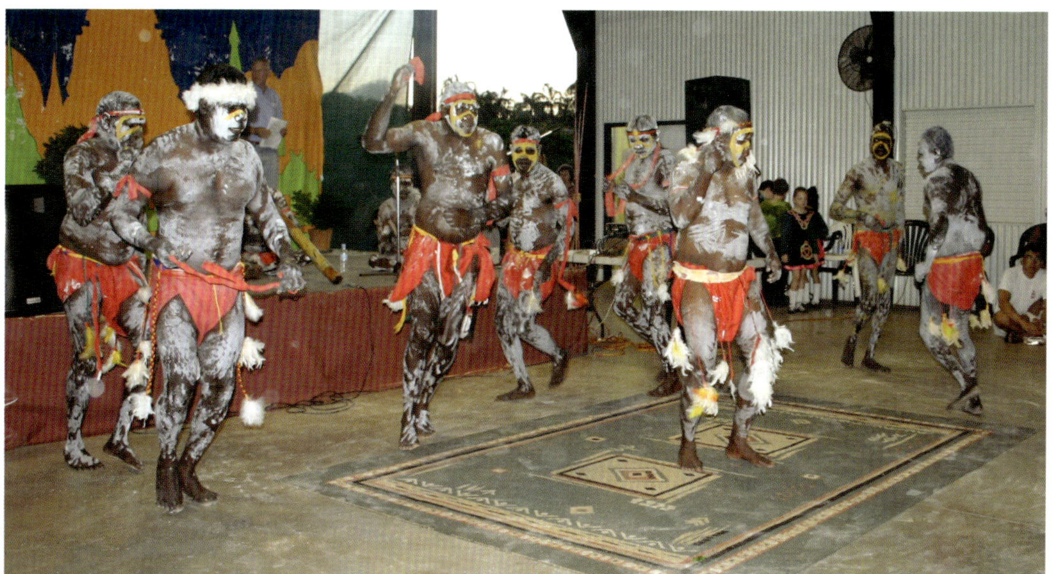

Arnhem Land dancers wearing simple armbands and tassels from their heads and waists. Some carry thin strips of cloth, replacing traditional strings, similar to the early Tasselled Figures above. Dance troupe One Mob, Different Country. Northern Territory. 2007.

BENT KNEE FIGURES

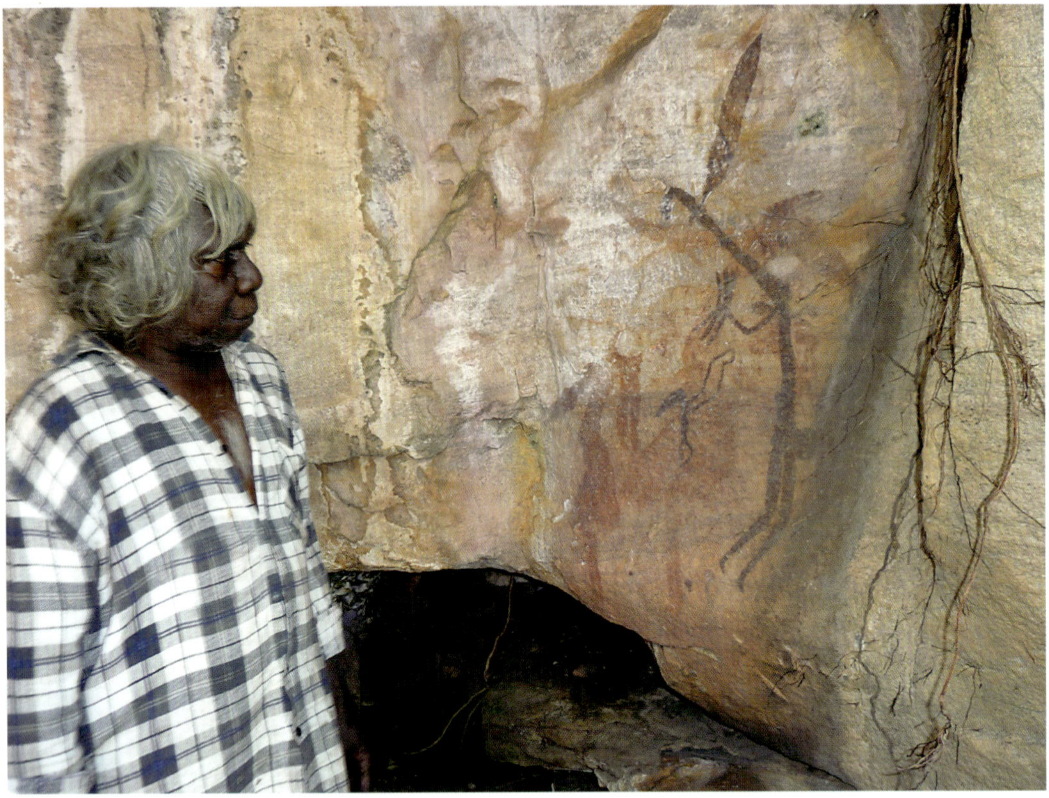

Gwini elder, Kevin Waina, with Bent Knee Figures near Kalumburu, northern Kimberley.

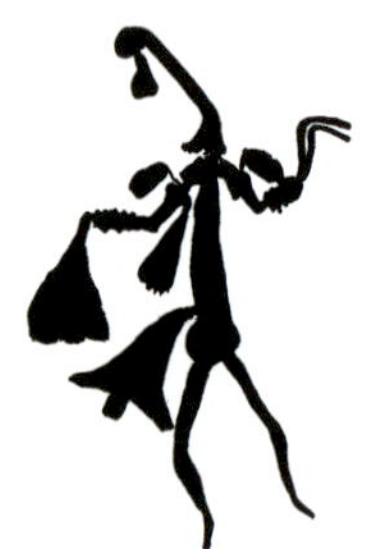

Bent Knee Figures form a second distinctive type of Bradshaw Figure with the following general characteristics:

- Most survive with monochromatic solid infill, painted in deep reds, brownish reds and purple hues. Occasional examples reveal gaps of banded body decoration, indicating they were originally painted in more than one colour, probably with white pigment.
- The majority wear a tall conical headdress, known locally as *ngadari*, made from rolled-up sheets of paperbark (*Melaleuca* species). Protruding sticks, feathers, and paired bird wings are also worn on the head.
- Triangular shapes representing feather and leaf bunches are worn from the waist and carried in the hands. Other waist appendages include hanging

branches, small oval shapes representing pearl shell ornaments, and large rounded items. Tassels are absent.

- Upper arm protuberances, appearing similar to epaulets worn over the shoulders, are unique to Bent Knee Figures. These were made by tucking folded leaves, emu feathers and other materials into the upper arm bands.
- Multiple forearm bands are frequently worn, giving the forearm a thickened ribbed appearance.
- One or two short curved boomerangs are carried in each hand. Other weapons which would have been used at the time, such as spears and clubs, are absent. The spearthrower is absent.
- The majority of figures adopt graceful poses with their legs bent at the knees, depicting traditional Aboriginal dancing positions.
- In a similar fashion to the earlier Tasselled Figures, Bent Knee Figures are mainly depicted with a combined perspective, as if partly turned to one side. Occasionally artists painted full-profile and full-frontal forms.
- Female figures are rare, and are recognised by the presence of breasts, lack of elaborate headdress, and lack of accoutrements. They are depicted shorter and fatter than their male counterparts. All Bent Knee Figures wearing long headdresses and carrying boomerangs represent male performers in ceremonies.
- When human-animal associations occur, the animals are depicted disproportionately larger than life, in relation to the human figures.

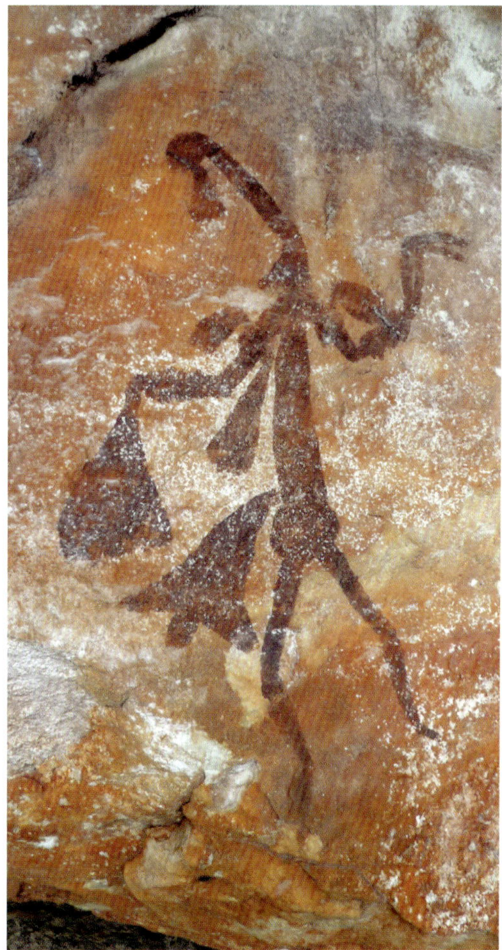

A Bent Knee Figure wearing a tall conical headdress *(ngadari)*, decorations attached to the upper arms, and triangular feather or leaf bunches hanging from the waist and upper arm. Two boomerangs are carried in one hand and a triangular feather or leaf bunch in the other. Painted in an uncommon frontal pose. Central Kimberley.

The bent knee position gives the figures the appearance they are floating and adds an ethereal quality to the art. However, its significance is realised when one observes traditional Aboriginal dance, where performers typically strut over the corroboree ground with their knees similarly bent.

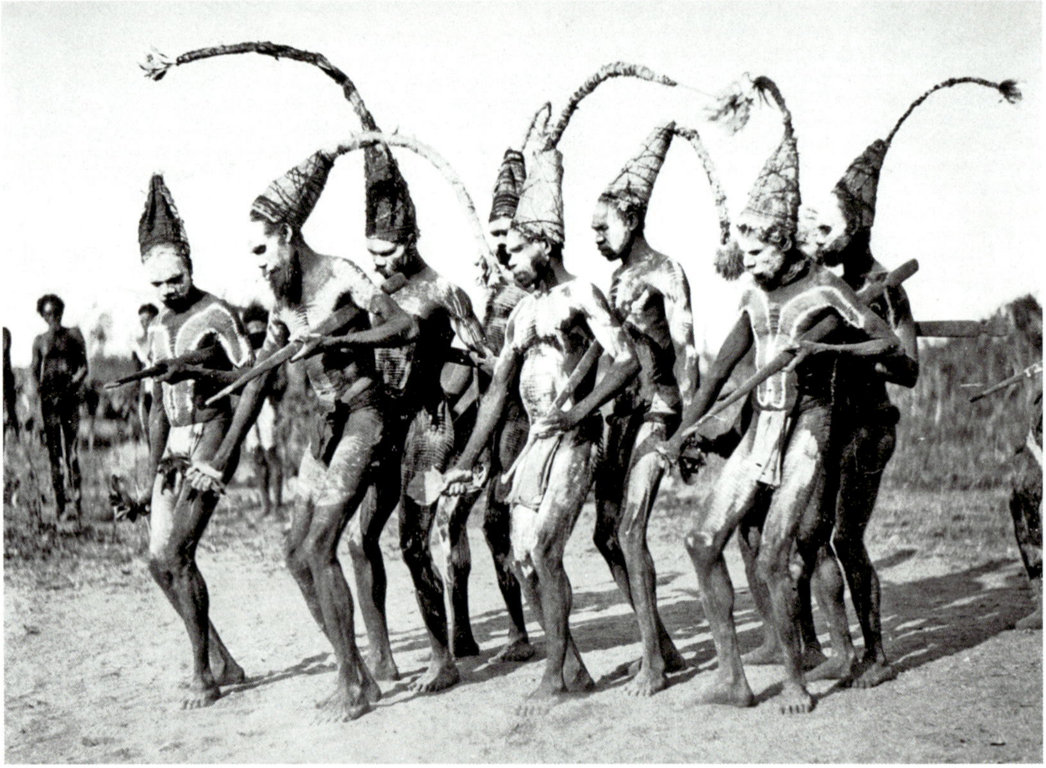

▲ Kimberley men performing a corroboree, wearing the long conical *ngadari* headdress and with knees bent, similar to Bent Knee Figures. Drysdale River Mission, northern Kimberley, circa 1920s or 1930s. (Photograph courtesy of Battye Library, State Library of Western Australia, 51235P / 71508P.)

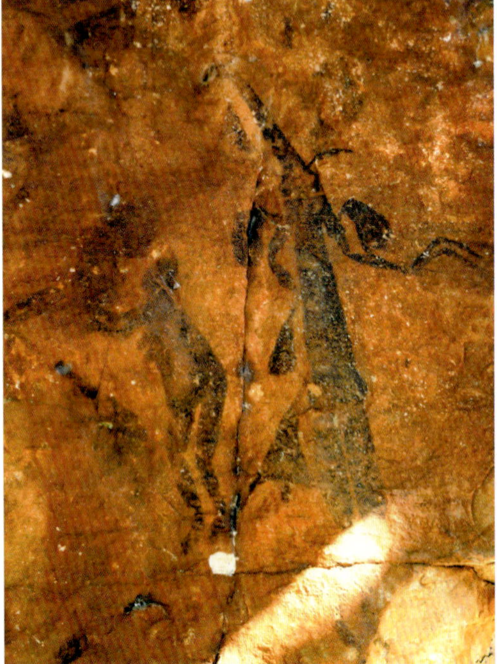

► Two Bent Knee Figures, one wearing an unusual arc-shaped headdress, each carry two boomerangs in one hand and a triangular feather bunch in the other. Located in the same shelter as the cover photograph. Roe River Valley, central Kimberley.

◄ An uncommon depiction of a *female* Bent Knee Figure (left) associated with a ceremonially-dressed male. The female is distinguished by her breasts, fuller body shape, and short stature, and lacks a headdress or other accoutrements. Height of male figure 47 cm.

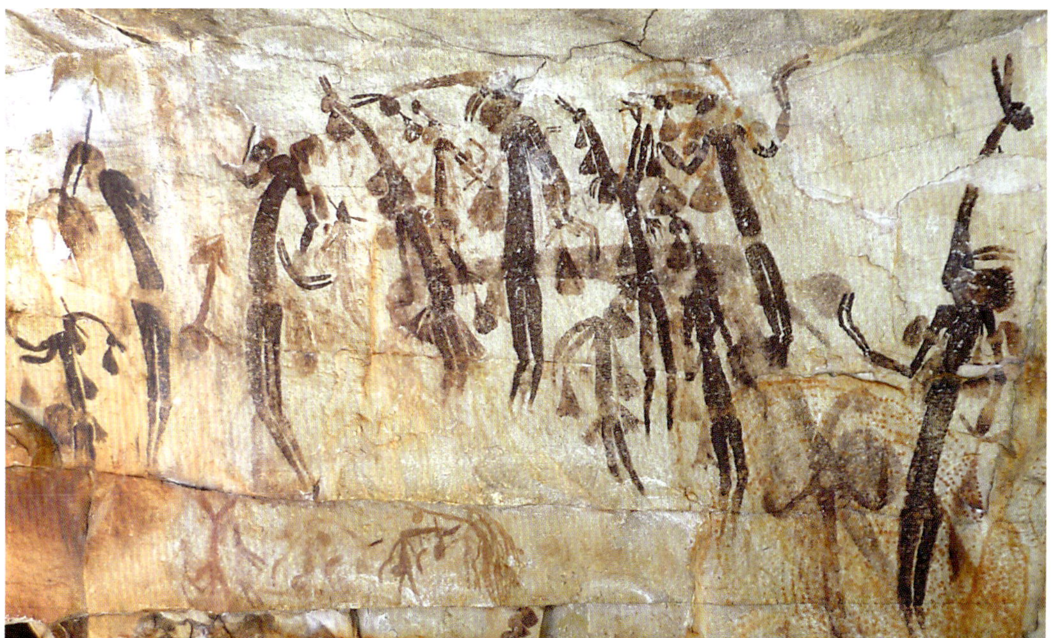

A group of Bent Knee Figures wearing tall conical headdresses with attached feathers and sticks, upper arm protuberances, hanging feather bunches and strings, a variety of dancing aprons, and thick forearm bands. They carry short boomerangs and hanging bunches of feathers or leaves. Mitchell River Valley, northern Kimberley.

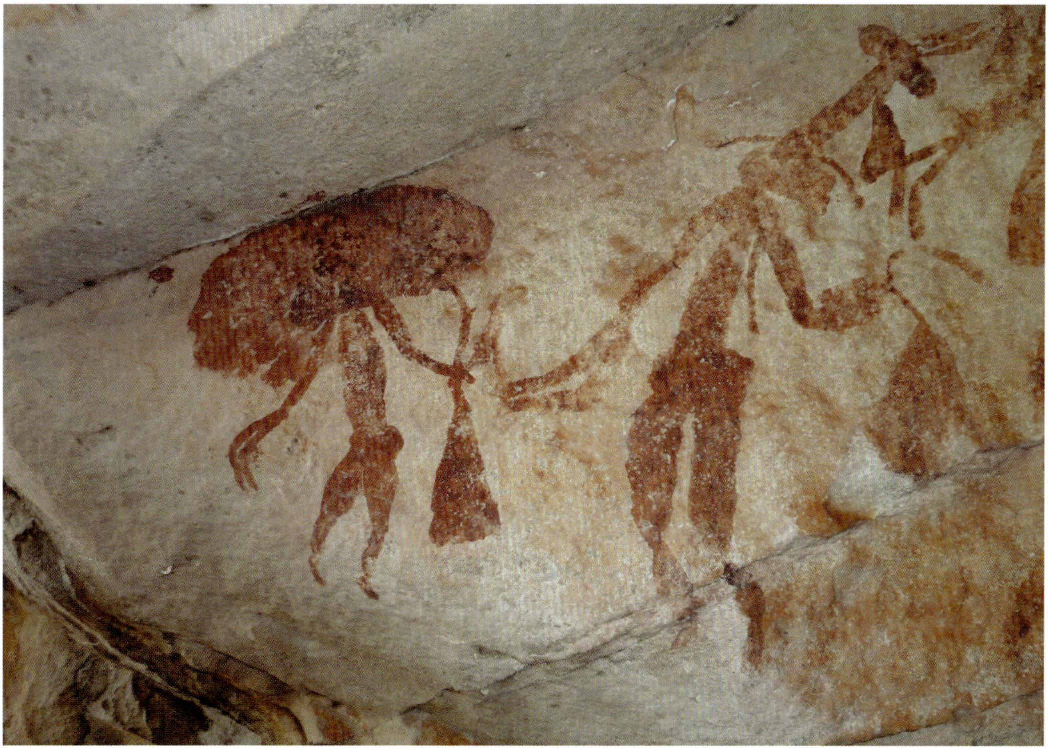

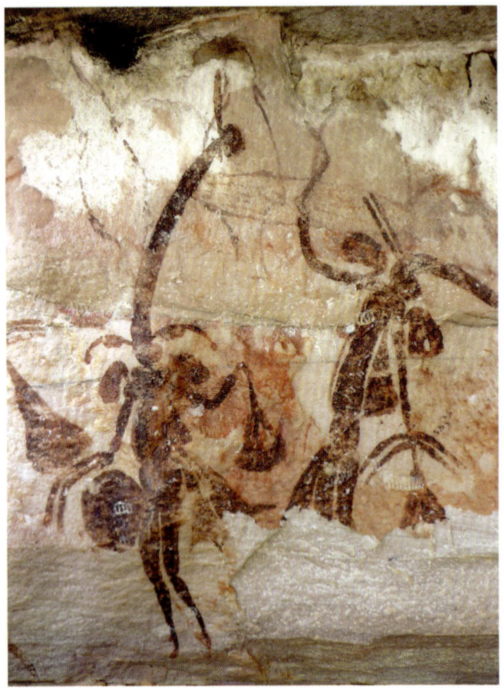

Bent Knee Figures wearing tall conical headdresses *(ngadari)*, upper arm decorations, hanging feather bunches, and rounded and triangular waist appendages. They carry boomerangs and ceremonial bunches of feathers or leaves. Height of left-hand figure 77 cm. Lawley River Valley, northern Kimberley.

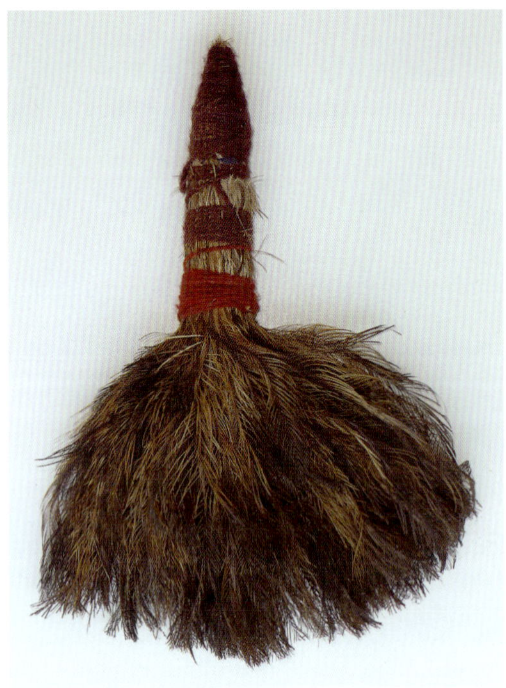

A ceremonial emu feather bunch carried and worn during ceremonies in Central Australia. Collected by the author in the 1980s.

Emu Feather bunches *(yululu* or *maltara)*

Perhaps one of the most enigmatic accoutrements worn by Bent Knee Figures is their triangular waist attachment, often with three points along the lower edge. This is most likely to represent a bunch of emu feathers gathered at one end and spread fan-like at the other, tied to a hair belt worn around the waist. Amongst Gwini people of the northern Kimberley, emu feather pendants are known as *yululu*, and stuck together with native beeswax and bush string.

Historic photographs show men wearing emu feather bunches during ceremonies held in Western Australia, Northern Territory, Queensland and South Australia, and I have three emu feather bunches amongst my collection of Aboriginal artefacts.

One historic photograph, taken probably in the 1890s, shows Dieri tribesmen (from the far north of South Australia) wearing this decoration during a dance performance. Emu feather bunches, known locally as *maltara*, hang down from their waists in a similar fashion to that seen on Bent Knee Figures and the occasional Straight Part Figure. The Dieri men also wear bunches of emu feathers tied to the ends of their headdresses, and carry ceremonial poles with emu feathers tied to the ends.

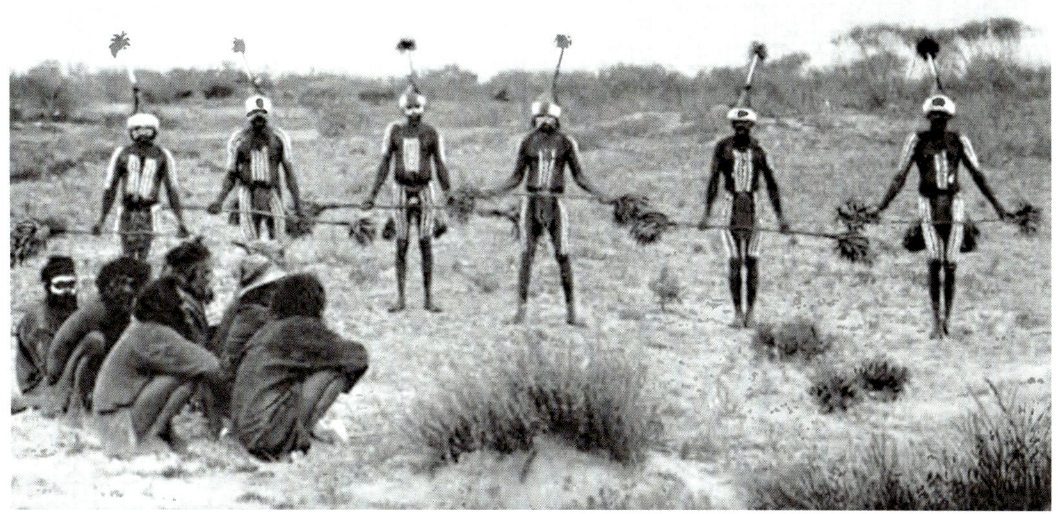

Men wearing tall headdresses, body paint, and emu feather bunches *(maltara)* hanging from their waists. Bunches of emu feathers are also tied to their headdresses and the ends of ceremonial poles. Dieri tribe, circa 1890. (Photograph from *The Native Tribes of South-east Australia* by A. W. Howitt, 1904, page 331.)

Clearer photographs of emu feather bunches worn attached to thick waist belts follow. In one, a Marranunga man from the Northern Territory bends forward, revealing a spray of emu feathers tied to the back of his waist. Overleaf, two Kimberley men stand sideways to the camera in order to display the items they wear. The man in front wears an emu feather bunch tied to the back of his waist, while the man behind wears a rounded upper arm decoration. These two items are worn by the accompanying Bent Knee Figures. Both men also wear a pearl shell tucked into their thick human-hair-string belts.

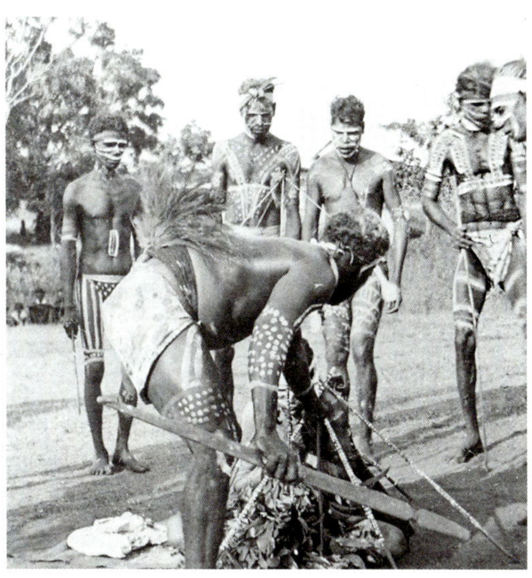

A man decorated for a funeral ceremony, wearing a triangular spray of emu feathers in his hair string belt. Marranunga tribe, Anson Bay region, Northern Territory, circa 1940. (Photograph by Jessie Litchfield, courtesy of the Northern Territory Library, Mayse Young Collection, 200/353.)

The photographs show different arrangements of emu feather bunches,

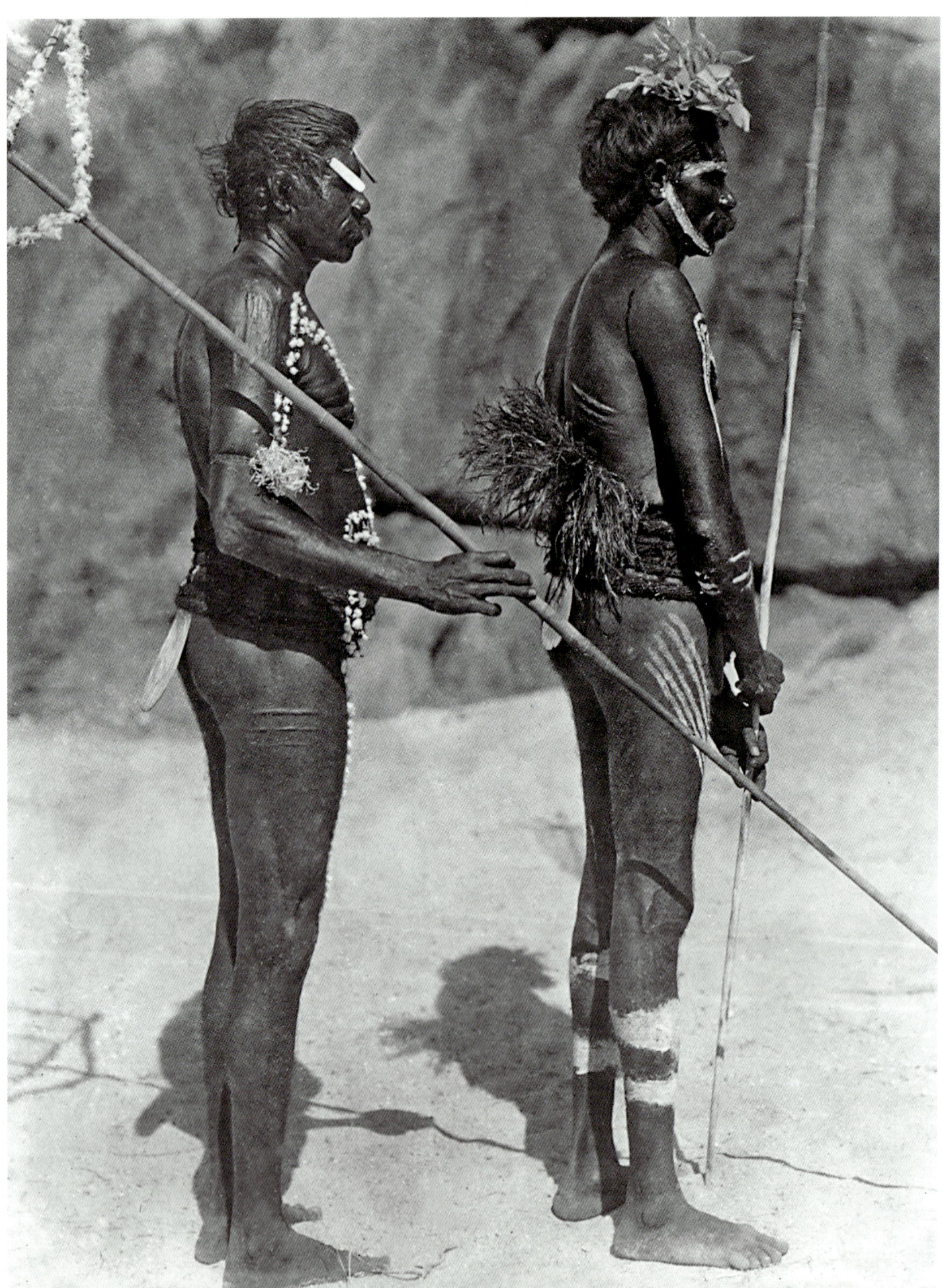

Bardi men wearing an emu feather bunch, rounded upper arm decorations, and forehead projections similar to adornments present on the accompanying Bent Knee Figures. Sunday Island, Kimberley coast, Western Australia, 1916. (Photograph by Herbert Basedow, courtesy of the Mitchell Library, State Library of New South Wales.)

sometimes hanging down, sometimes ruffled up. The emu *(Dromaius novaehollandiae)*, Australia's large flightless bird, is renowned for its three large toes on each foot. With this in mind, it is possible that performers sometimes gathered the lower border of the decorative item into three points, symbolic of the three large toes of an emu, and this might explain the three points appearing on the triangular waist attachments worn by Bent Knee Figures.

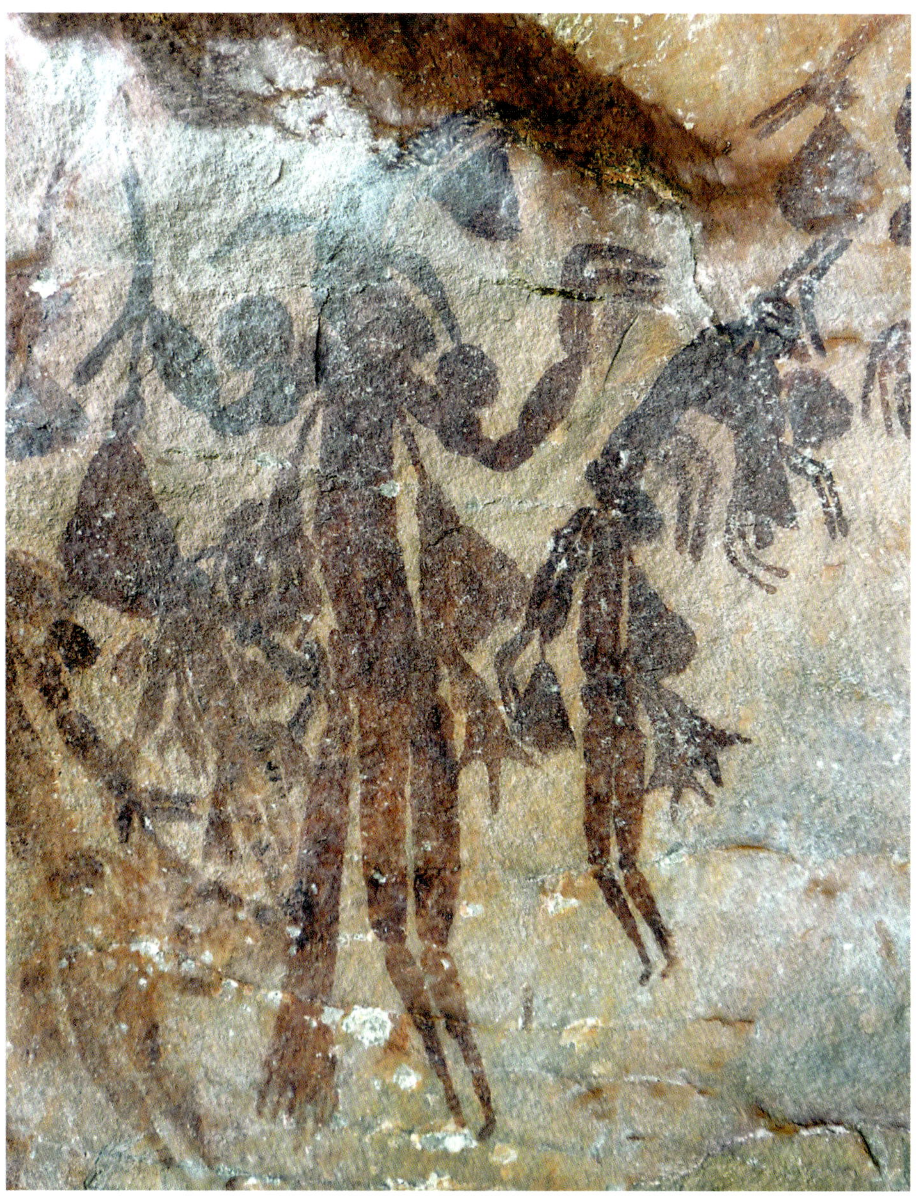

Bent Knee Figures wearing rounded upper arm decorations, triangular waist attachments with three points, forehead projections, and other ceremonial regalia.

KIMBERLEY DYNAMIC FIGURES

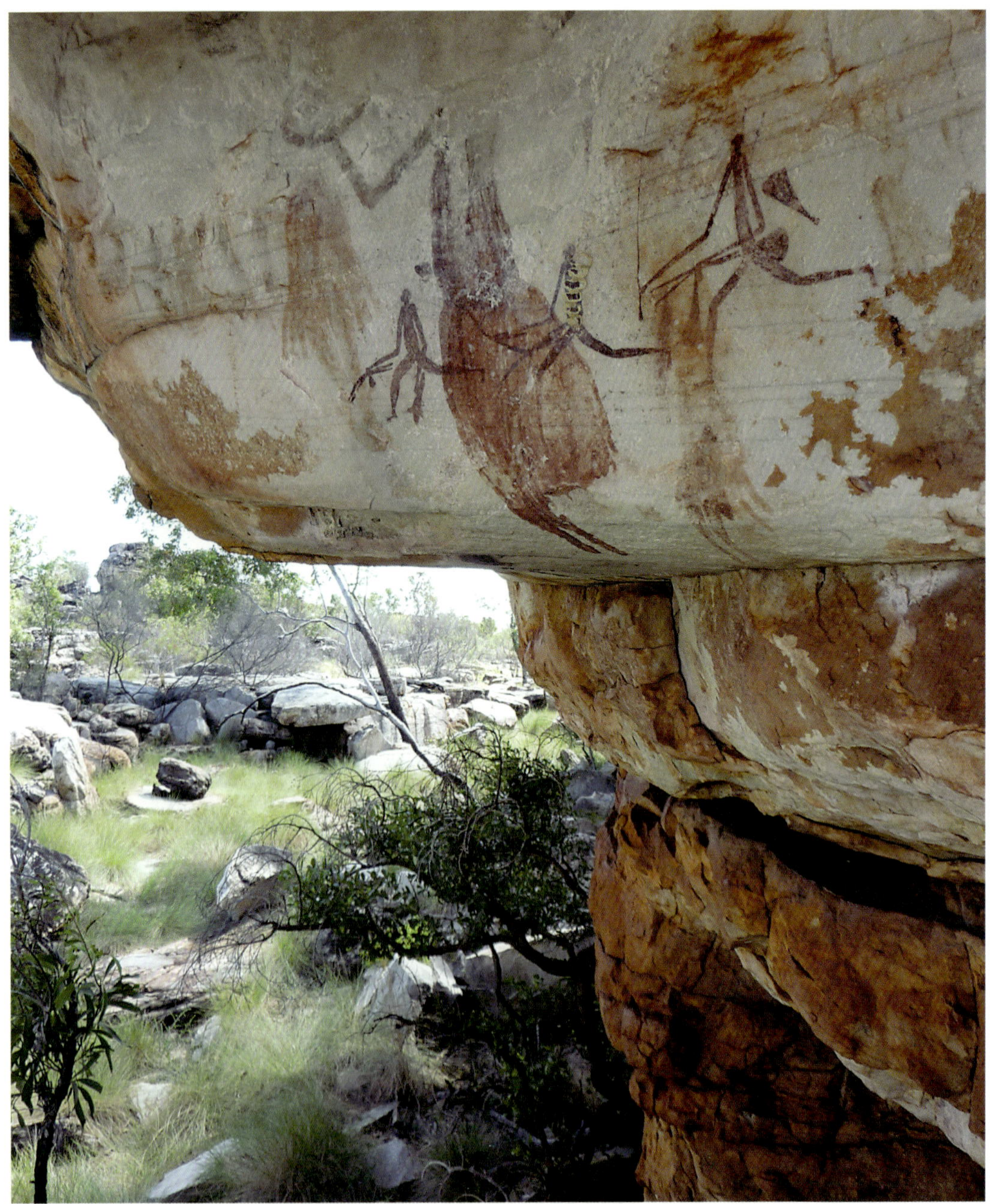

Three running Kimberley Dynamic Figures painted over earlier Tasselled Figures. They carry long boomerangs, small globular spirit bags, a club and a long wand or spear. Height of running figure nearest camera 24 cm. Northern Kimberley.

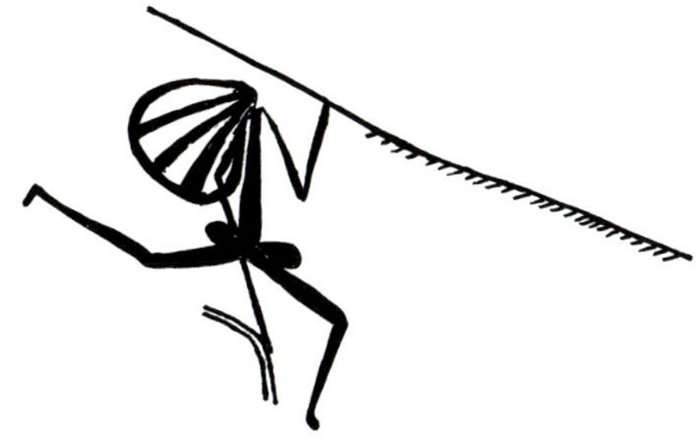

With so many elaborately decorated, ceremonially dressed human figures represented in the art, we may wonder whether artists occasionally depicted people carrying out more mundane, day to day activities. A significant group of early paintings consists of unadorned or minimally adorned human figures which appear to be engaged in a range of activities, including running with widely-outstretched legs, seated cross-legged, hunting kangaroos, and dancing. These are often smaller than the earlier figures and painted on the under-surfaces of rock ledges and overhangs. They generally appear brighter than the other Bradshaw Figures, being painted in a vivid orange-red colour, and are most common in the northern Kimberley, though they extend 180 kilometres into the central region.

The term *Kimberley Dynamic Figure* was chosen because of the similarities between these paintings and those of the Kakadu / western Arnhem Land region to the east, where artists have painted a distinct style of human figure, known as *Dynamic Figures* or *Dynamic Mimi*, also engaged in running, sitting and hunting activities. Kimberley Dynamic Figures and Arnhem Land Dynamic Figures both appear to predate the invention of the spearthrower, and are likely to be contemporaneous.

The characteristics of Kimberley Dynamic Figures are:

- Human figures appear unadorned or minimally adorned.
- Most figures appear monochromatic with solid infills. However, gaps on some figures indicate that artists occasionally used more than one colour.
- Running figures appear in groups, carrying long boomerangs, small globular spirit bags (used to hold ochre, quartz crystals and other precious items), clubs and spears.
- Spearthrowers are absent.
- Seated figures may occur in isolation or accompany running and dancing figures on the same panel. They are depicted side-ways with their knees bent up, or from the front with their legs crossed or knees bent and legs drawn under the body.
- When human-animal associations occur, the animals are depicted with natural sizes in relation to the human figures.
- Unlike the earlier artists who mainly painted on vertical panels facing outwards from the shelters, the artists of Kimberley Dynamic Figures often chose sloping ceilings and the under-surfaces of rock overhangs and ceiling steps to place their art.

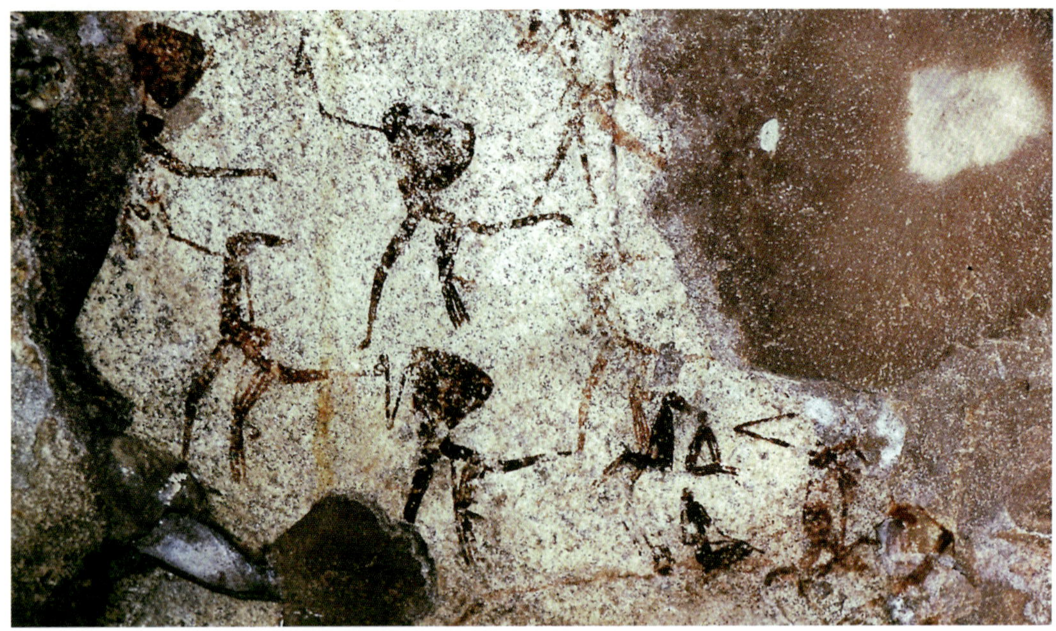

Running and seated Kimberley Dynamic Figures, in a hill-top shelter discovered by the author in the far northern Kimberley in 1992. The running figures wear large headdresses and carry boomerangs and small spirit bags. Their upheld arms once carried spears painted in less stable pigments. Height of lowest running figure 20 cm.

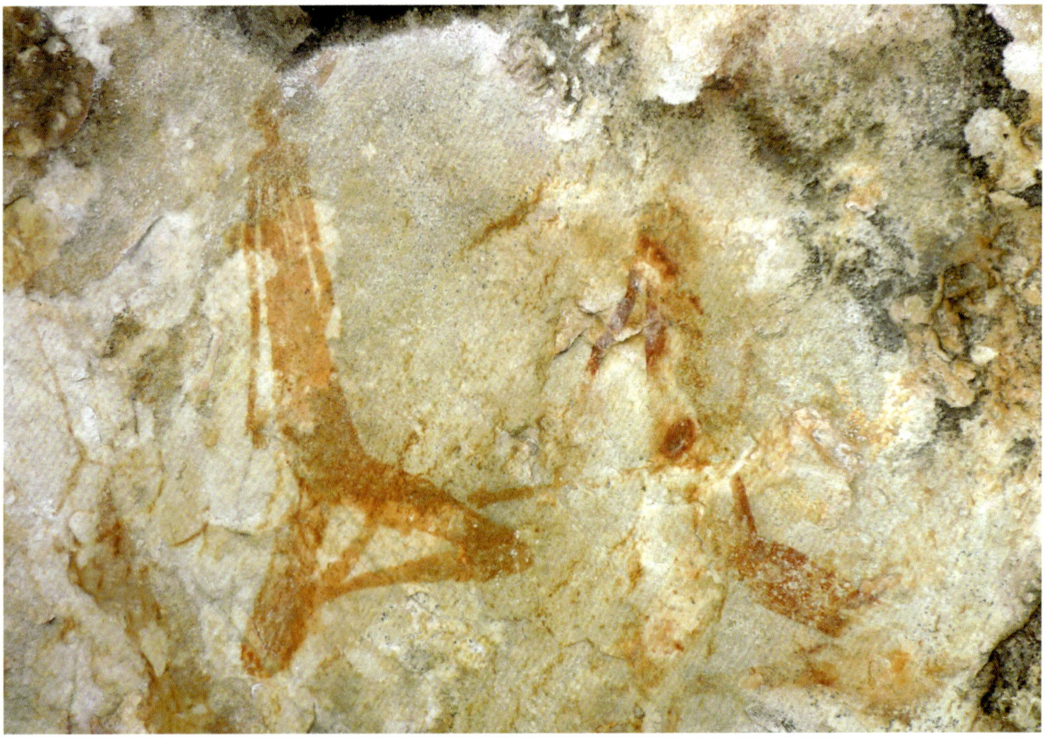

Kimberley Dynamic Figures seated with legs crossed. Height of left figure 48 cm.

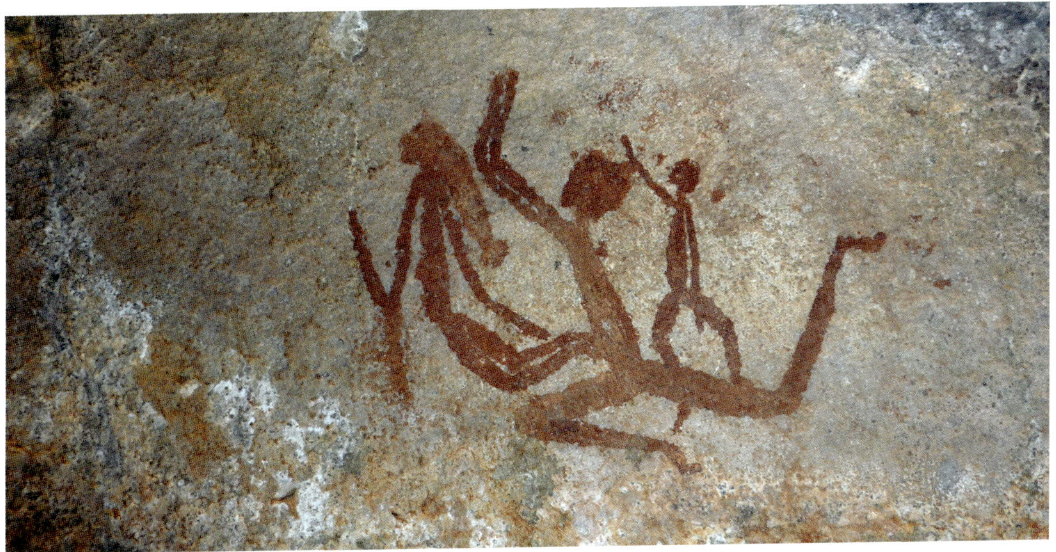

Kimberley Dynamic Figures engaged in dancing, painted on the undersurface of a low rock overhang, near the mouth of the King Edward River, northern Kimberley. Height of central figure 12 cm.

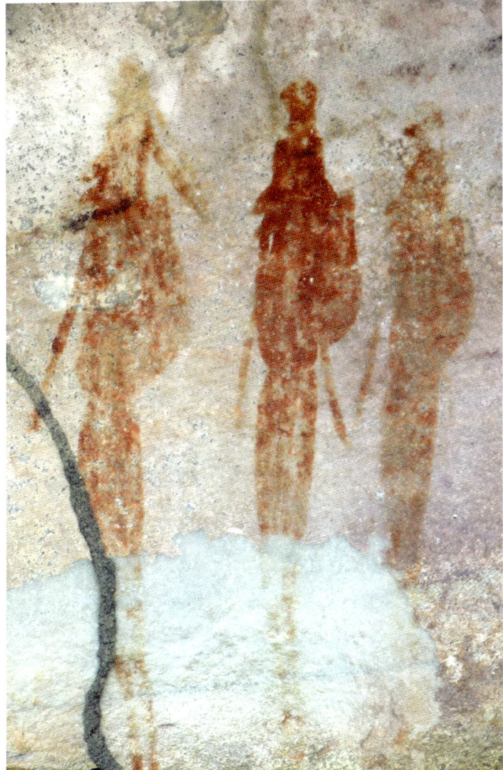

Women carrying large dilly bags over their backs. Kimberley Dynamic Figures, northern Kimberley.

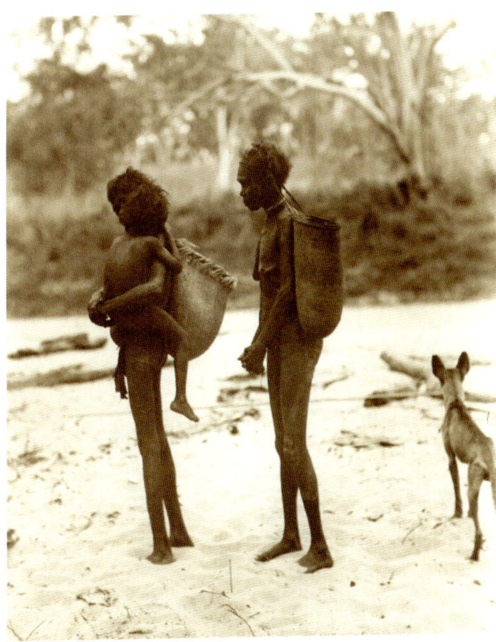

Aboriginal women carrying large dilly bags over their backs match the scene depicted in the ancient Kimberley paintings. Herbert Basedow took this photograph on the Liverpool River in Arnhem Land, Northern Territory, in 1928 and recorded that the bags were used when fishing and hunting. (Photograph courtesy of the Mitchell Library, State Library of New South Wales. Pic Access 5669, Box 1, No. 19.)

STRAIGHT PART FIGURES

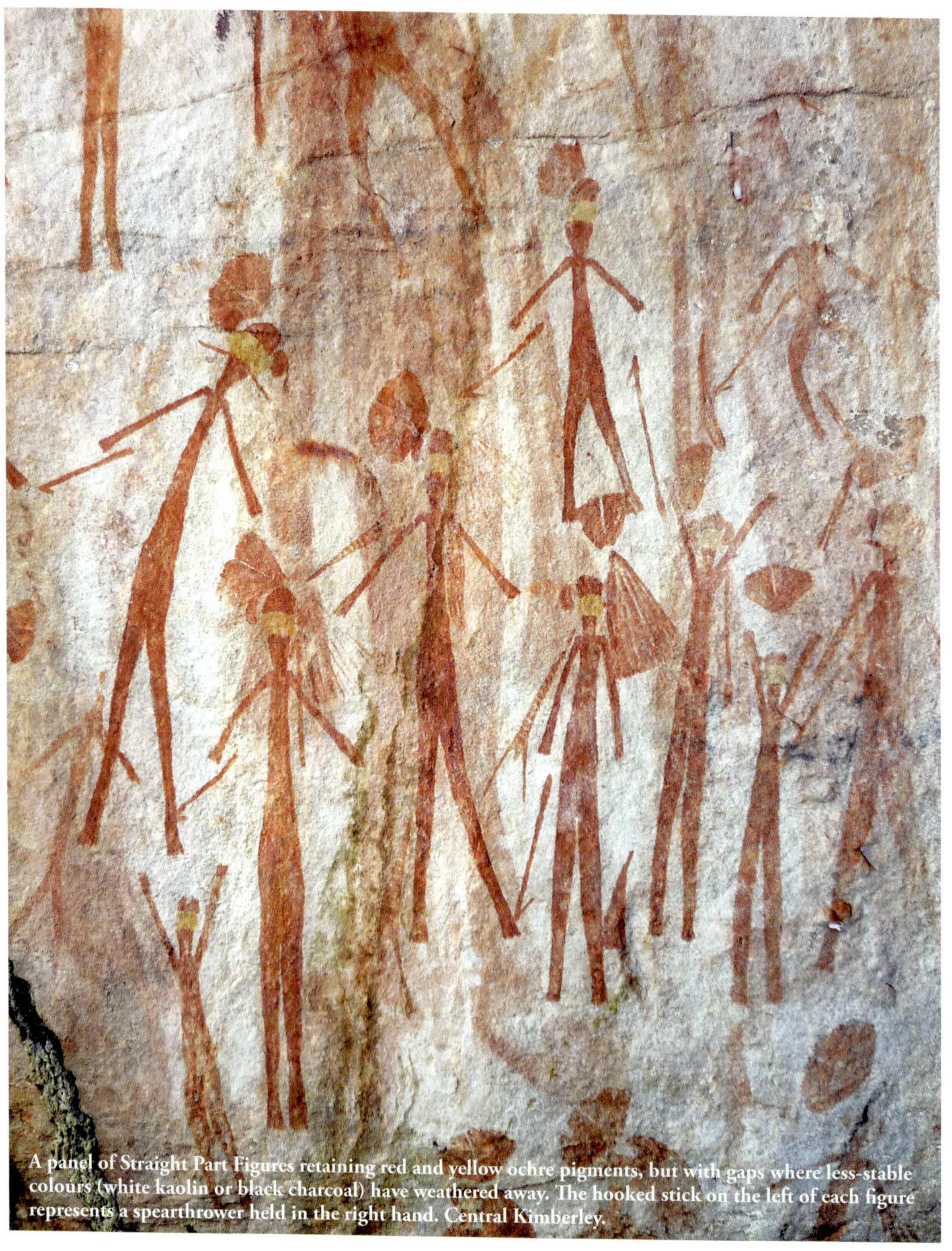

A panel of Straight Part Figures retaining red and yellow ochre pigments, but with gaps where less-stable colours (white kaolin or black charcoal) have weathered away. The hooked stick on the left of each figure represents a spearthrower held in the right hand. Central Kimberley.

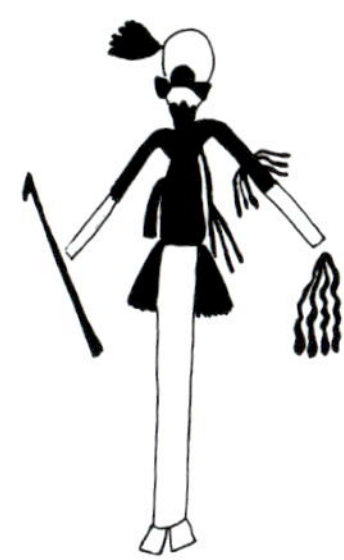

Midway through the Kimberly rock art sequence, artists changed their style of painting human figures from curvaceous muscular forms to rigid forms with straight body sections. Technical aspects of the paintings also changed, from predominantly monochromatic figures to polychromatic figures.

During this time, cultural changes occurred. Spearthrowers were invented or introduced, appearing as hooked sticks held in the figures' hands. A radically new headdress style evolved, with layers of paperbark now rolled into a cylinder, rather than the previous conical type. Local Aborigines have described this headdress to the author as a *barrel* or *bucket* headdress, or shaped like a *bishop's hat*. Its local name in the northern Kimberley (in Gwini language) is *ngumuru*, pronounced *noo-moo-roo*. Sprigs of leaves and other items attached to the frame of this headdress produce a striking appearance.

The important corroborees being portrayed by the artists across the region changed. Performers now held spears and spearthrowers during their dances, and stood erect, possibly shuffling in their dance steps. While some carried spears and spearthrowers, other performers carried hanging strings, ceremonial bags, and boomerangs, but generally with a spearthrower in one hand.

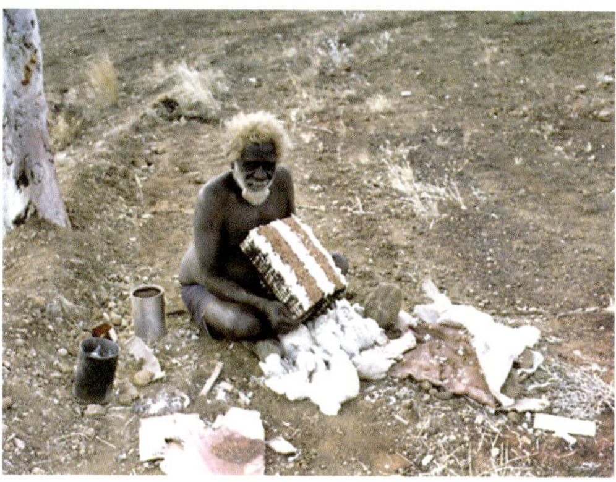

Mick Rallah preparing a bucket headdress, known locally as *kumundungu,* for a Mantiwar ceremony in Halls Creek in 1979. Modern materials, cardboard and kapok from a pillow, have replaced the traditional bark, plant down and bird down formerly used to make this item. (Photograph by Kim Akerman.)

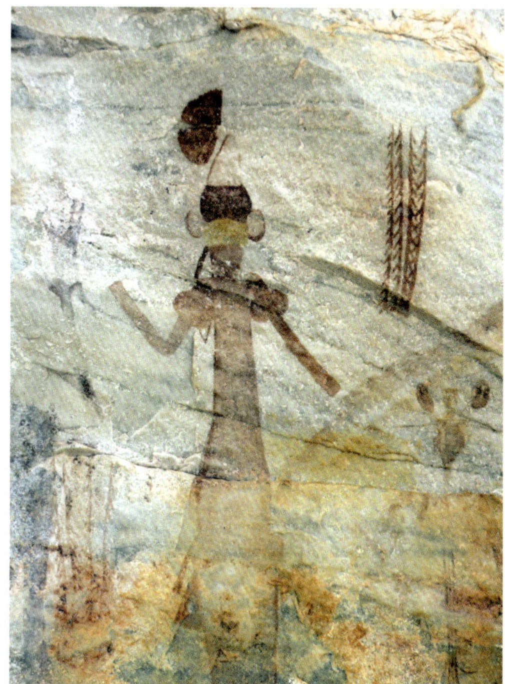

A Straight Part Figure retaining red and yellow pigments. Loss of white pigment has resulted in gaps along the forearms and spear shafts. Central Kimberley.

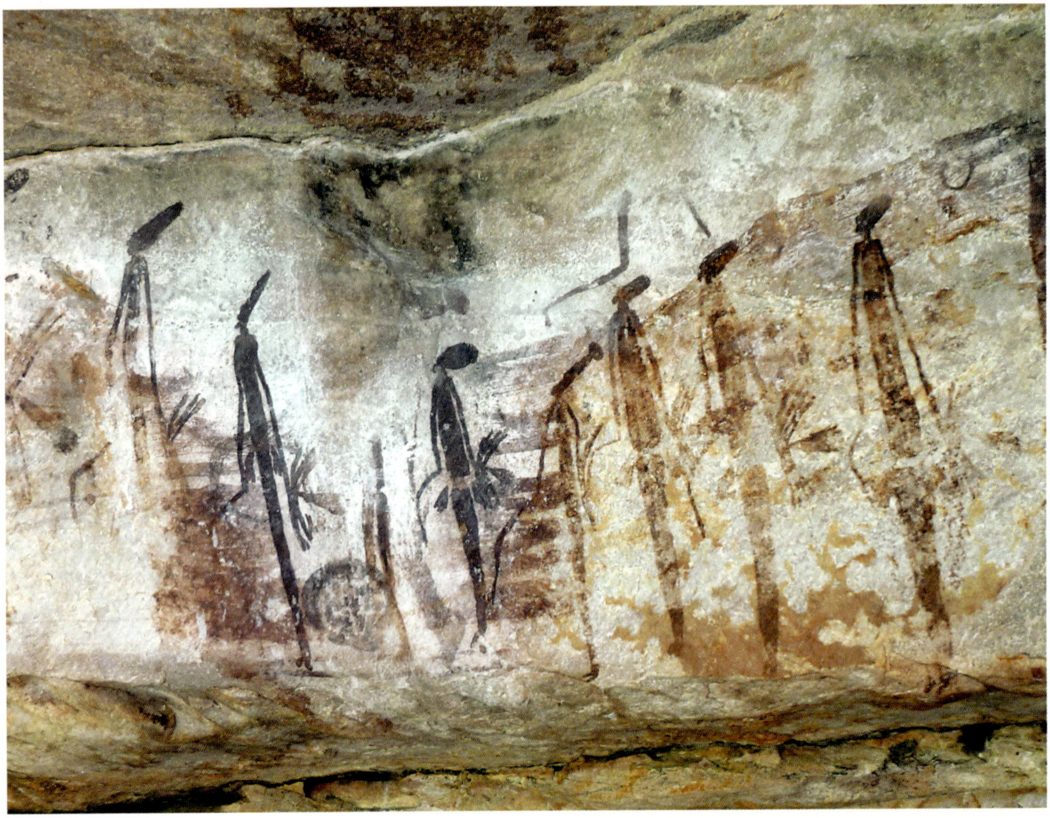

Early Straight Part Figures carrying boomerangs and small bunches of feathers or leaves. They have gaps of missing pigment at their waists, and pre-date the introduction of the spearthrower, which is common on later figures from this Period. Height of tallest figure 56 cm. Located in the valley of the lower Mitchell River, northern Kimberley.

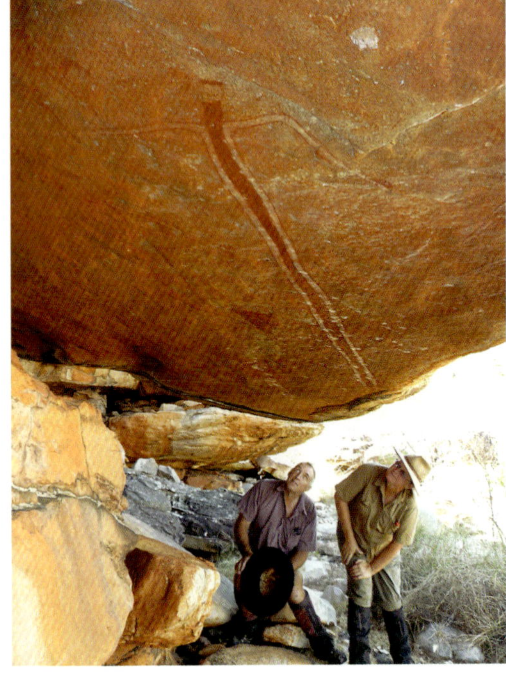

The tallest known Straight Part Figure, 230 cm long, with its discoverers, Lee Scott-Virtue and Dean Goodgame. Lower Mitchell River Valley, northern Kimberley.

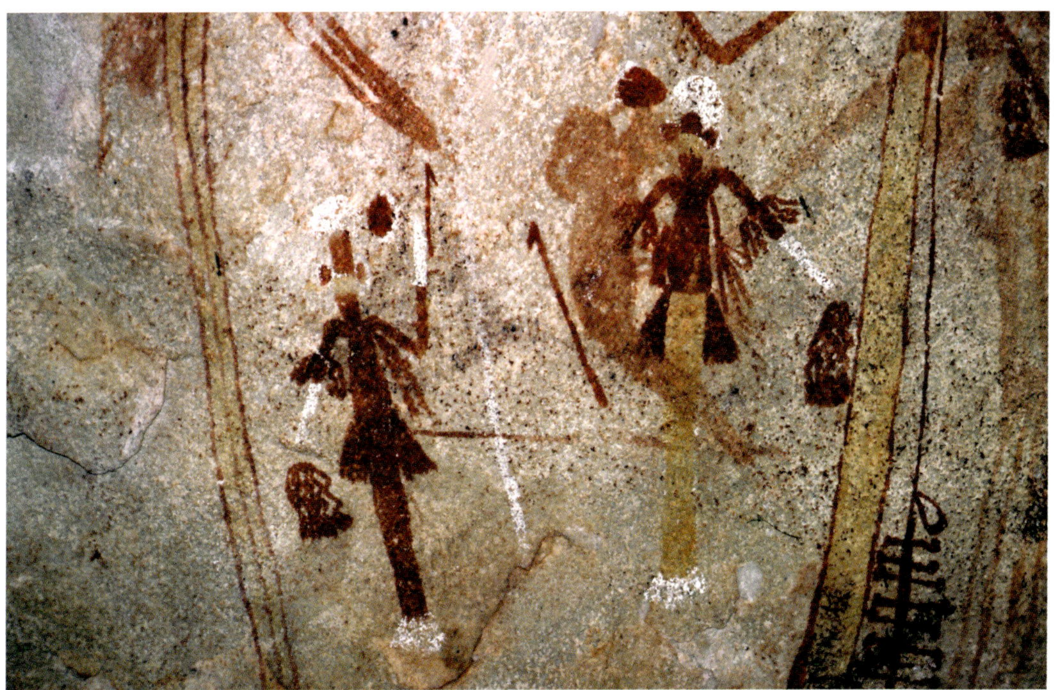

Two small Straight Part Figures placed amongst taller forms, painted in red, yellow and white. The left figure wears a bucket-style headdress, while the right figure wears a rounded variation of this. Sprigs of leaves are attached to these headdresses. Hanging strings and triangular leaf or feather bunches from the waist are also worn. Each figure carries a spearthrower in one hand and a bunch of hanging strings in the other. Heights 23 and 24 cm.

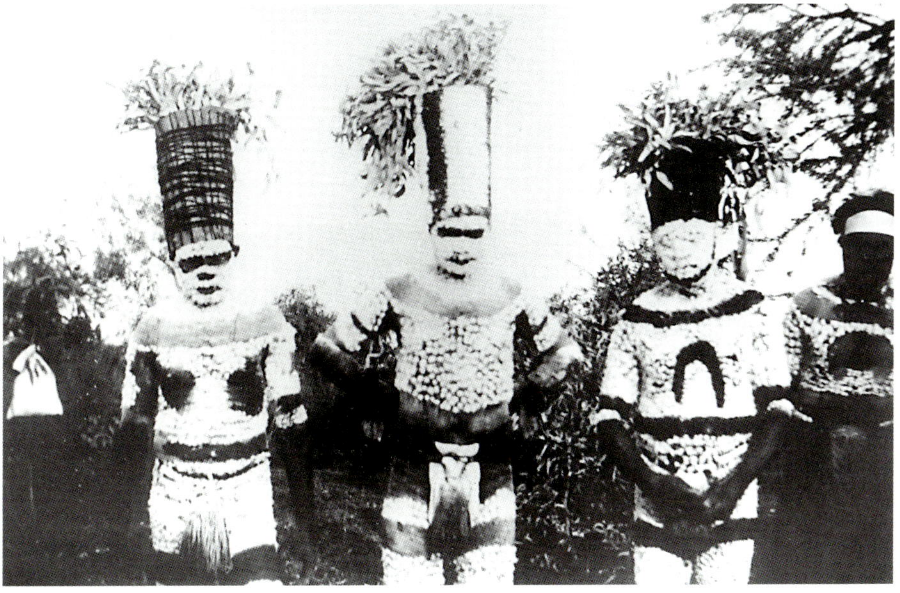

Three men dressed for a corroboree, wearing thick layers of bird or plant down body decoration, triangular waist attachments attached to their belts, bucket-style headdresses made from rolled-up paperbark, and sprigs of leaves. Brunette Downs, Northern Territory, 1935. (Photograph courtesy of the Northern Territory Library, James S. White Collection, PH 290/77.)

The general characteristics of this new art form, named *Straight Part Figures* after their dominant attribute, include:

- Frontally-aligned human figures, painted with straight sections in multiple colours – red, yellow and white. Limb musculature is absent, but some examples have a rounded paunch.
- Due to their age, the less stable white and yellow pigments have weathered away on the majority of figures, leaving gaps of missing pigment. These gaps are most common on the head, headdress, forearms, lower legs, belt line and spear shafts. Of the three main colours used, white is the least stable pigment and the first to disappear.
- The dominant headdress is the bucket-like *ngumuru* with a range of attachments. Less common headdress styles include tapering, conical, rounded and arcuate forms.
- The spearthrower is held in one hand, in a position consistent with the performer waving it about during his dance, rather than it being used offensively to launch spears. Early (older) Straight Part Figures lack the spearthrower.
- The range of paintings during this period includes ***Profile Straight Part Figures***, ***Parallel Line Figures***, ***Pre-Wandjina Figures*** and ***Oval-head Attenuated Figures***.

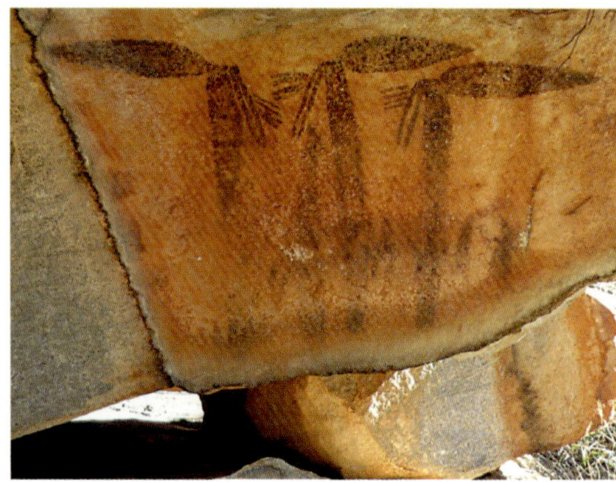

Profile Straight Part Figures wearing tapering headdresses and lacking spearthrowers. Central Kimberley.

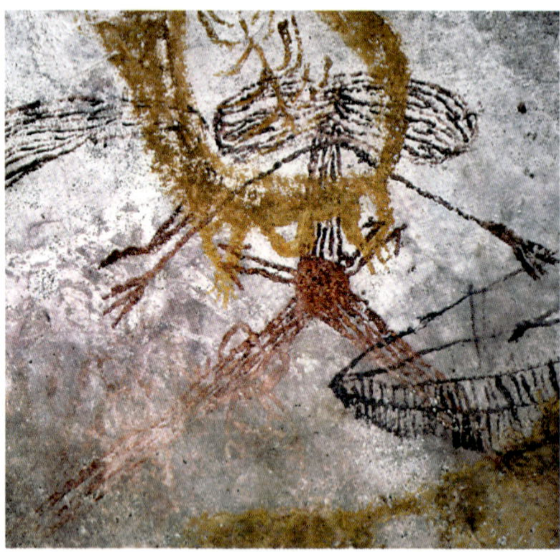

A Parallel Line Figure with outstretched arms and legs, carrying four spearthrowers in its belt. A yellow echidna from the later Painted Hand Period is painted over this.

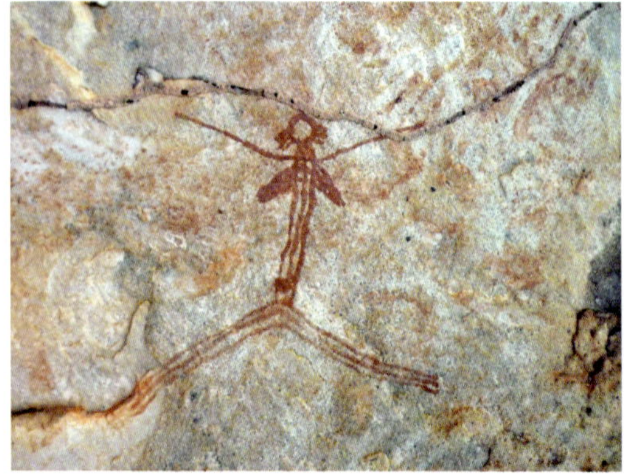

A rare female Parallel Line Figure, 26 cm tall, from the north-west Kimberley.

During the Straight Part Figure Period, new deities – mythical Ancestral Beings or gods – appear in the art. These include a range of Pre-Wandjina Figures, Oval-head Attenuated Figures, and other part-human, part-plant forms.

Pre-Wandjina Figures

Pre-Wandjina Figures wear an arcuate or horseshoe-shaped headdress, similar to that seen on the later Wandjina deities. However, their body form is completely different, being extremely attenuated and consisting of long parallel lines. Their overall shape, being bulbous at one end, and with a series of lines emanating from this, suggests they represent mythical ***Yam Men*** or ***Plant People,*** where the head represents a bulbous root vegetable and the lines represent its shoots and above-ground vine. Cleverly, the central line represents a human trunk and divides some way down into two legs. Parallel lines on either side of the central trunk represent the arms and generally finish below where the trunk divides into legs.

In a similar fashion to other paintings from the Straight Part Figure Period, the majority of Pre-Wandjina Figures survive with only their red pigment, and have gaps where less stable white and yellow pigments were originally used. Well-preserved examples reveal that their faces were generally painted white, similar to the later Wandjina figures.

In addition to being precursors of the later Wandjina deities, some Pre-Wandjina Figures retain traces of adornment from the earlier Tasselled Figures when they wear tassels hanging from the sides of the headdress.

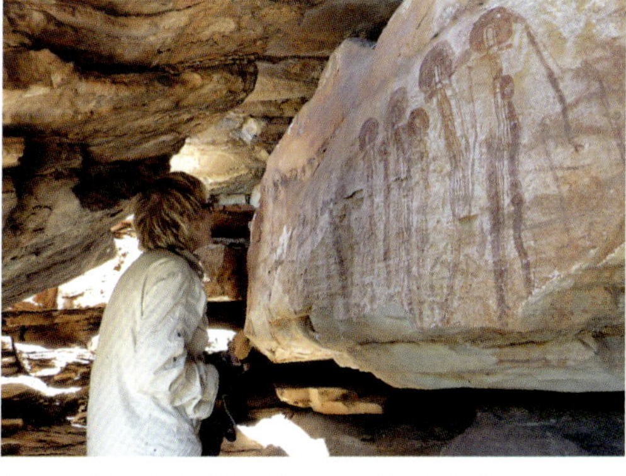

A row of Pre-Wandjina Figures with their discoverer, Ann Welch. Central Kimberley.

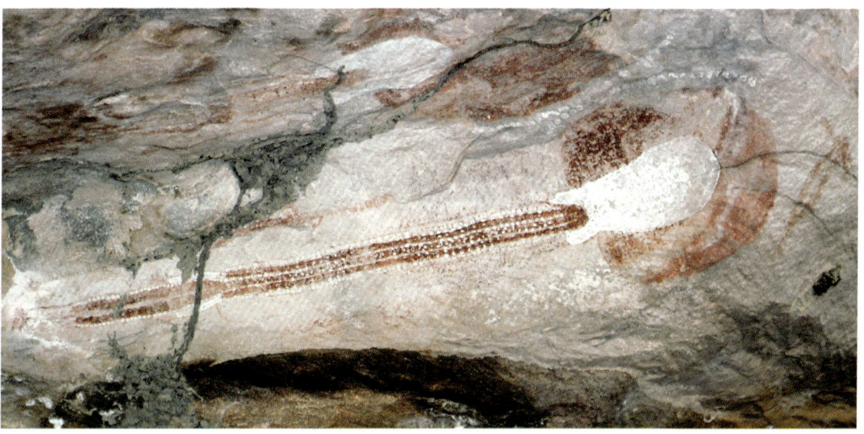

A Pre-Wandjina figure where white pigment is retained on the face, trunk and limbs. Length 113 cm. Central Kimberley.

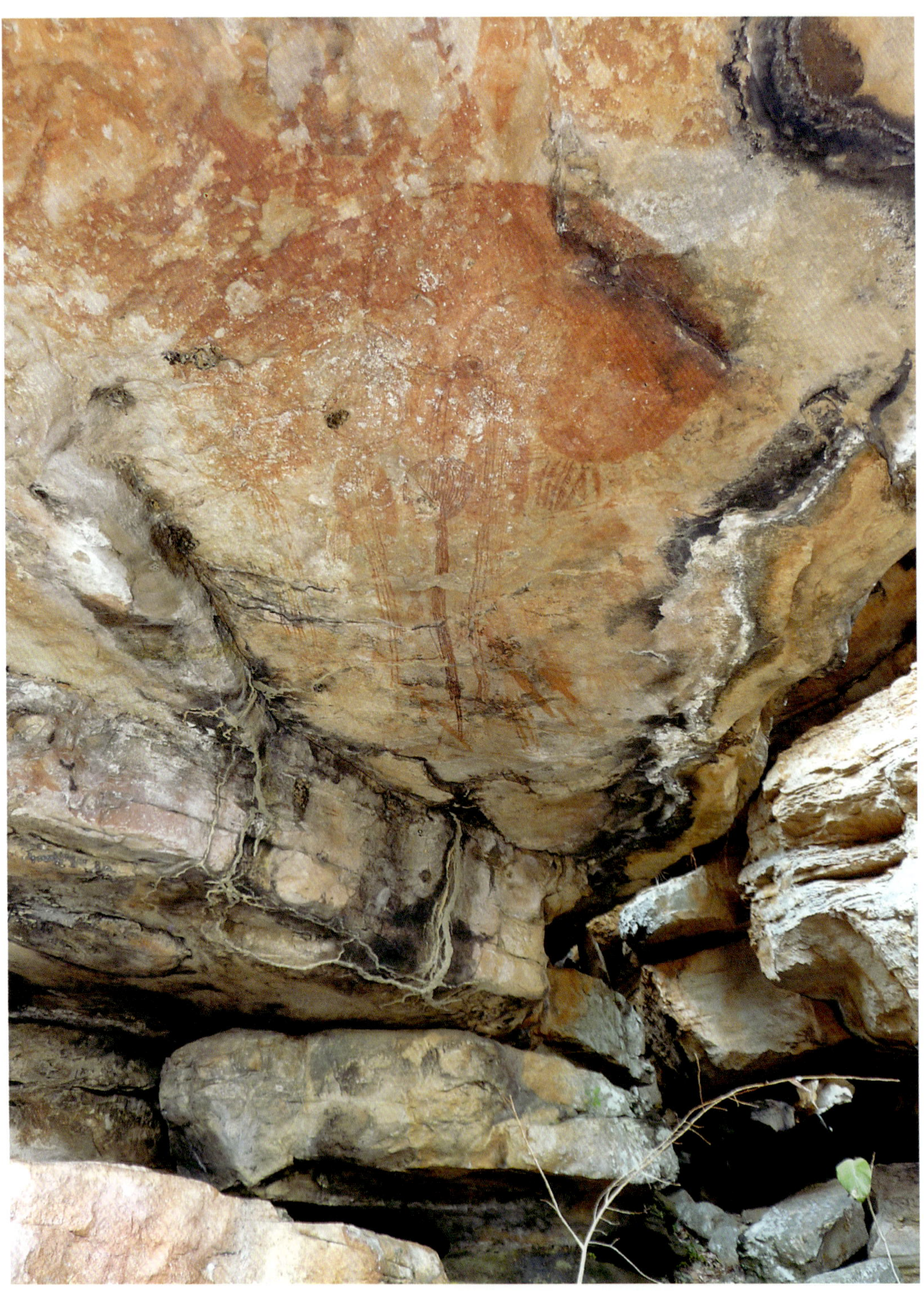

A shelter ceiling containing the largest-known Pre-Wandjina Figure, with a headdress width of 120 cm. Tassels hang from its sides. Smaller Pre-Wandjina Figures and Straight Part Figures also adorn the ceiling. Central Kimberley.

Oval-head Attenuated Figures

As with Pre-Wandjina Figures, Oval-head Attenuated Figures have a bulbous head at one end and a series of parallel lines extending from this, representing both the shoots of a yam (or other bush food) and the trunk and limbs of a human. These Plant People appear throughout the central and northern Kimberley, often painted on shelter ceilings, and generally with only red pigment surviving. Remarkably well-preserved examples, painted alongside Pre-Wandjina Figures, were discovered by the author on the ceiling of a deep shelter positioned above a scree slope at the base of high cliffs in the central Kimberley.

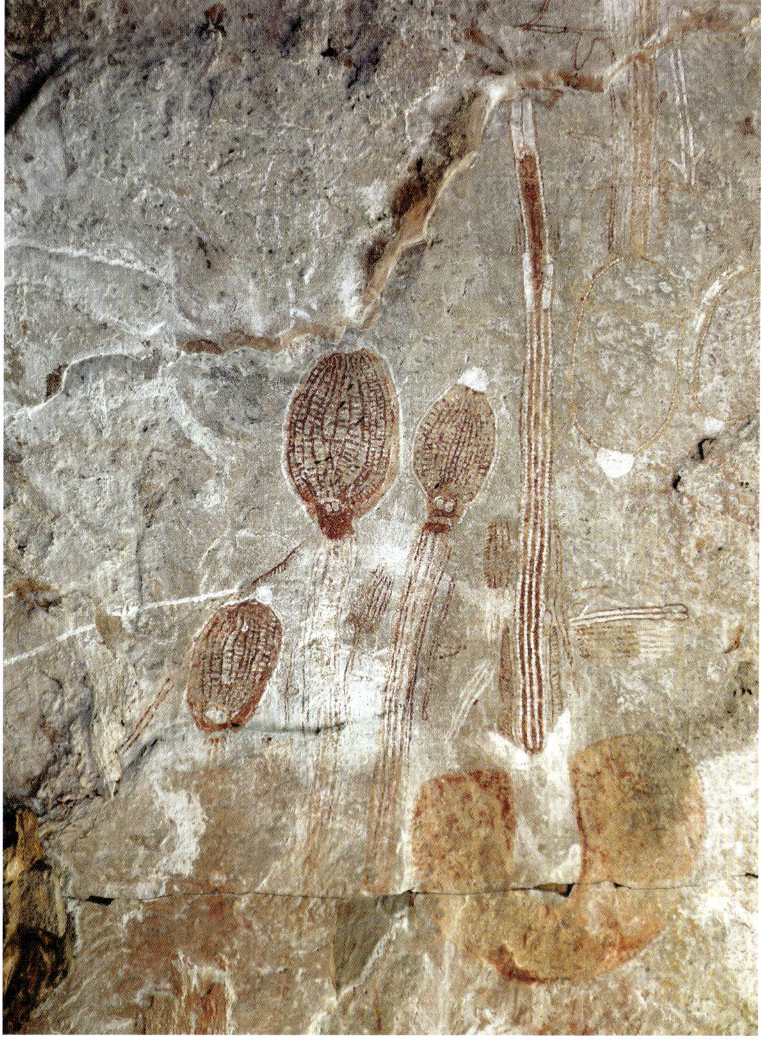

Three Oval-head Attenuated Figures, each with a set of two eyes, showing remarkable detail and preservation on a well-protected shelter ceiling. To the right is a Pre-Wandjina Figure with an arcuate, Wandjina-like headdress. (Turn the page upside down to appreciate this figure.)

THE PAINTED HAND PERIOD

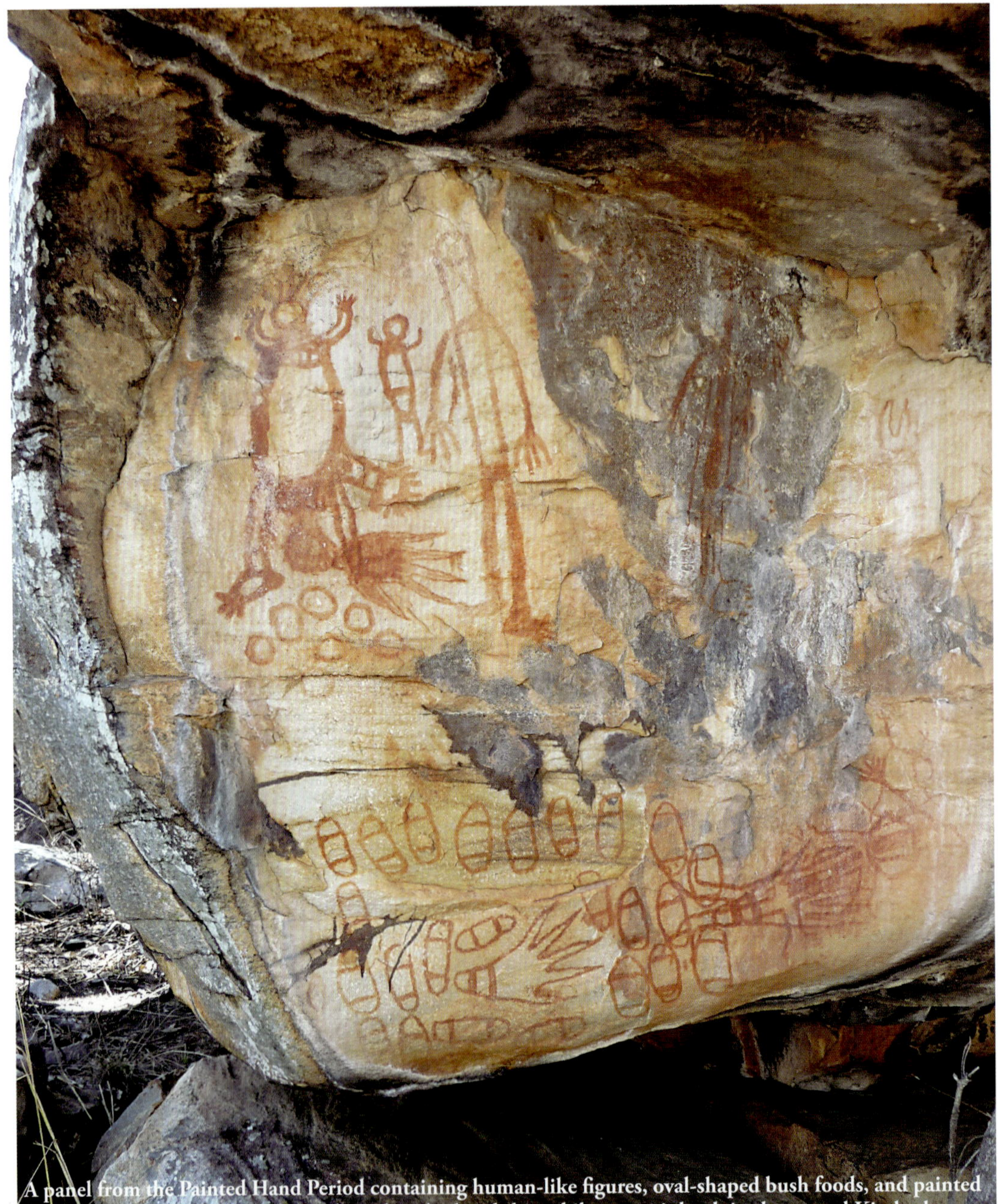

A panel from the Painted Hand Period containing human-like figures, oval-shaped bush foods, and painted hands with long fingernails, located one hundred and thirty kilometres inland, in the central Kimberley. Features of this art period include the bright orange-red colour, crude depiction of motifs, simple outline of the subjects, and use of transverse lines crossing within the body of the subject.

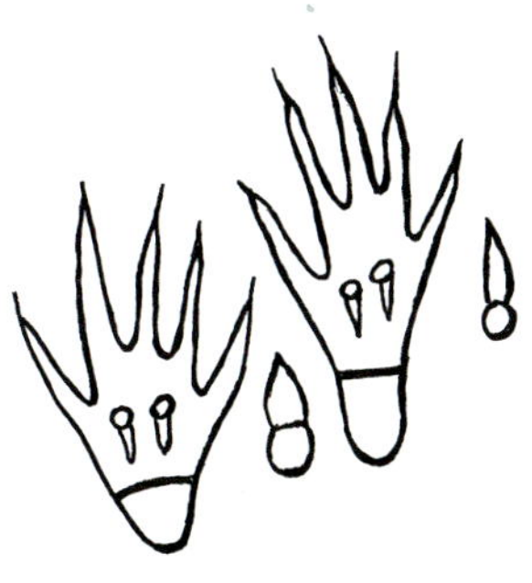

The Painted Hand Period marks a further shift in artistic style, technique in the application of pigments, and choice of colours, from the earlier Bradshaw Figures. During this time, artists changed from more refined art styles to less refined, more elementary representations of their subjects. Departing from the use of fine lines, they now employed thick bold outlines to paint their subjects in simple, stylised, more abstract forms. A new style of infill also emerged, with the placement of transverse lines across the frame of the outline, resulting in subjects appearing segmented. Grid patterns were also employed. In some examples, blocks of colour were used, drawing from the influence of the Straight Part Figure Period. Lastly, the choice of colour for the majority of paintings during this time was a bright orange-red, similar to the colour chosen by artists of the Kimberley Dynamic Figure Period.

The subjects chosen by artists during the Painted Hand Period include animals (crocodiles, lizards, snakes, echidnas, macropods (kangaroos and wallabies), possums, thylacines, turtles and fish), plants (fruit, berries, vines, roots, yams), human-like figures, animal tracks (particularly macropod tracks) and human hands. This art style appears throughout the quartzite regions of the central and northern Kimberley, stretching some three hundred kilometres north-south and two hundred kilometres east-west.

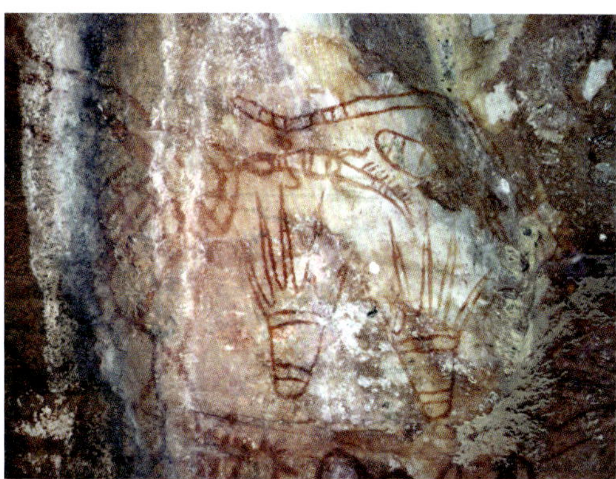

A snake, crocodile, oval bush food, and two painted hands with long fingernails.

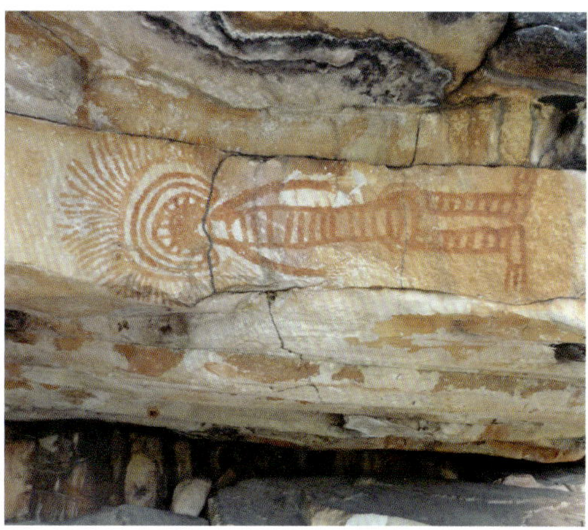

A human figure painted in the horizontal position wearing an arcuate Wandjina-like headdress with radiating lines. Length 116 cm. Painted Hand Period.

Unlike *hand stencils* (where pigment is sprayed from the mouth over a hand placed on the rock surface) and *hand prints* (where wet pigment is applied to the palm of the hand and this is then pressed onto the rock surface), the *painted hands* from this Period are freehand drawings depicting the human hand, close to life-size.

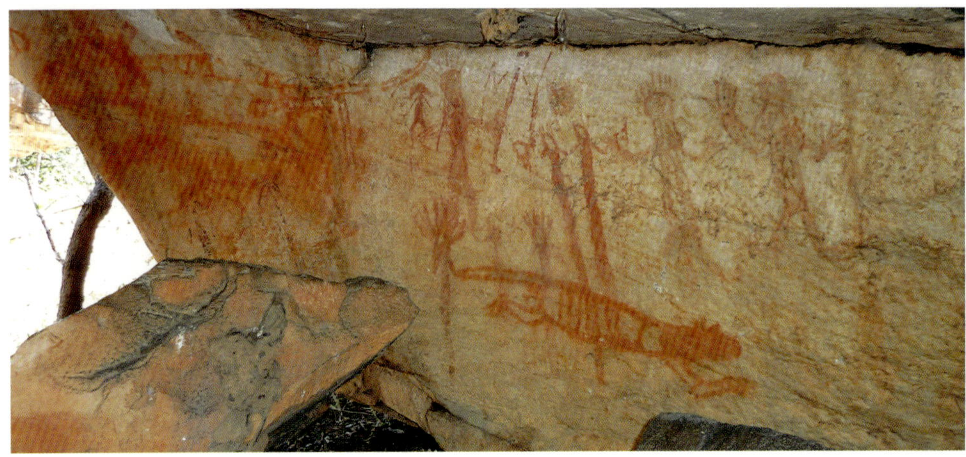

Two thylacines (Tasmanian tigers) painted over earlier Straight Part Figures. The animals are identified as thylacines by their dog-like body shape, stiff tails and stripes. Note the running pose with widely-outstretched legs on the lower right figure. Roe River Valley. Top left thylacine 86 cm long. Lower right thylacine 62 cm.

Artists from this period generally produced story panels composed of several different motifs. In the central Kimberley, painted hands with long attenuated fingers and fingernails often appear alongside bush foods.

The presence of long fingers and long fingernails is interpreted by local Aborigines in different ways. For some, they signify the devil and the paintings are regarded as a warning of evil. For others, the long fingers and fingernails are regarded as being useful for digging into the ground to reach yams and other edible root vegetables. The paintings are thought to represent the hands of the artists, showing others the food available in their clan estates.

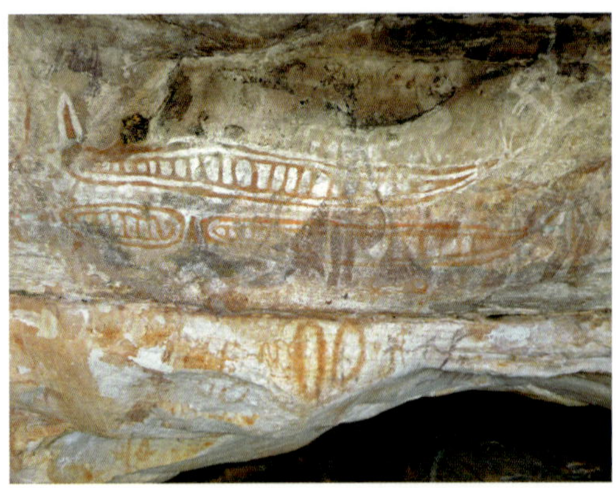

Two long yams painted with bold white outline and thick orange-red transverse lines giving them a segmented appearance. Their shoots are at the right and feet-like projections representing tubers are to the left. Painted Hand Period art, painted over earlier Bent Knee Figures. Length of upper yam 95 cm. Northern Kimberley.

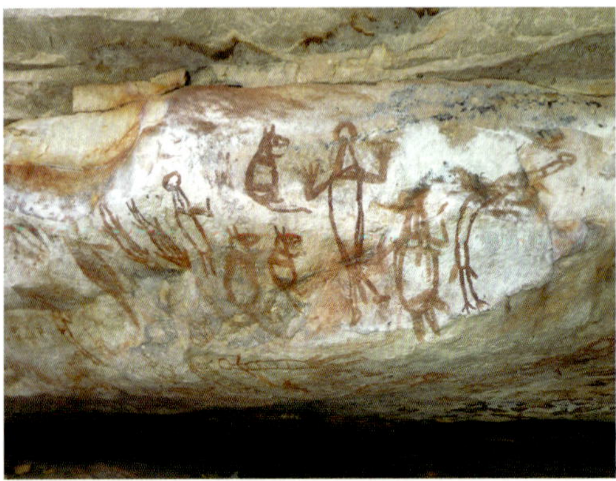

A panel of art from the Painted Hand Period containing fish, macropods and human-like figures, located in the valley of the lower Mitchell River, near the northern coastline. The designs are simple with bold outlines. Transverse lines across the frame of the outlines give the subjects a segmented appearance.

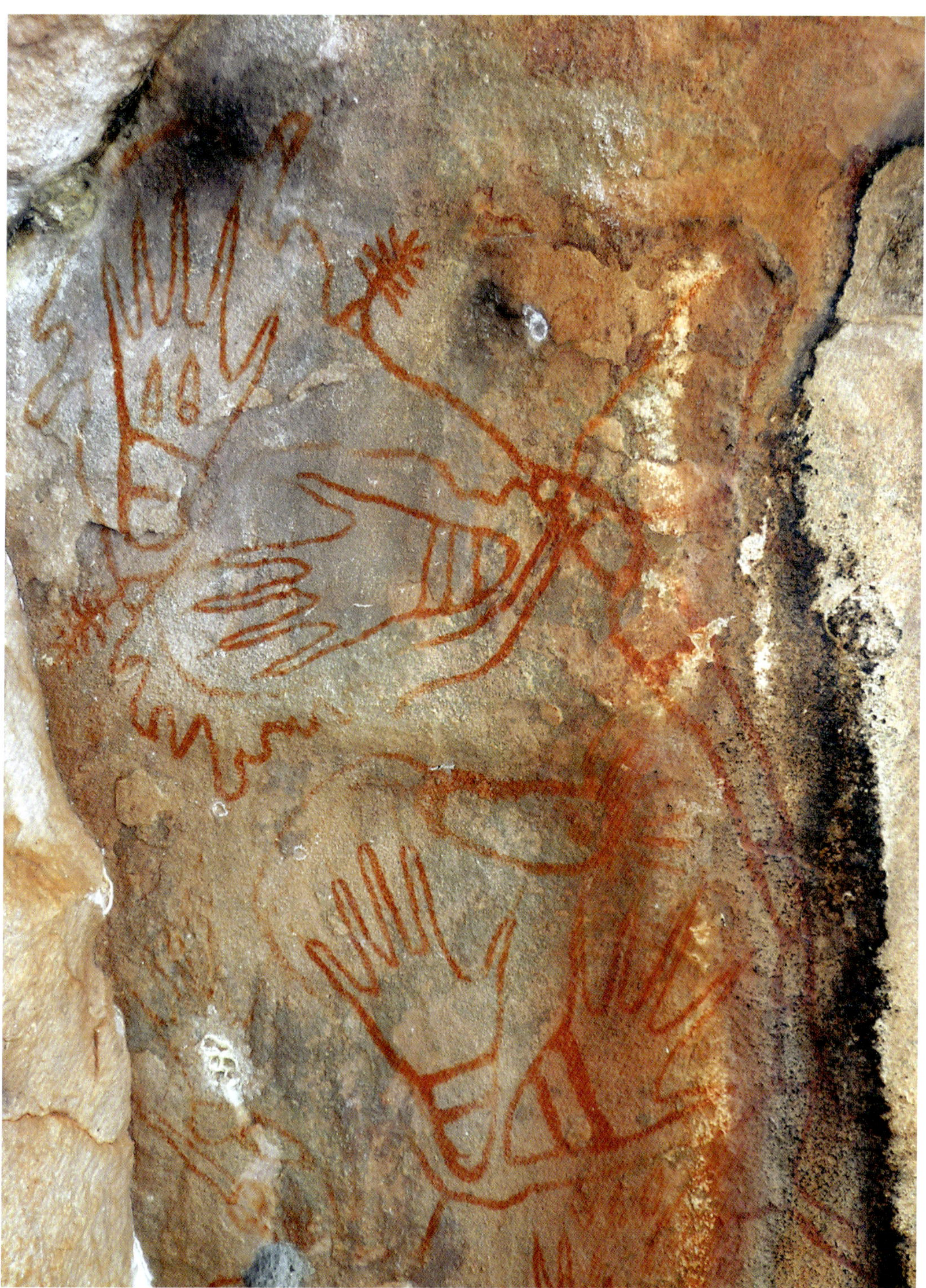

Painted hands with long fingernails, surrounded by yam-like motifs with meandering lines representing yam-vines or yam-roots. The two small motifs within the upper hand are kangaroo paws. Central Kimberley.

Wandjina Paintings

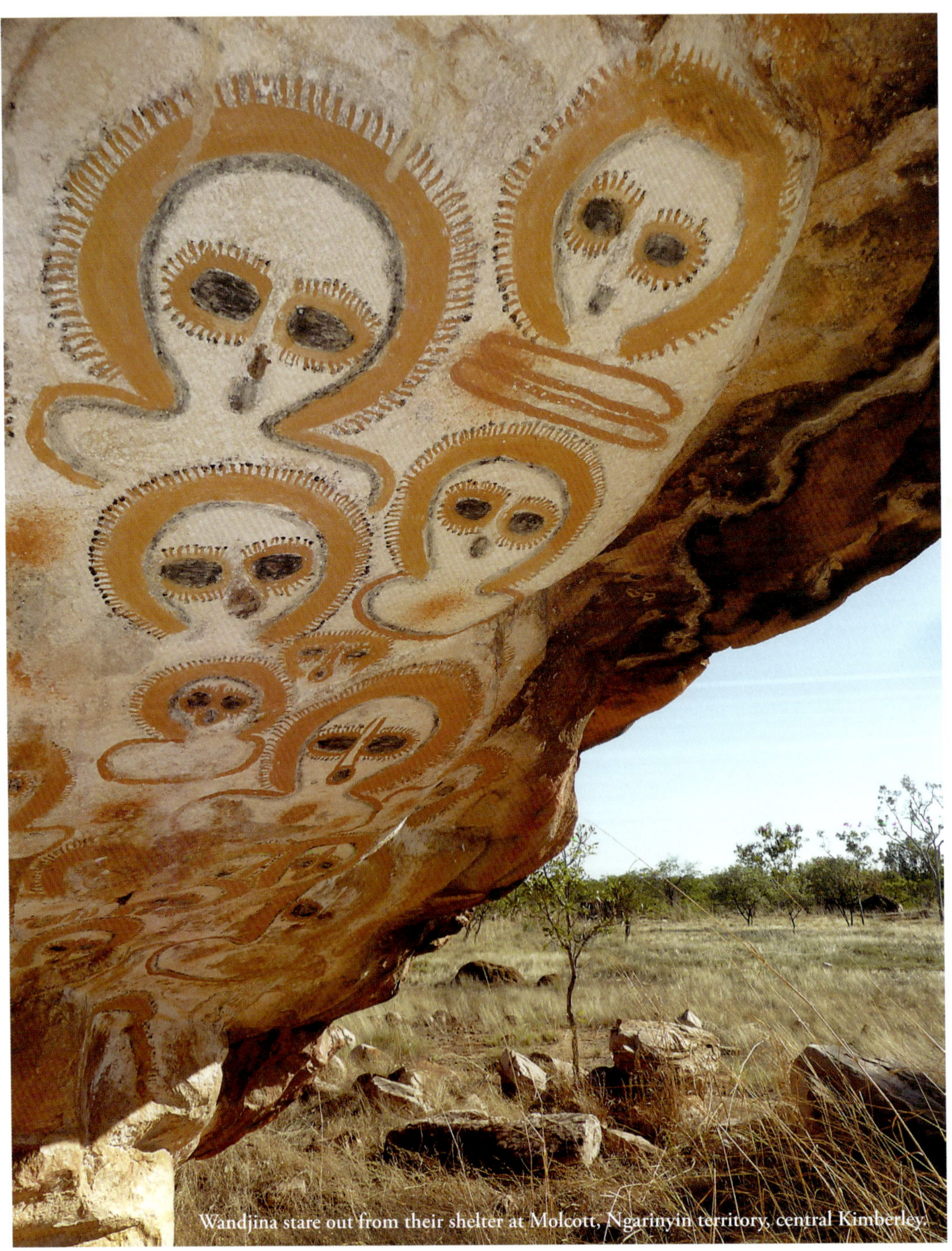

Wandjina stare out from their shelter at Molcott, Ngarinyin territory, central Kimberley.

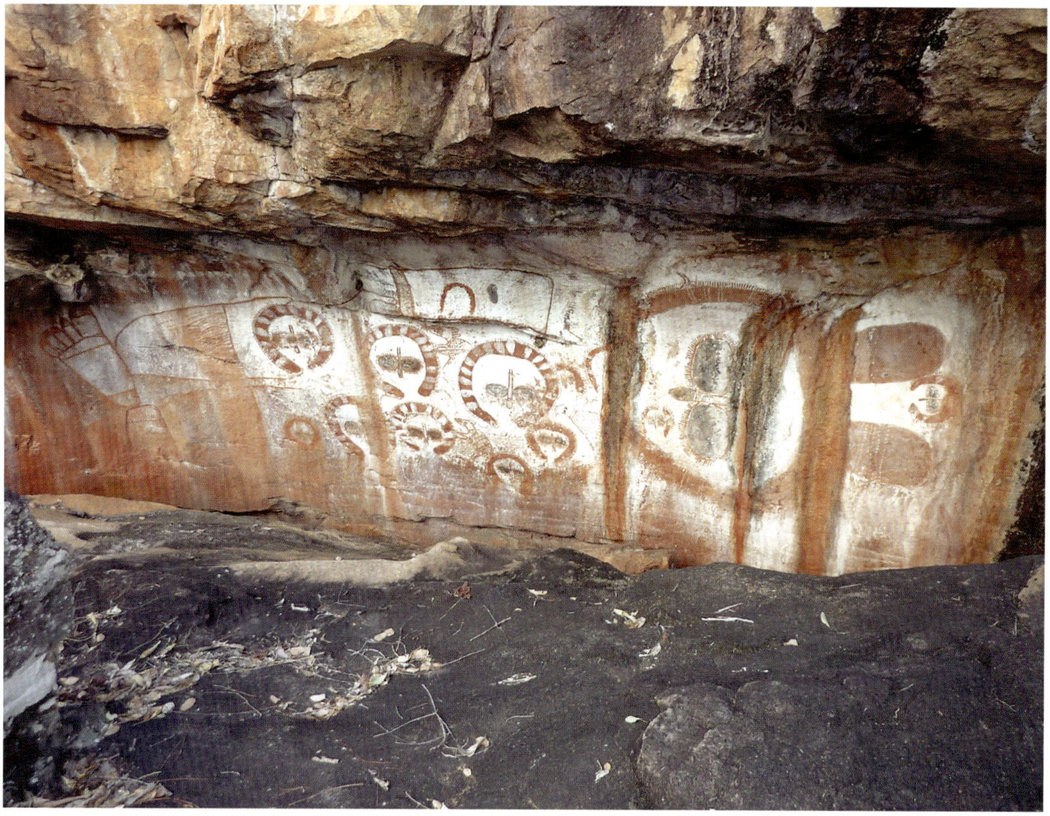

A five-metre-long Wandjina resting in his shelter at Ai-angari in the central Kimberley. Smaller Wandjina heads painted across his body represent his family and followers.

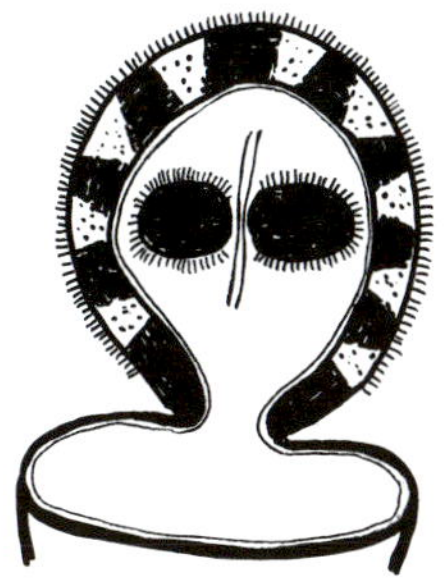

At Ai-angari in the central Kimberley, lies a five-metre-long Wandjina with a simple headdress of two male-black-cockatoo tail feathers. After travelling through the land during *Lalai* (the Creation Period or Dreamtime), this great Wandjina became tired and lay down to rest in the shelter. He painted his "shadow" and remains here to this day, resting on his side, as a painting. Smaller Wandjina faces painted across his body represent other Wandjina who accompanied him in his travels.

In a crevice below the painting, and tucked under a rock, lies a large baler shell *(Melo amphora)*, representing the Wandjina's drinking vessel. This is forty-two centimetres long, and its central whorl has been removed to enhance its use as a water carrier.

A nearby Wandjina painted on a vertical rock face is said to represent a Wandjina woman, *mulu-mulu*, who has toughened skin. The *mulu-mulu* went hunting and captured two boys whom she planned to cook and eat. She carried

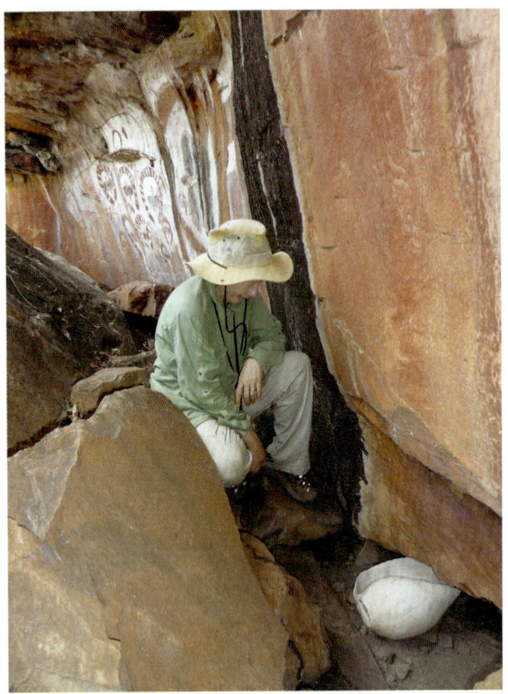

The baler shell water container *(nyalega)* representing the Wandjina's drinking vessel.

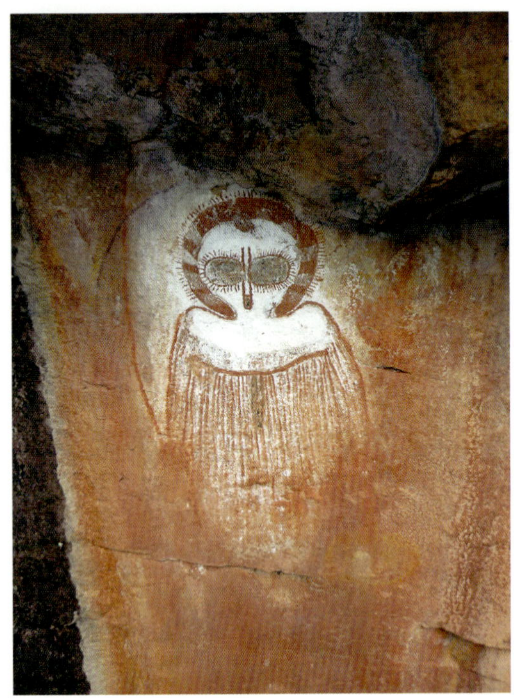

The Wandjina described as a *mulu-mulu*, at Ai-angari.

them to the Ai-angari waterhole, and while she collected lily roots they escaped and ran back to their camp. The *mulu-mulu* followed them, and when the men threw their spears at her, they bounced off her tough skin. Eventually a spear was thrown at her weakest spot – her feet – and she fell down dead.

Wandjina are mythical Ancestral Beings that travelled through the Kimberley region during *Lalai* (the Creation Period or Dreamtime). When they came to their shelters they placed their self-images as paintings and remain to this day. Wandjina are responsible for bringing the annual clouds and wet season rains. Without the Wandjina, there would be no rain.

Each *clan* (small land-owning group) and *tribe* (larger language group) has its own Wandjina site and version of associated legends. *Wandjina* is a collective term, and the Wandjina at each site also have their individual names and characteristics. Two common types of Wandjina paintings are the *Galaru-style* and the *Namarali-style*.

Galaru-style Wandjina are multi-coloured with a red or yellow arcuate (horseshoe-shaped) headdress, a bright white face, and black charcoal eyes. Often only their heads or upper bodies are depicted. Galaru is the name of an important Wandjina for Ngarinyin people in the central Kimberley.

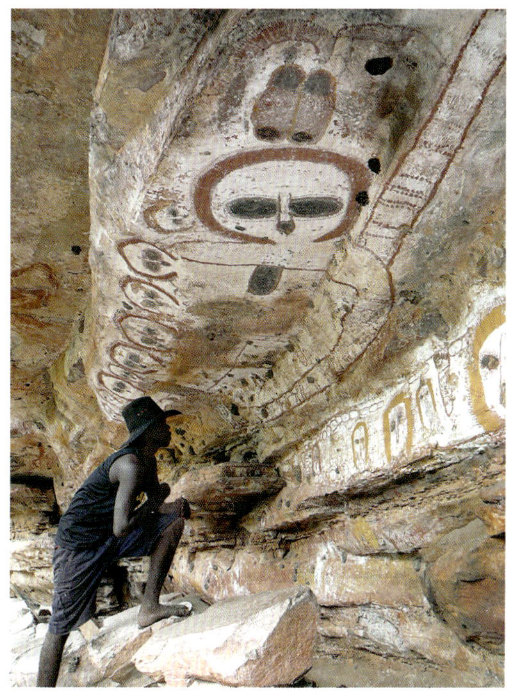

Ngarinyin man, William Tataya, with the Wandjina called Galaru at Wanalirri in the central Kimberley.

Namarali-style Wandjina have circular headdresses with radiating lines, are often monochromatic (painted in one colour), and the complete body is always depicted. Namarali is the name of an important Wandjina for Worora people in the north-west.

There are hundreds of Wandjina paintings throughout the Kimberley, with many variations and unique features. Some outstanding examples, including the smallest and largest Wandjina heads known to the author, are shown on the accompanying pages.

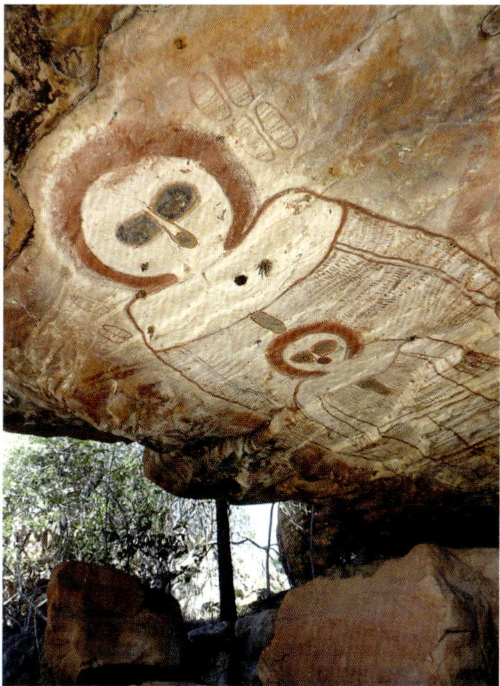

Two Galaru-style Wandjina stare out from their shelter near the Manning River in the central Kimberley.

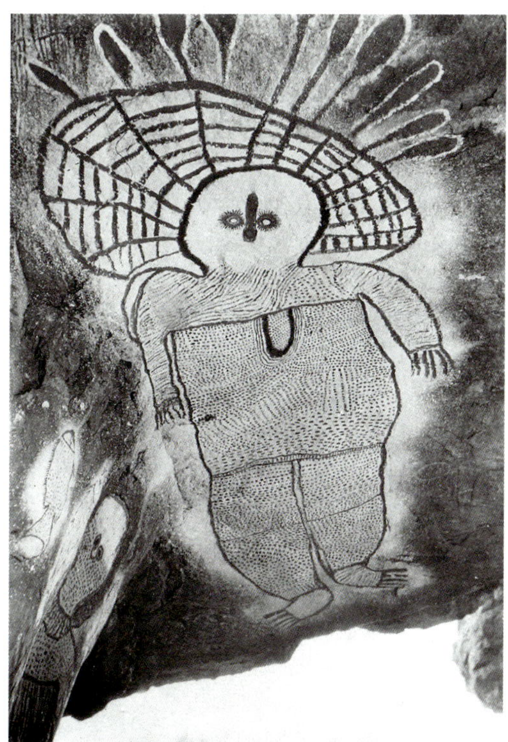

The Wandjina named Namarali at Kundiringurrim, Worora country, north-west Kimberley, circa 1929. (Photograph by J. R. B. Love. Courtesy of the State Library of South Australia, PRG 214-44-B46.)

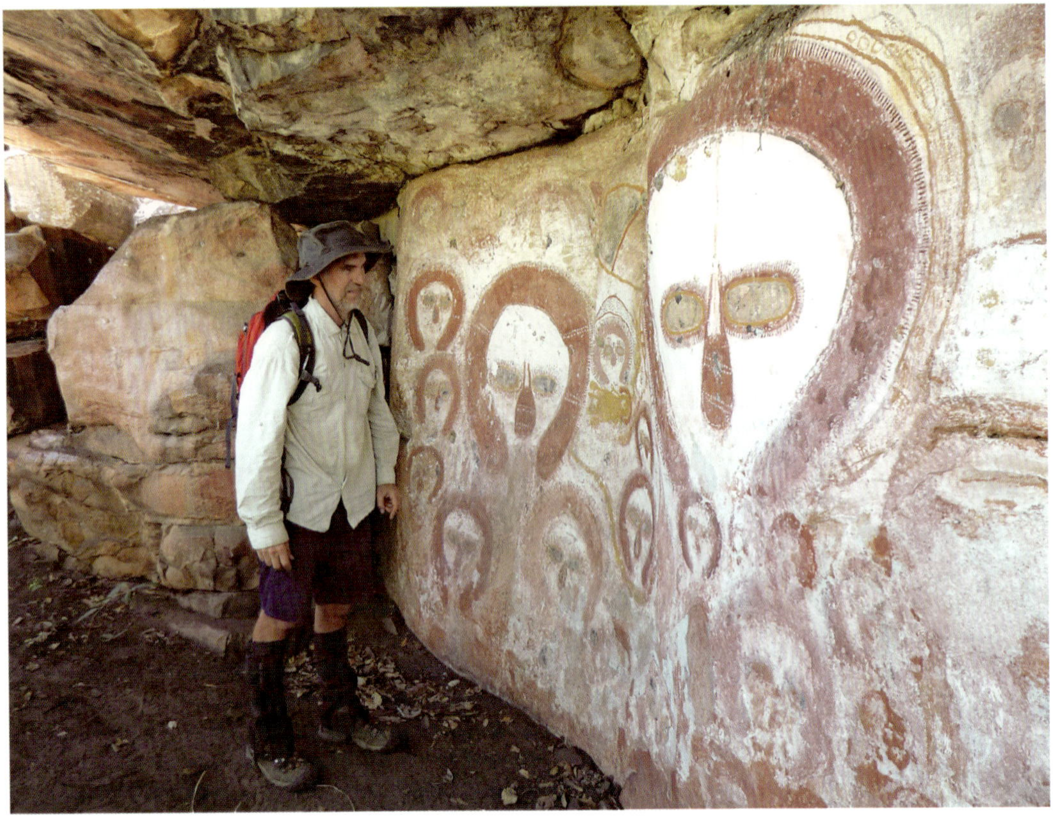

The Big-head Wandjina with a yellow snake around its headdress visible nearest camera. (Two snakes are out of sight on the far side.) The width of the head with snakes is 137 cm. Two feathers extend laterally from the head, bringing its total width to 237 cm. Western Kimberley. (Photograph by Michael Rainsbury.)

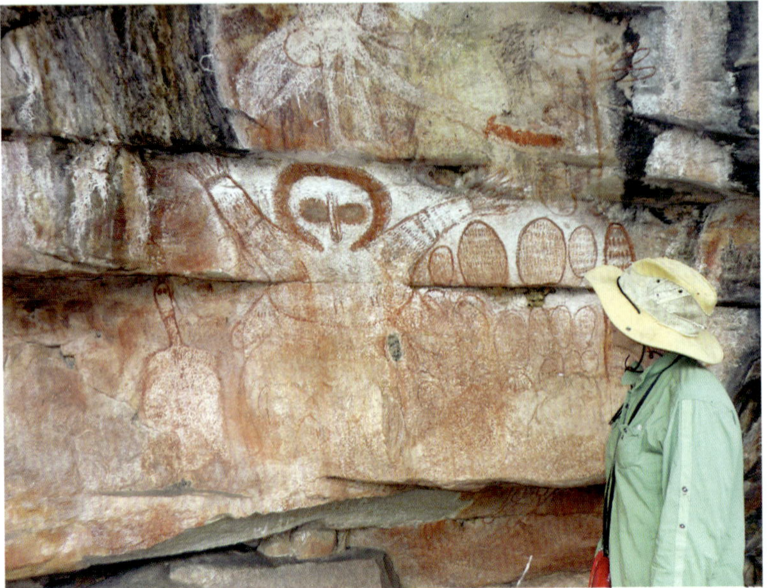

A female Wandjina with raised arms and breasts to the sides. Central Kimberley.

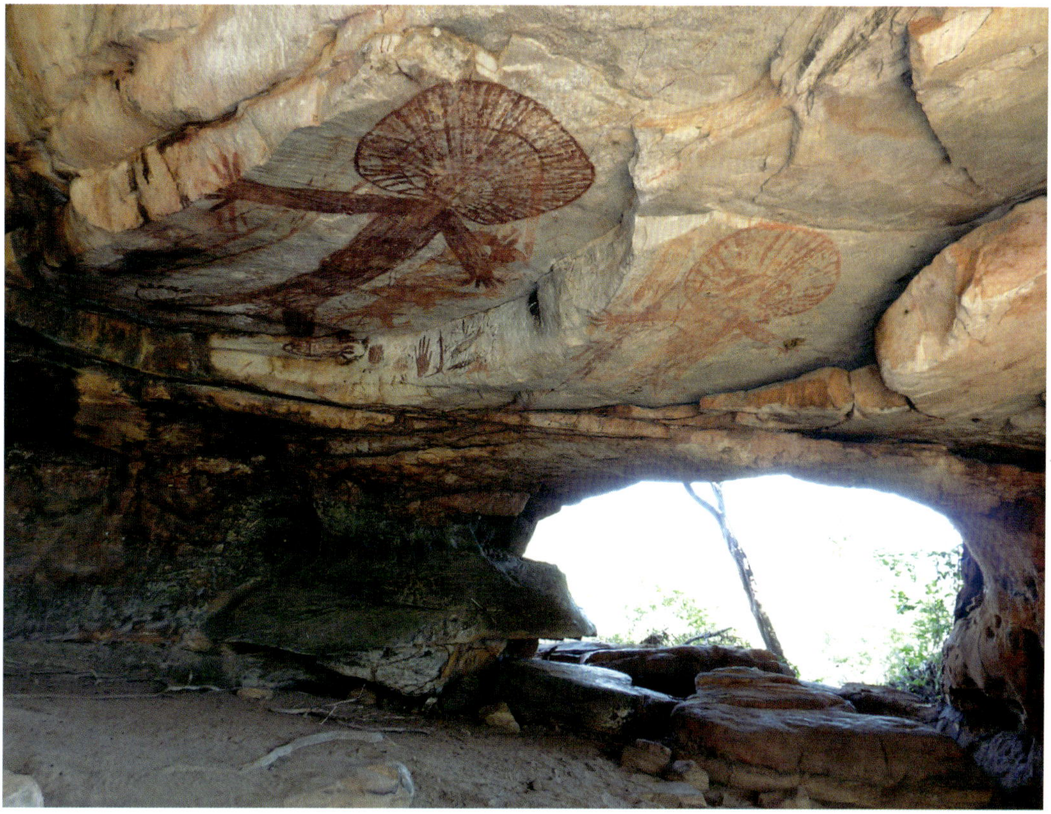

Two Namarali-style Wandjina peer down from the ceiling of their tunnel-like shelter beside the Mitchell River, northern Kimberley.

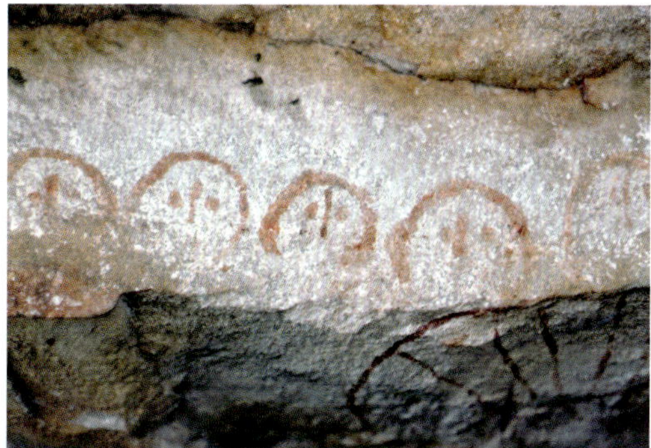

The smallest Wandjina recorded are these tiny heads, measuring two centimetres wide, in the central Kimberley.

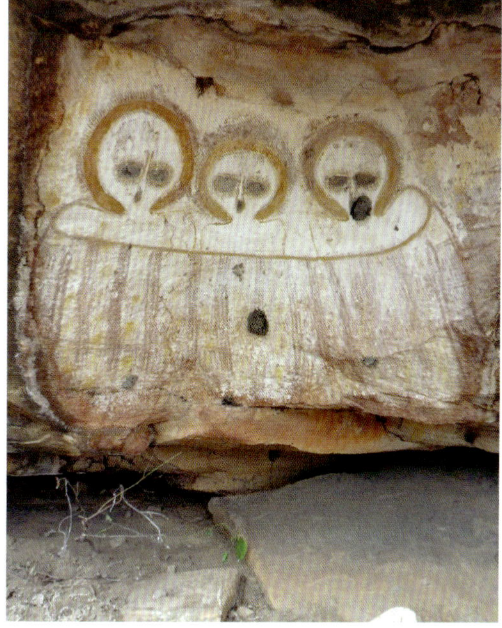

Joined Wandjina sharing the one neck line and body. Central Kimberley.

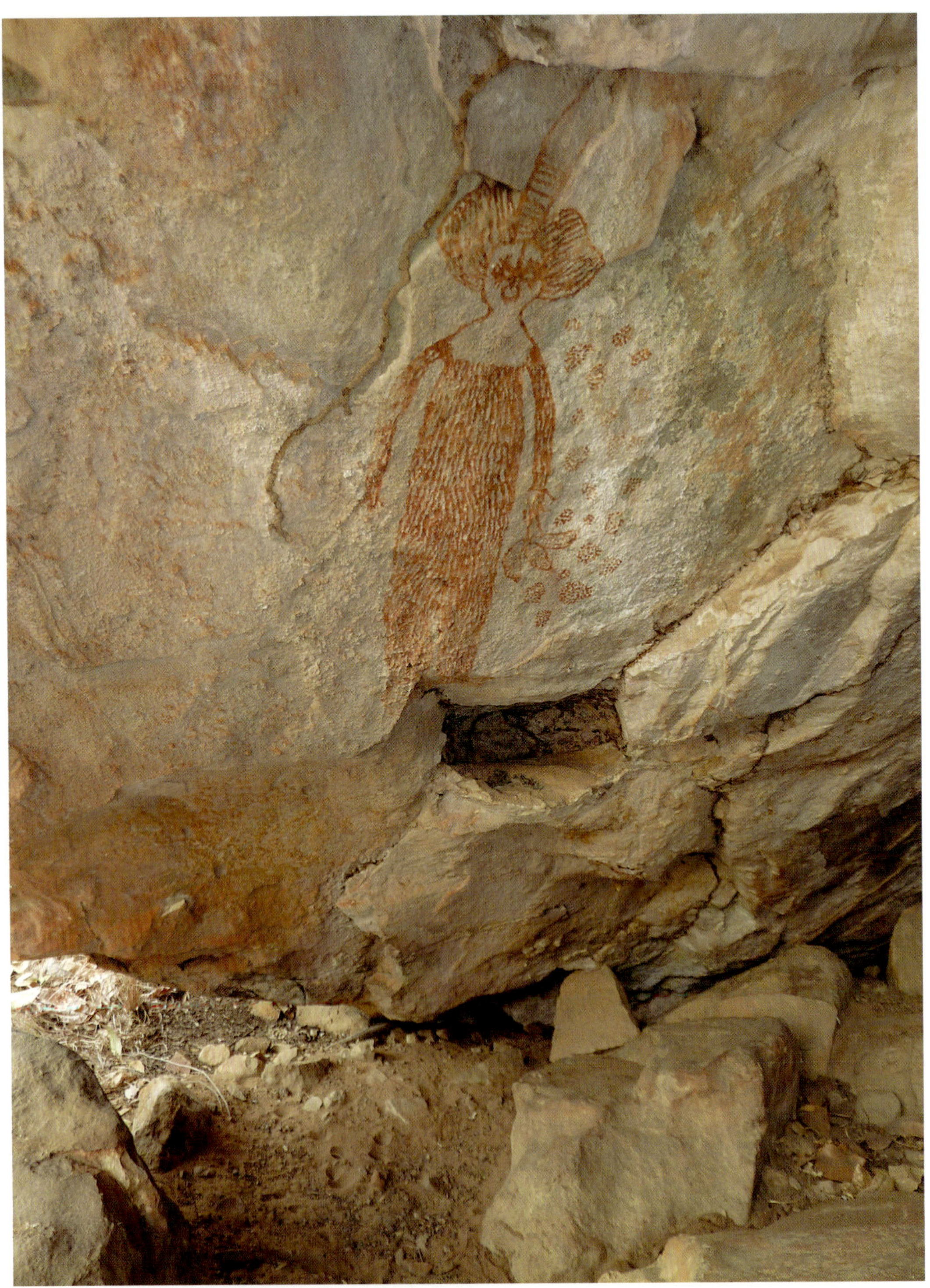

A full-body Wandjina wearing a long central feather in its headdress, and carrying bush foods. Dotted motifs to the right may represent more bush foods. Height 70 cm.

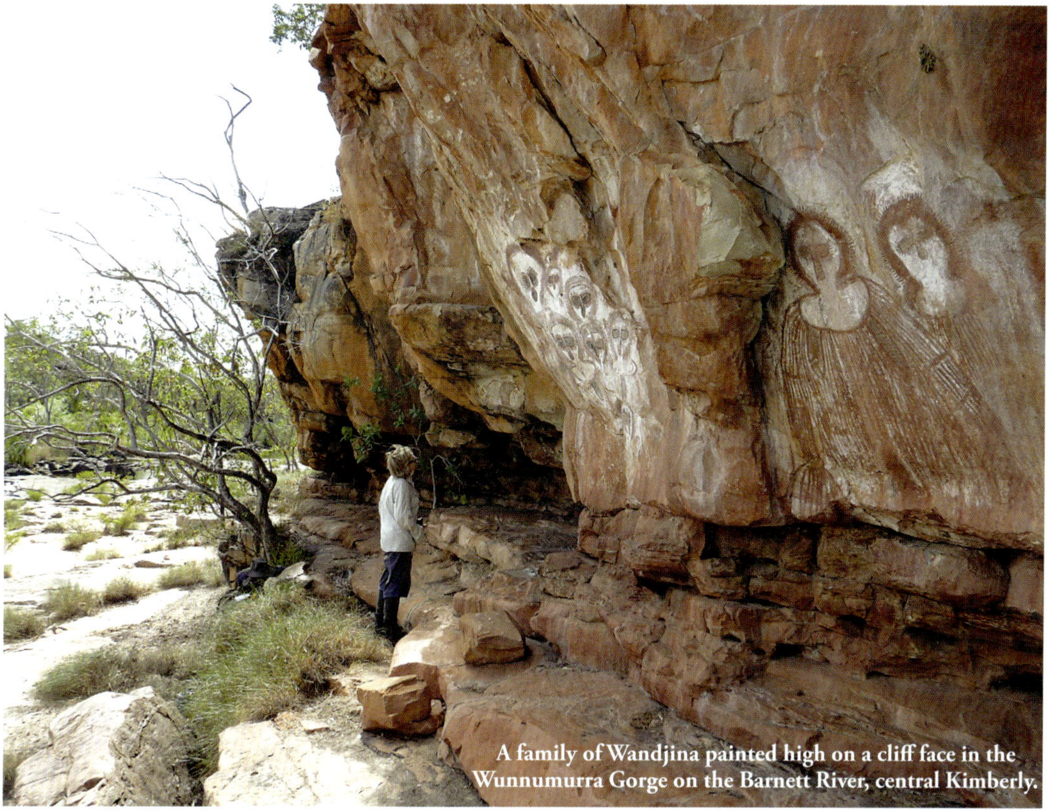

A family of Wandjina painted high on a cliff face in the Wunnumurra Gorge on the Barnett River, central Kimberly.

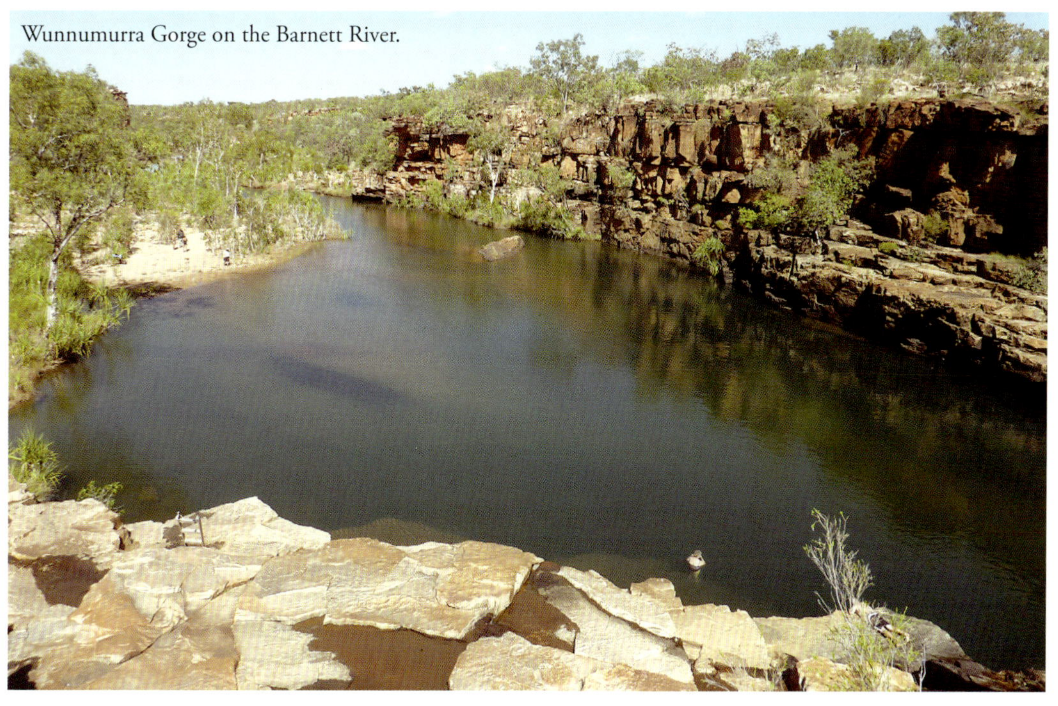
Wunnumurra Gorge on the Barnett River.

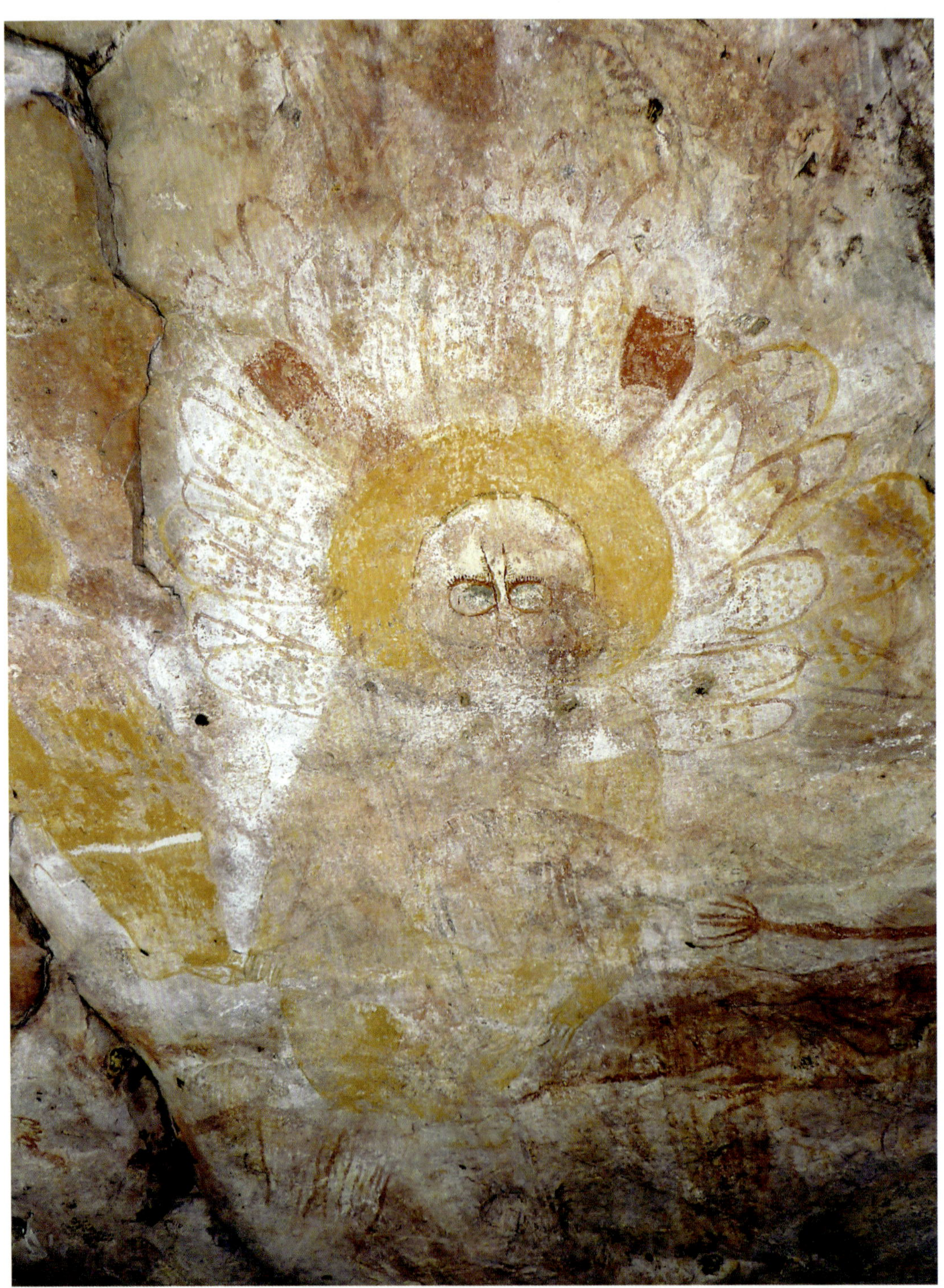

A Galaru-style Wandjina which has been repainted several times, wearing a large multi-layered feather fan headdress. Some of the feathers have two dots representing two eyes, and symbolise mythical snakes. Two feathers have central red bands, representing the tail feathers of the male black cockatoo. Central Kimberley.

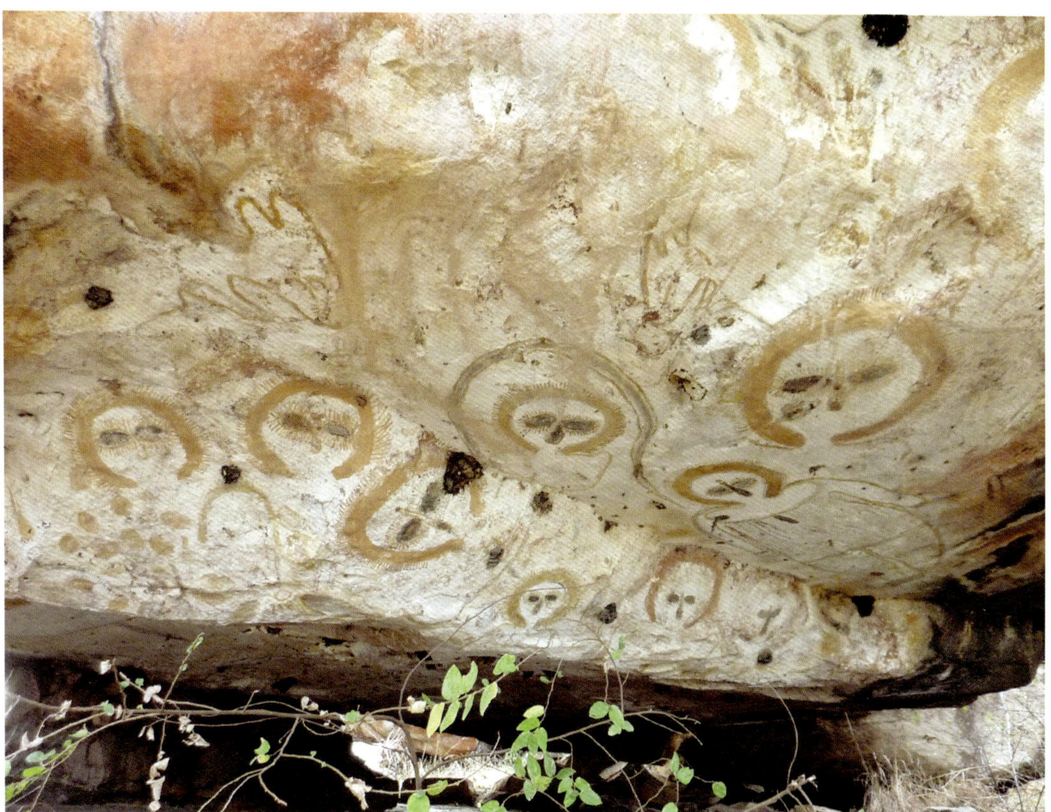

A ceiling and ceiling step adorned with Wandjina and marsupials. The black snake-like line encircling the central Wandjina represents a bolt of lightning. Central Kimberley.

Significance of the Wandjina image

Each component of the Wandjina image holds special significance for Aboriginal custodians. These include:

- The arcuate layers on Wandjina headdresses signify rainclouds, rain, the rainbow and lightning.
- The red and black feather decoration *(djangal)* worn over the head of some Galaru-style Wandjina represents the tail feathers of the male black cockatoo, which in turn represent flashes of lightning. (A flash of red is seen on the tail feathers when the birds take flight.)
- Zig-zag and fork-like motifs associated with Wandjina images represent bolts of lightning. Lightning is also represented by long straight lines emanating from Wandjina and snake-like lines curving around the head.
- White blotches and patterns sprayed over the headdresses of some Wandjina signify *ondolon*, rain clouds.
- Red paint on Wandjina signifies blood within its body.
- White paint on Wandjina signifies water within its body.
- Decorative body paint *(djili)*, when composed of long red lines or dashes,

represents falling rain.

- An oval motif across the chest represents *rangu*, the Wandjina's heart or source of power.
- Bright colouring on Wandjina paintings reflects the degree of strength held by each individual. A freshly-painted Wandjina is considered strong and healthy. A faded painting indicates the Wandjina has become weak.

Traditionally, faded Wandjina were repainted at the end of the dry season, with the belief that such retouching would strengthen the Wandjina and ensure a good wet season. As a result of this practice, Wandjina paintings are often thick with multiple layers of pigment. When they fade, earlier versions of the paintings sometimes become visible below.

The **lack of mouth on Wandjina paintings** is explained in several ways by local Aborigines. The author has been told that the Wandjina has no mouth because it does not speak and only makes the noise of the wind. Other accounts describe the mouth being closed by a bolt of lightning, by the Rainbow Serpent, or for other reasons. People say that adding a mouth (that is, changing the Wandjina's image) will anger the Wandjina, who will create great storms and floods.

Although much attention has been drawn to the lack of mouth on Wandjina paintings, research by the author reveals there is a general lack of mouth on Aboriginal human-like figures painted by Aborigines across northern Australia. Rather than holding some special meaning, the lack of mouth appears to follow an artistic convention when depicting human faces viewed from the front. When artists wish to indicate their subjects are singing or calling out, they paint the human face in profile with an open mouth.

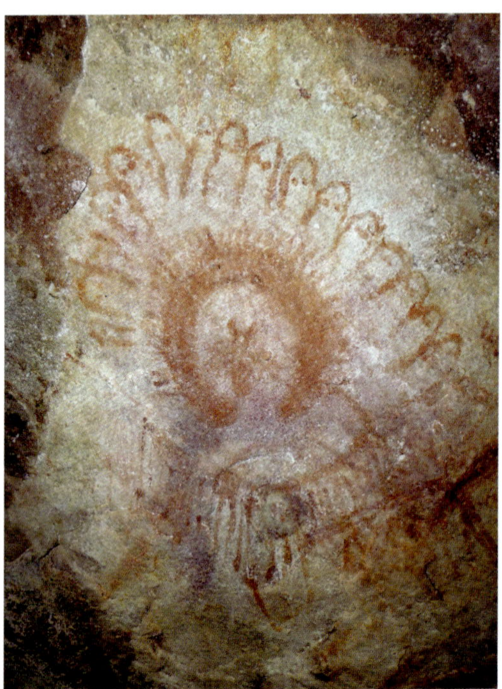

This Wandjina's headdress incorporates the heads of sixteen snakes, each with two eyes. The painting is located on the undersurface of an overhang on an isolated boulder on an elevated section of plain in the central Kimberley. Width of motif 32 cm.

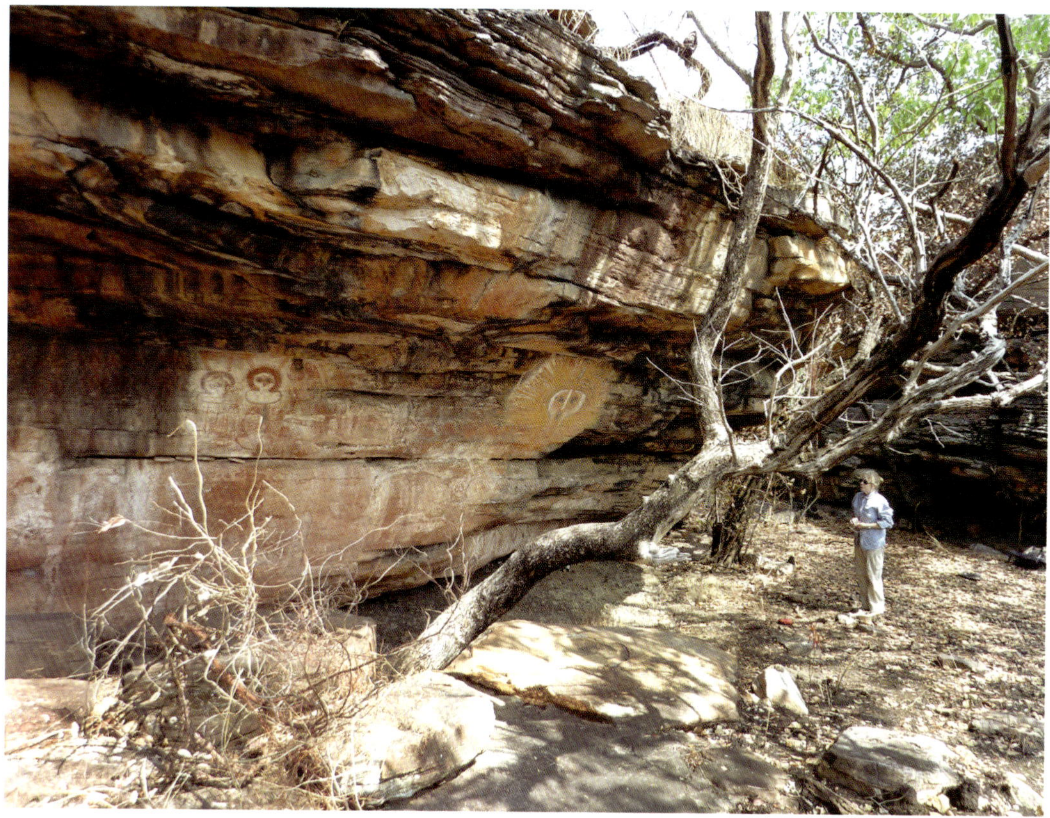

Brad, the Rising Sun Wandjina, painted in a bright yellow pigment, mimicking the glowing rays of a golden sun. Bradwodingari, central Kimberley.

Origins of the Wandjina image

There are those who believe that Wandjina figures are of recent origin, arriving in the Kimberley within the past few hundred years, and depicting people wearing robes. In fact, a beeswax representation of a Wandjina, because it contained carbon material, was able to be carbon-dated at 3,800 years old. In round terms, it is safe to say that the Wandjina Period dates back 4,000 years.

Elements of the Wandjina image can be found amongst the earlier paintings. Arcuate or horseshoe-shaped headdresses are found amongst the preceding Tasselled Figures, Straight Part Figures, and human figures from the Painted Hand Period. The fashion where two feathers project from the heads of Galaru-style Wandjina is seen on early Tasselled Figures and Bent Knee Figures. The fashion where radiating lines with end blobs are incorporated into the headdresses of Namarali-style Wandjina is seen on early human figures. These and other Wandjina features have their origins in the costumes worn for ceremonial occasions. A chart on the page opposite illustrates these points. This was produced by the author for a talk presented at an international rock art conference held in Alice Springs in 2000.

Although the components of the Wandjina image have largely disappeared from Kimberley culture, they have survived into the twentieth century in central Australia one thousand kilometres away. An example here illustrates an Aboriginal man from the Aranda tribe in central Australia wearing a large headdress with an arcuate component similar to the Galaru-style Wandjina. From this, thirty feathers, each with a tuft of white down in their end, project outwards, similar to the design of the Namarali-style headdress. Incredibly, the feathers used in this decoration have the same characteristic black and red colours of those depicted on Galaru-style Wandjina. They are the tail feathers of the male black cockatoo.

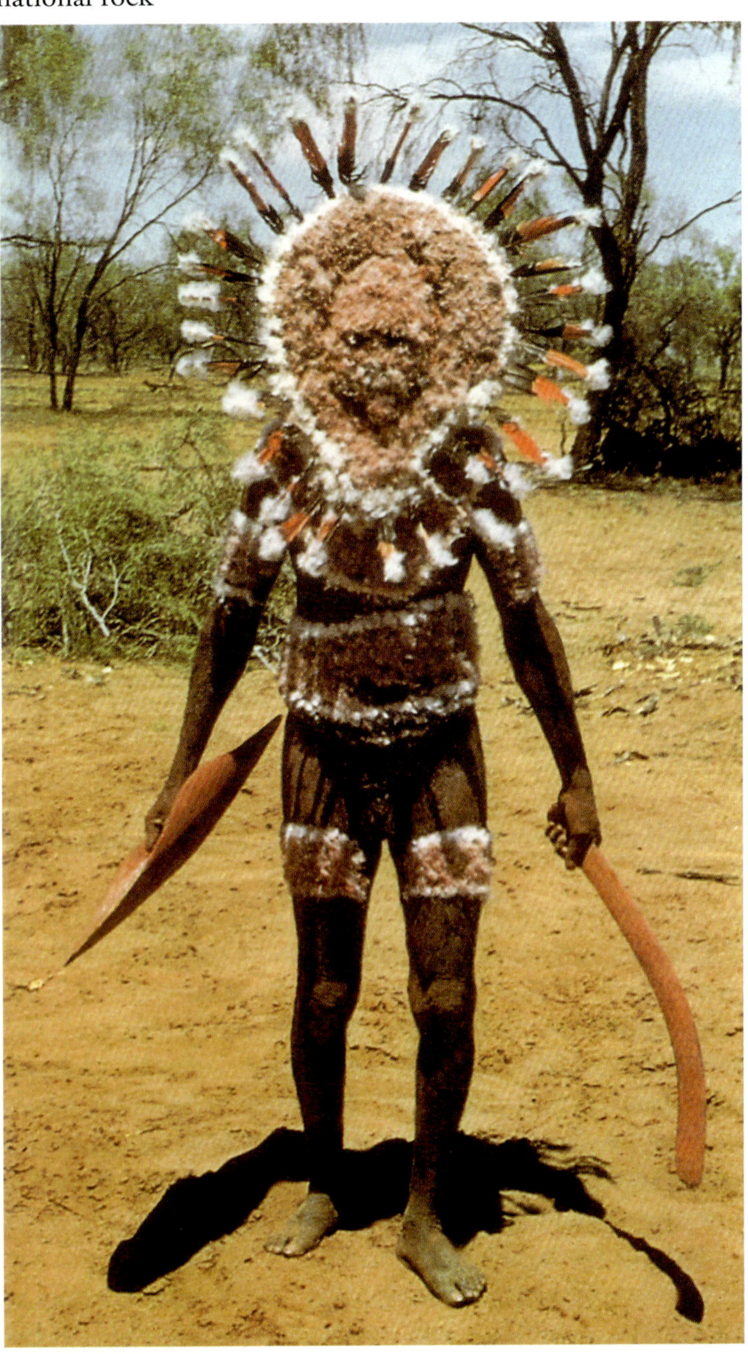

An Aranda man from central Australia wearing an arcuate headdress with thirty radiating black cockatoo feathers. (Photograph by Ted Strehlow, circa 1949.)

ORIGINS AND CONNECTIONS OF THE WANDJINA IMAGE

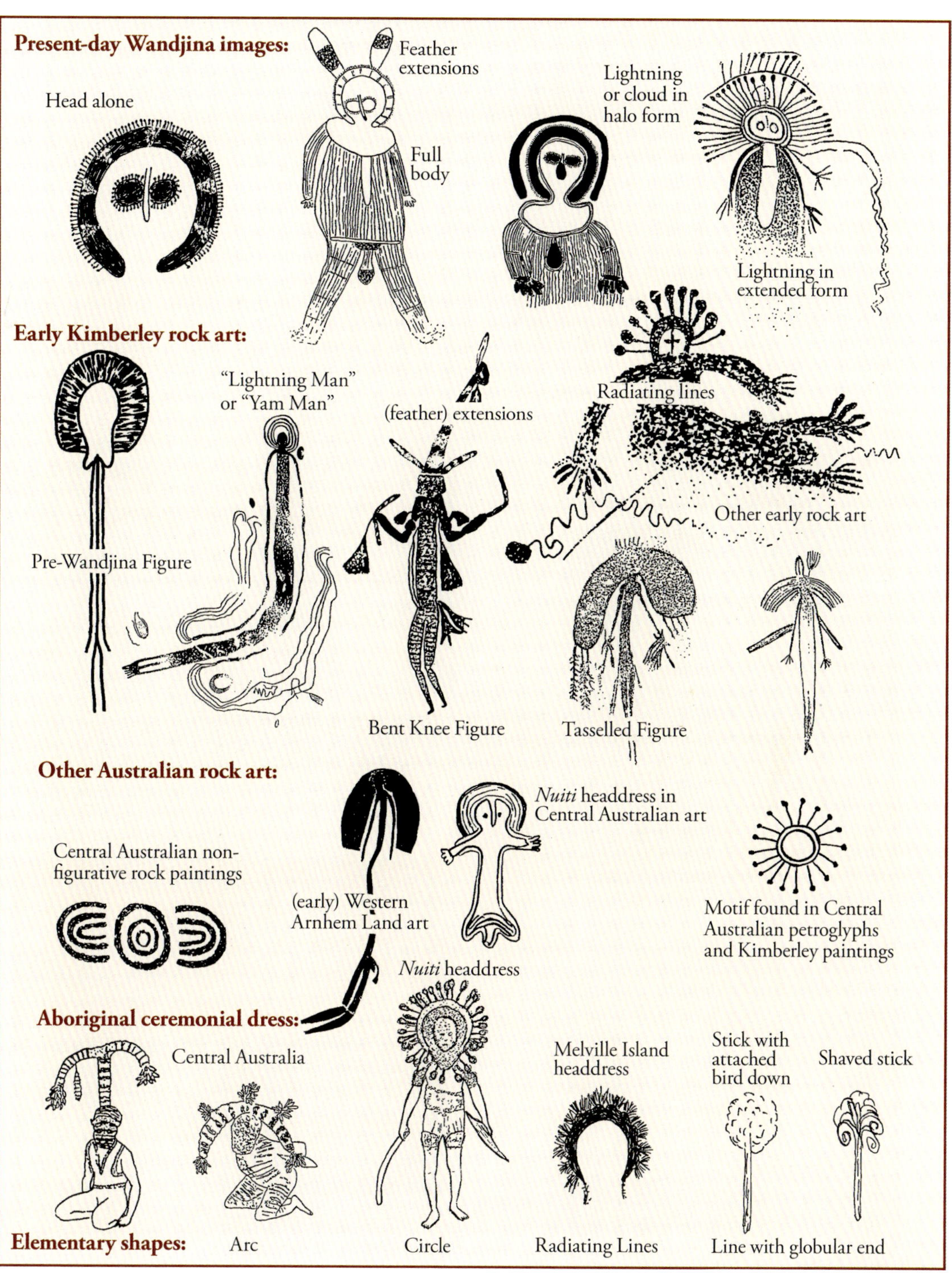

(Dr David M. Welch)

As places of worship, Wandjina and the totemic sites (discussed in the next chapter) often contain significant archaeological features resulting from ritual activities, day-to-day living, and burial practices. Features appearing *within* Wandjina and totemic sites include:

- Human bone deposits. These are secondary burials placed on rock ledges, in crevices and amongst stone piles. (The primary burial is when the body is first placed on a wooden platform, in a tree, or buried, and the flesh allowed to decay from the bones.)
- Smooth rounded polished stones, representing parts of the Wandjina and associated totemic plants and animals. For example, a rounded stone might represent the Wandjina's kidney or the egg of a totemic animal.
- Small slabs of rock, sometimes containing paintings of Wandjina and other figures, wedged into narrow crevices.
- Stone piles representing offering platforms, deities, and for human burials.
- *Nyalega*, the baler shell water container, representing the Wandjina's drinking vessel.
- Stone anvils, artefacts, stored objects, lumps of pigment, and debris from human occupation.
- Pits, cupules, pounding hollows, abraded grooves, and smooth rubbed rocks, all resulting from ritual hammering, pounding and rubbing associated with the extraction of *kuranita* (rock dust) in order to increase individual plant and animal species. Multiple small chippings along rock edges may have served a similar purpose.
- In rare instances, large stone tablets are present, containing images of Wandjina.

Archaeological features associated with Wandjina and totemic sites

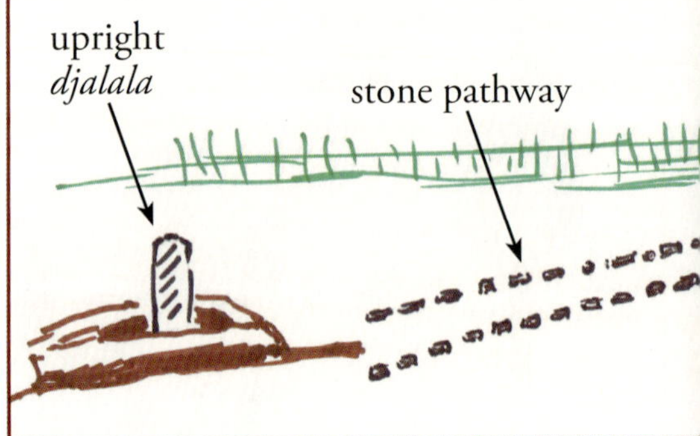

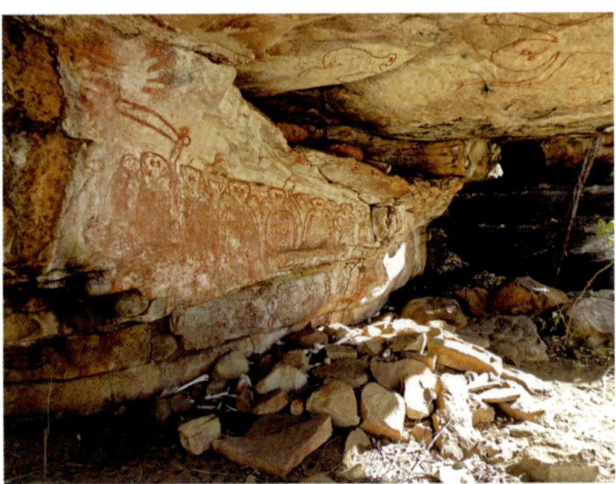

A stone pile serving as a burial mound for human bones painted with red ochre, within a rock shelter featuring human-like motifs representing totemic frogs, owls or some other totem. Central Kimberley.

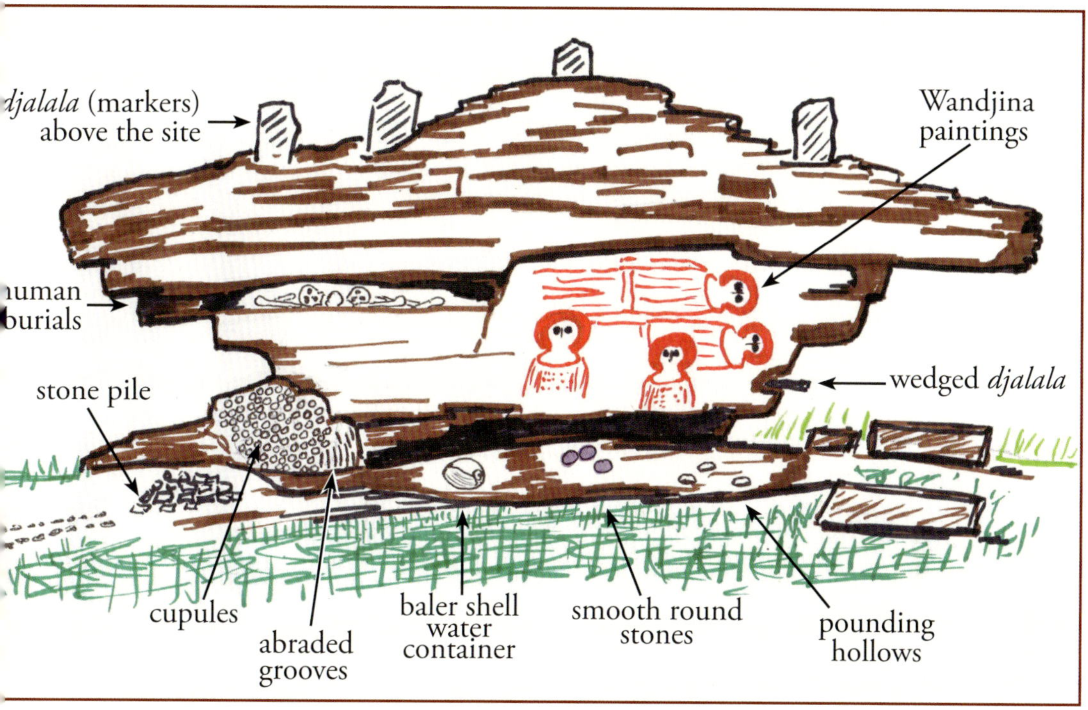

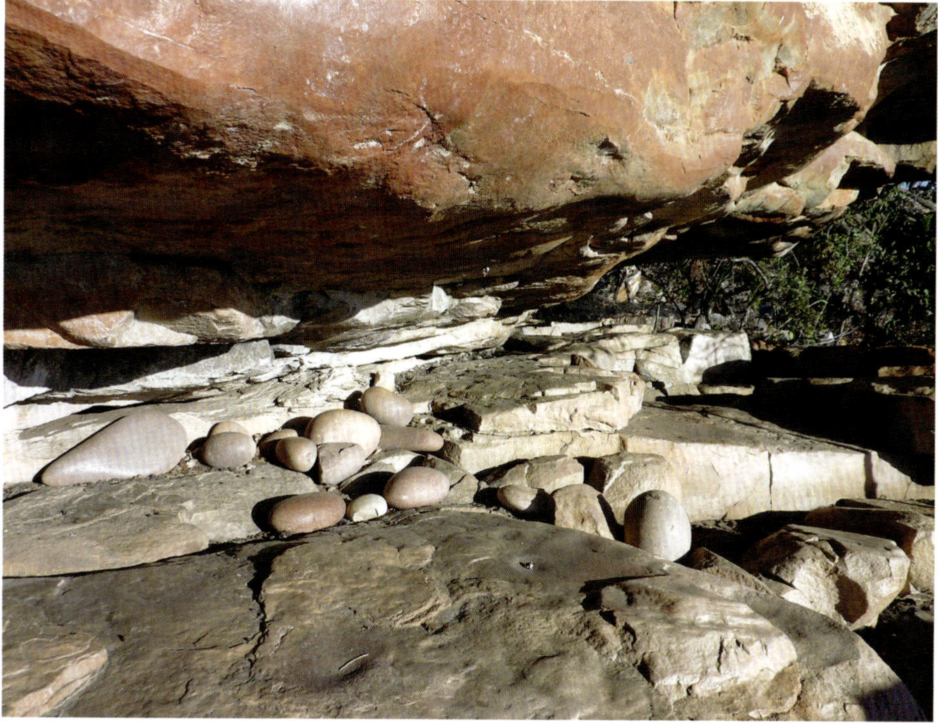

Sixteen smooth round river stones placed in a rock shelter. A two-metre-long Wandjina is painted on a ceiling high above. Lower Mitchell River Valley, northern Kimberley.

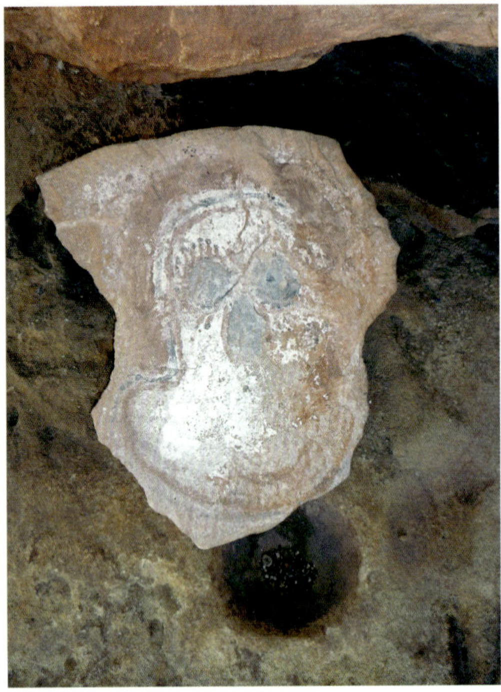

A Wandjina face painted on a thin piece of rock, thirty centimetres long, which was wedged into a crack below other Wandjina figures.

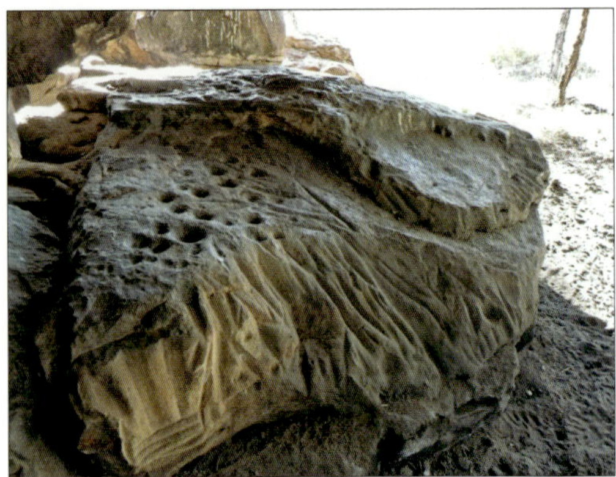

A rock shelf filled with man-made pits, cupules and abraded groves where people have pounded and rubbed the rock to extract its life-essence or *kuranita*, as part of their increase rituals. Central Kimberley.

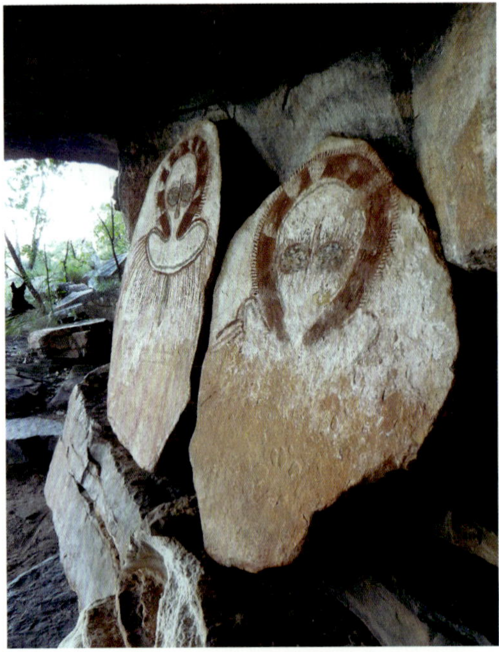

Large stone tablets painted with Wandjina images. Heights 88 cm and 82 cm. Central Kimberley.

Other features associated with Wandjina and totemic sites, but appearing *outside* the shelters, include:

- Marker stones (*djalala*, pronounced *ja-la-la*), consisting of upright stones, football-sized white quartzite blocks, and small stone piles. Thin upright stones also represent small Rainbow Serpents associated with a site, rising out of the ground.
- Simple stone pathways leading to or from the site. These represent the pathways taken by the ancestors when they first entered each site and should be followed when one enters such sites.
- Other stone arrangements, including natural rock tables with smooth rounded stones or bright white quartzite blocks placed upon them.

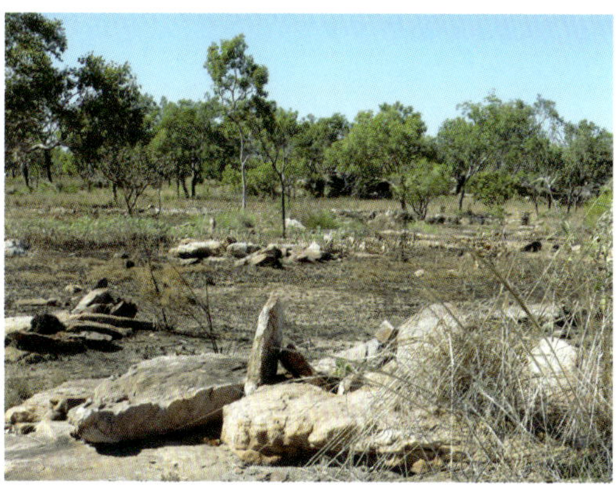

An upright stone *(djalala)* marking the route to a Wandjina site in the distant rocks.

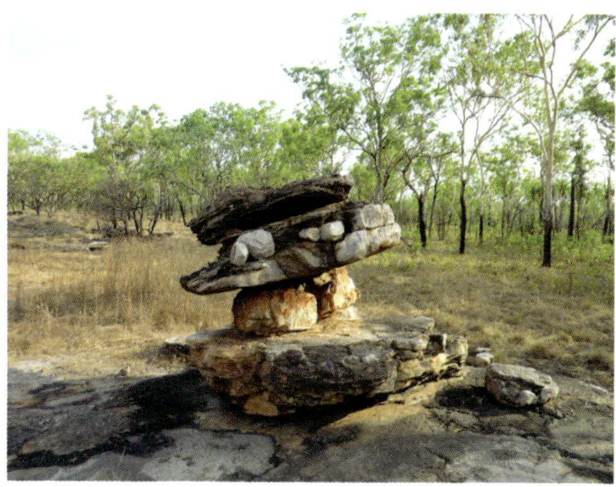

A rock table with bright white quartzite blocks, near Ai-angari, described on page 57.

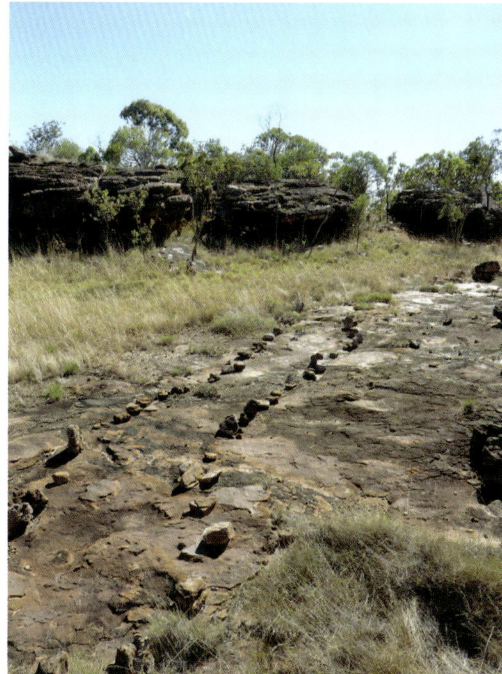

A stone pathway leads to low rocks containing a large horizontal Wandjina. The pathway is said to represent ants which followed the Wandjina into the shelter. The shelter also contains ochre pieces, human burials, and a sloping slab covered with cupules. Central Kimberley.

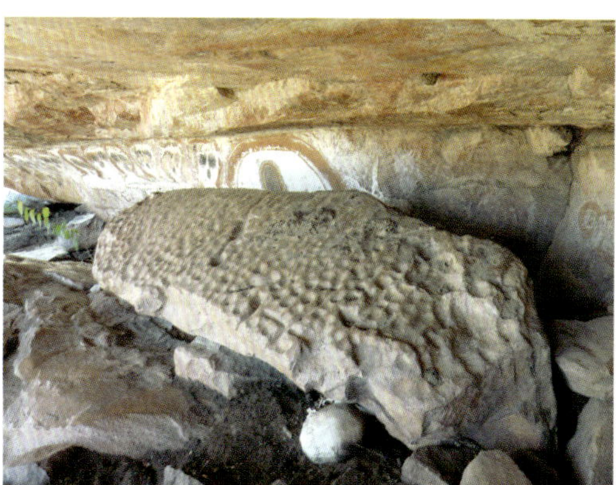

The sloping slab covered with cupules resulting from ritual hammering and pounding during increase rituals.

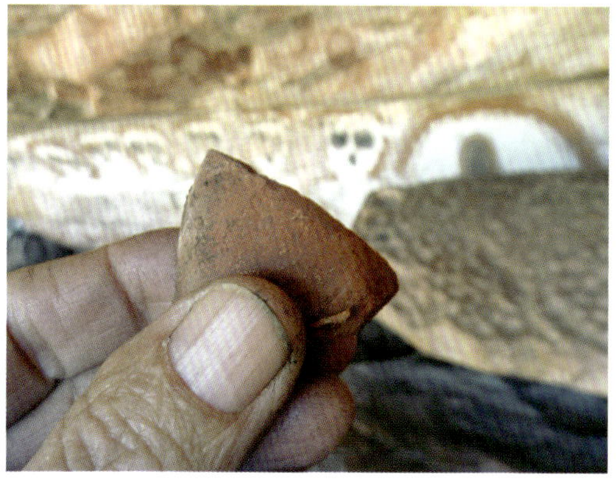

A piece of red ochre used to paint the Wandjina.

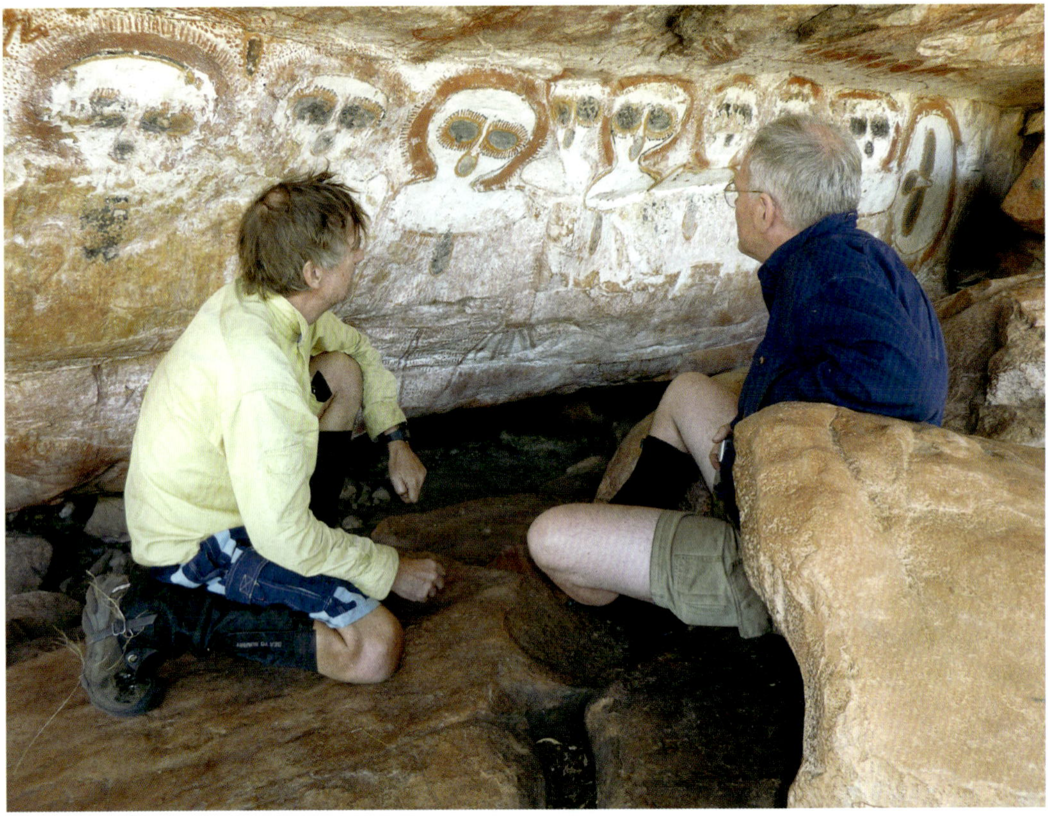

Also within the shelter are fantastic paintings of brightly-coloured Wandjina. The author (left) with Michael Rainsbury. (Photograph by Joc Schmiechen.)

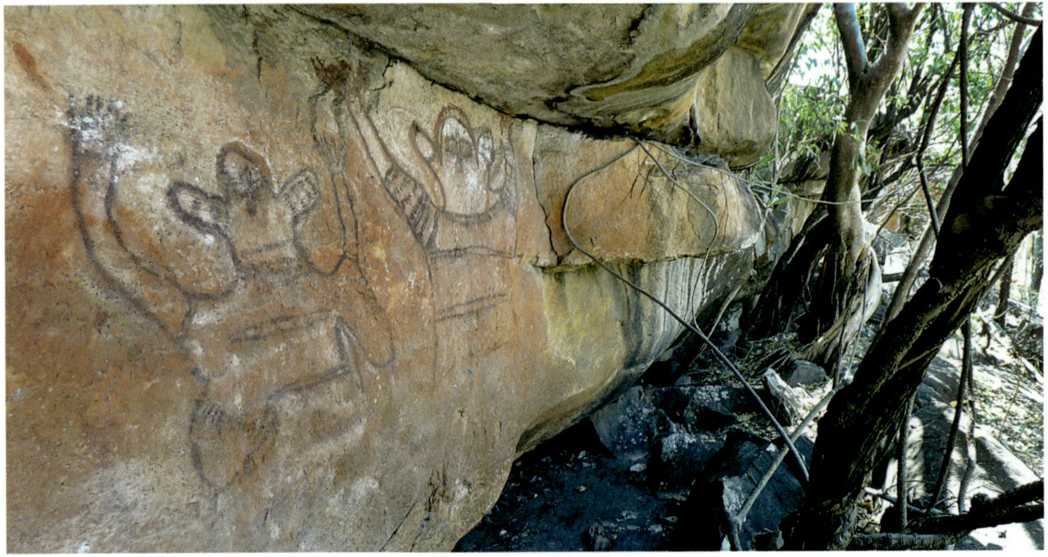

Male and female *agula* with prominent ears. Central Kimberley.

Other human-like deities and spirits from the Wandjina Period

In addition to Wandjina, the Kimberley rock shelters hold a range of similar human-like beings, but with distinctly different headdresses. Two important groups are *Bilateral Headdress Figures* and *Paddle Headdress Figures.*

Bilateral Headdress Figures (two-sided headdress figures) have two prominent extensions out to their sides. These can be large or small, symmetrical or asymmetrical, and often appear to form part of the head itself, resembling large ears.

The shape of this headdress might be based on tangible objects such as feathers or wooden boards placed on the head. Symbolically, it may represent a whirlwind or cyclone. Local Aborigines with whom the author consulted have given a variety of interpretations for these figures. Some are unsure, some suggest the figures represent *agula* (harmful spirits), and others see the figures as a type of Wandjina. In one instance, the headdress extensions were regarded as ears and the figure described as a bush spirit with good hearing. Ngarinyin man, Phil Krunmurra, described the figures as representing an insect that became a man and makes the wind.

Paddle Headdress Figures have a single paddle-like vertical extension from the head. This can be large or small, fat or thin, and again, may have its origins in the wearing of a tangible object such as a sacred wooden board.

Paintings from the Wandjina Period include a range of spirits, in particular ***agula*** (pronounced *ar-goo-la*, also spelt *argula*) who are regarded as harmful spirits arising from the deceased. Aboriginal people use the terms *devil* and *devil-devil* to describe them using English words, and they are believed responsible for one's mishaps and what we might call "bad luck". They can be invoked to threaten one's enemies. *Agula* paintings are characterised by being human-like with prominent or pointy ears and large genitals, and they are scattered across the Kimberley.

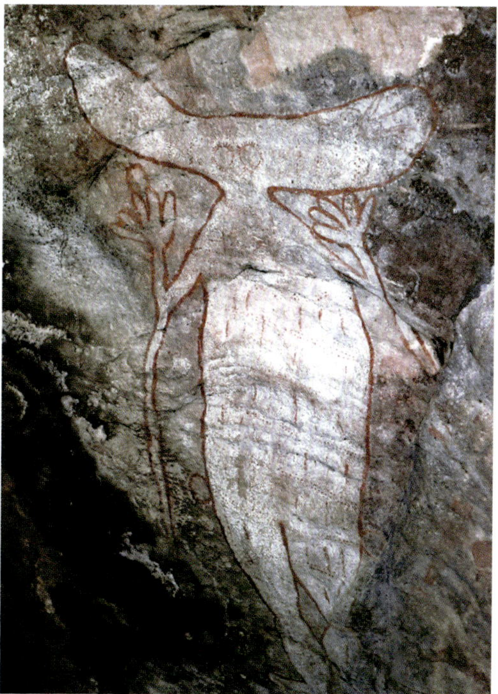

A Bilateral Headdress Figure with lines from each elbow representing ornamental strings. Height 112 cm. Central Kimberley.

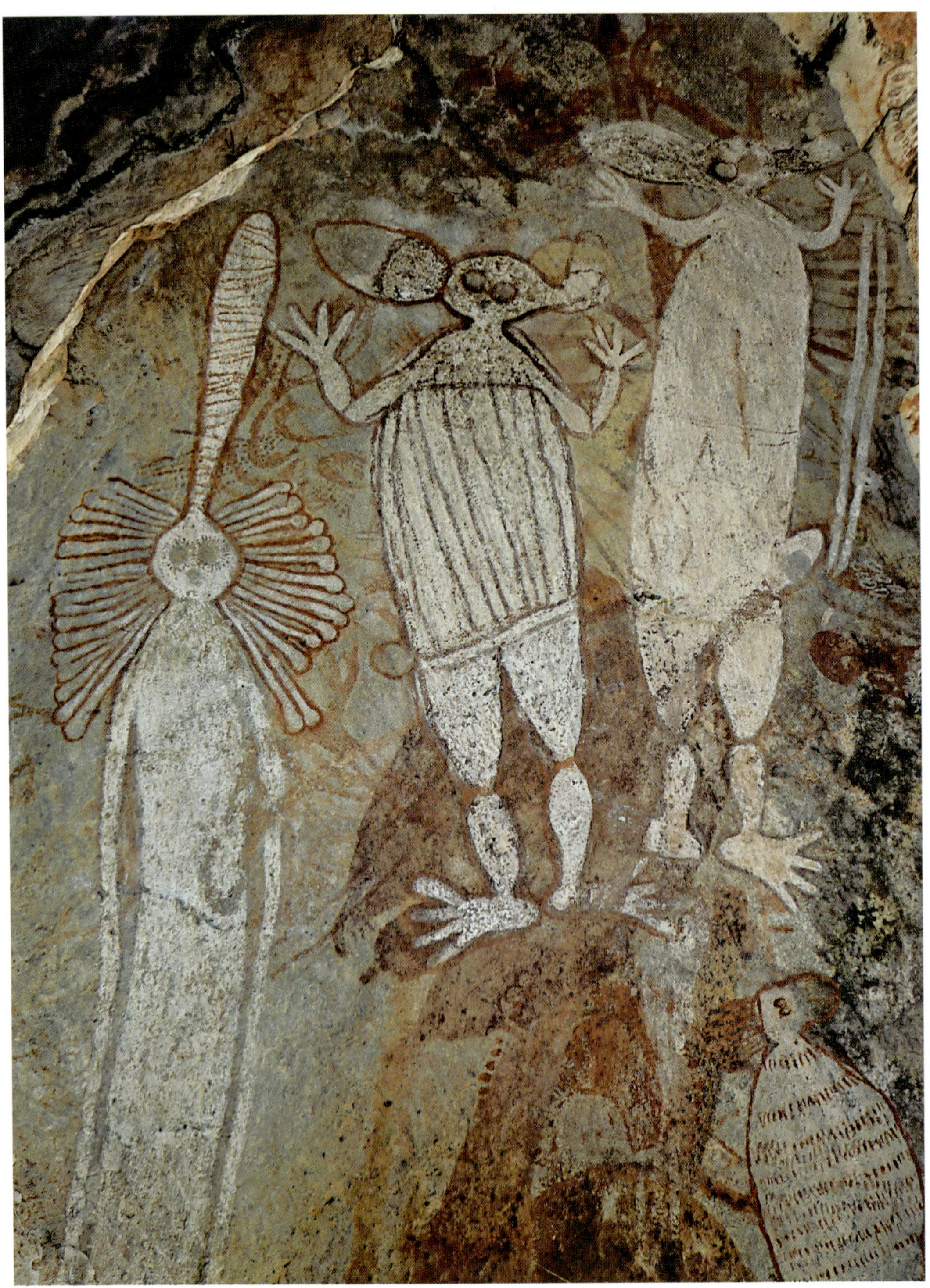

An attenuated Paddle Headdress Figure alongside two Bilateral Headdress Figures, painted across a shelter ceiling in the central Kimberley.

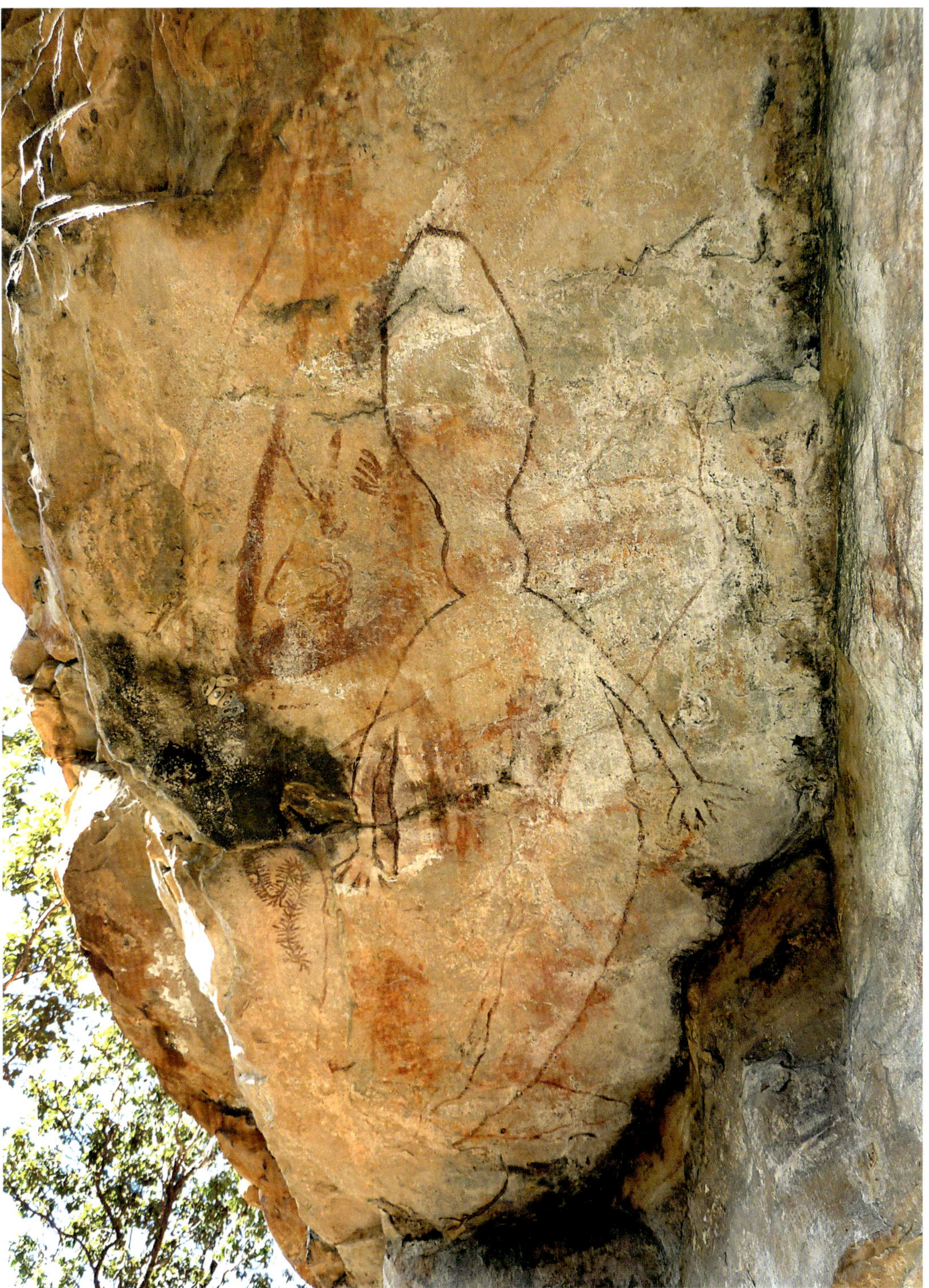

A Paddle Headdress Figure with a broad paddle-shaped headdress, painted on the undersurface of an overhanging rock. Central Kimberley.

TOTEMIC (DREAMING) SITES

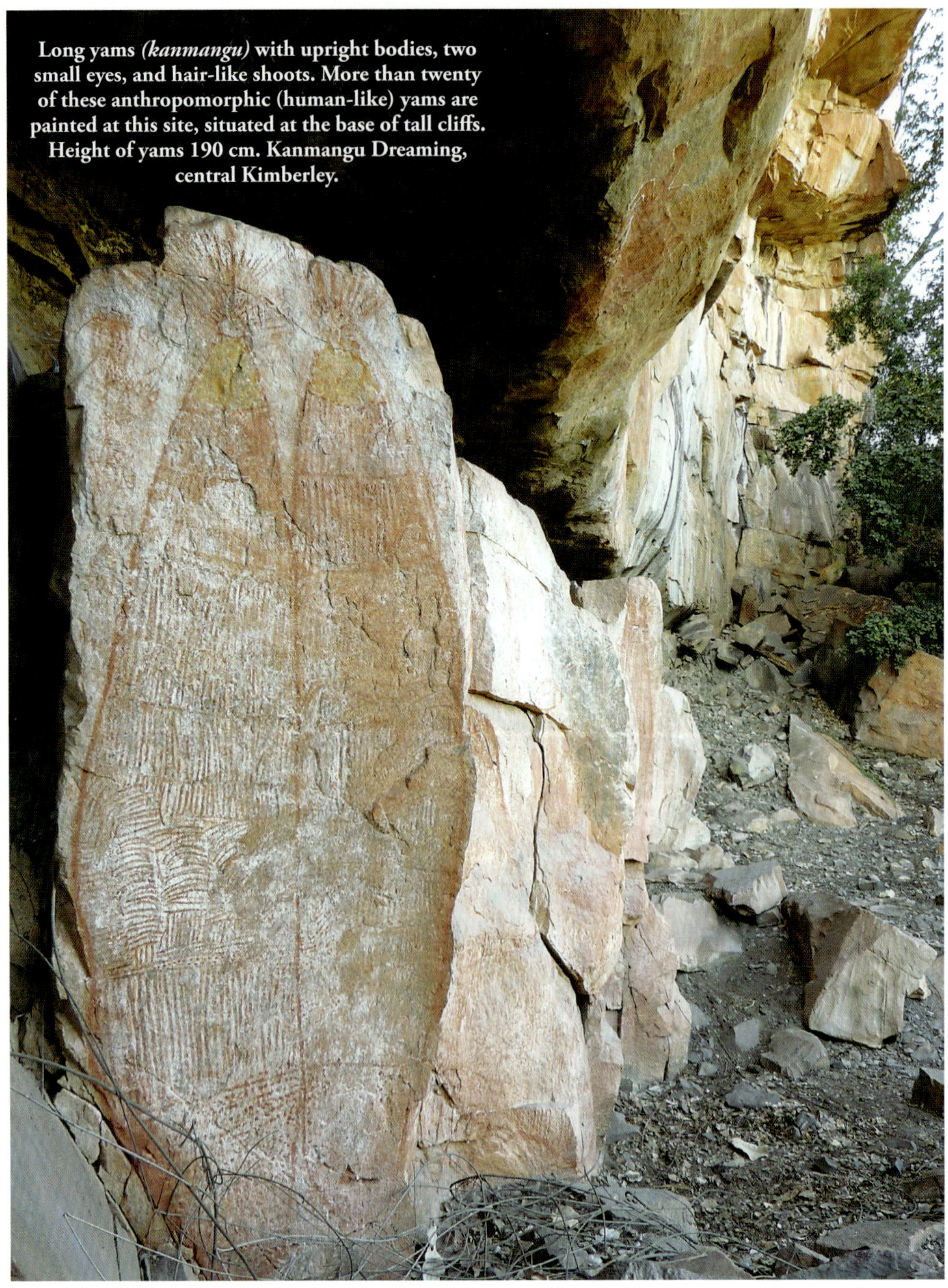

Long yams *(kanmangu)* with upright bodies, two small eyes, and hair-like shoots. More than twenty of these anthropomorphic (human-like) yams are painted at this site, situated at the base of tall cliffs. Height of yams 190 cm. Kanmangu Dreaming, central Kimberley.

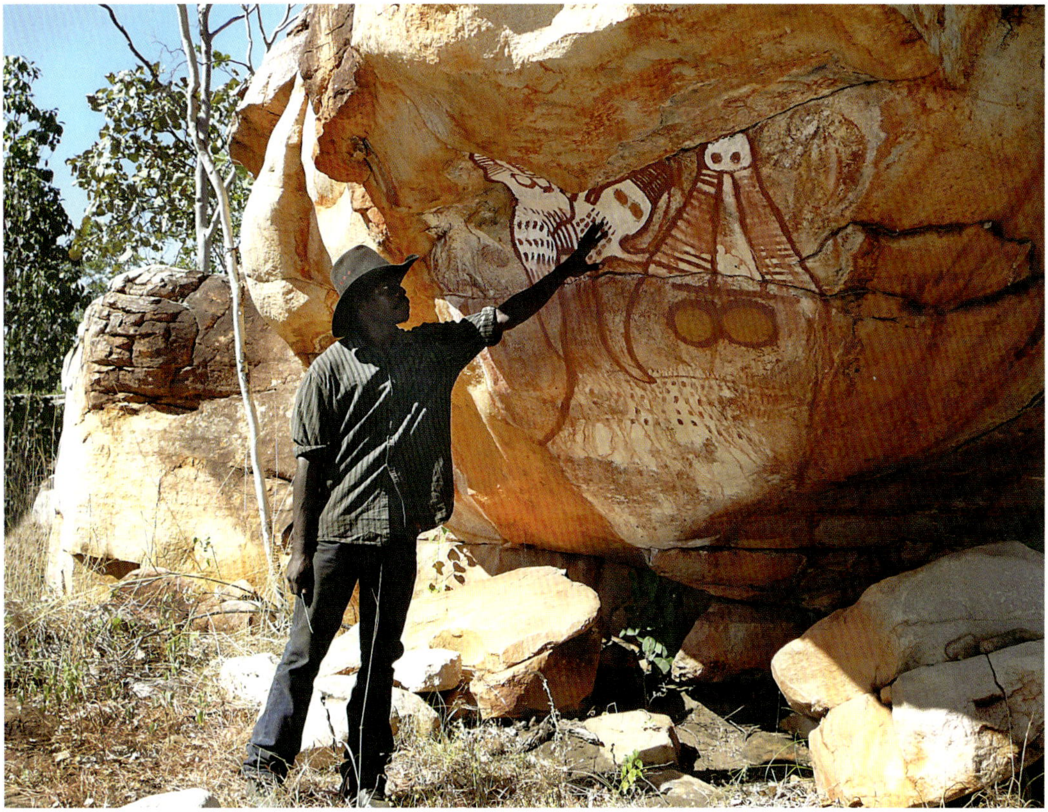

William Tataya at a Crocodile Dreaming site on Gibb River Station, central Kimberley.

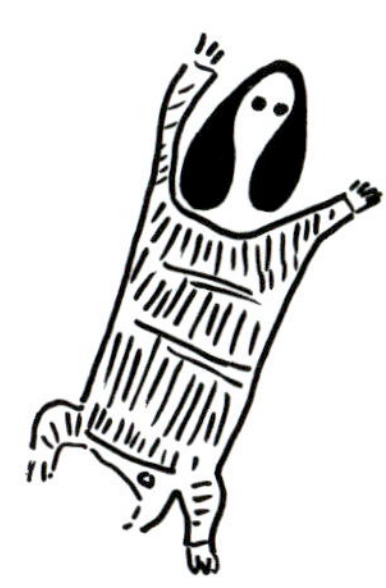

Many Wandjina paintings occur at totemic (Dreaming) sites celebrating a range of plants and animals. This chapter briefly outlines the nature of totems and totemic sites in Wandjina country.

Each member of Aboriginal society has one or more plants, animals, or inanimate objects which they regard as an emblematic leader, referred to as their *totem*. Each totem belongs to a *clan* (land-owning group) or *tribe* (language group) and is revered at a special place known as a *totemic site* or *increase centre*. Aboriginal people sometimes call these sites their *Dreaming* because they relate to the Creation Period, and it is believed that one can travel into the past at night when one dreams.

Totemic sites occur throughout Australia in the form of painted and engraved rock shelters, stone arrangements, and natural features such as trees and rock outcrops. In traditional times, it was the duty of clan leaders to regularly visit these sites, where they chanted, sang, rubbed or struck the rocks, and performed other rituals with the purpose of ensuring the continuing or increasing numbers of each species as a food source.

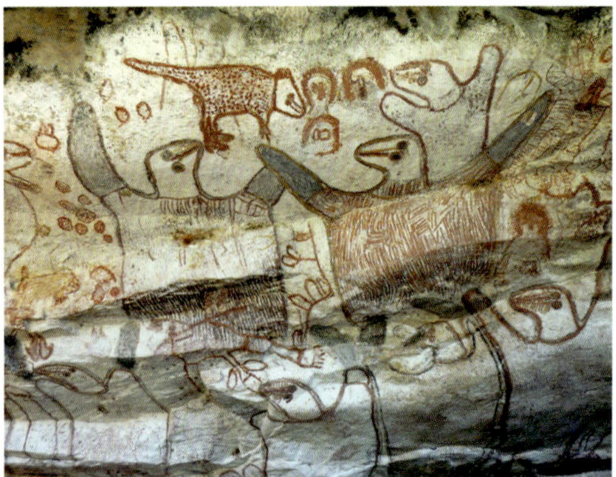

▲ An Eagle Dreaming site celebrating the wedge-tailed eagle *(warana)* and filled with paintings of eagles and Wandjina. Analogous to the eagle flying high in the sky, the site is located high on a hillside, looking over the valley below.

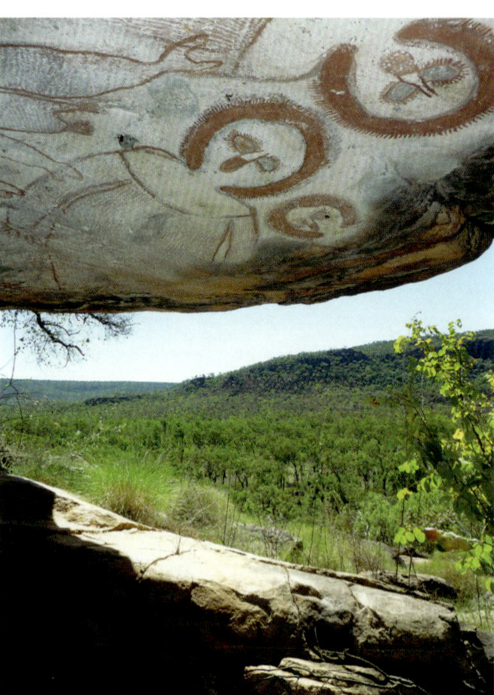

► Ceiling Wandjina at Eagle Dreaming, and view over the valley below.

▼ A Sugarbag-Wandjina Dreaming site, where a three-metre-long painting of a native beehive incorporates a Wandjina head into its left side. Central Kimberley.

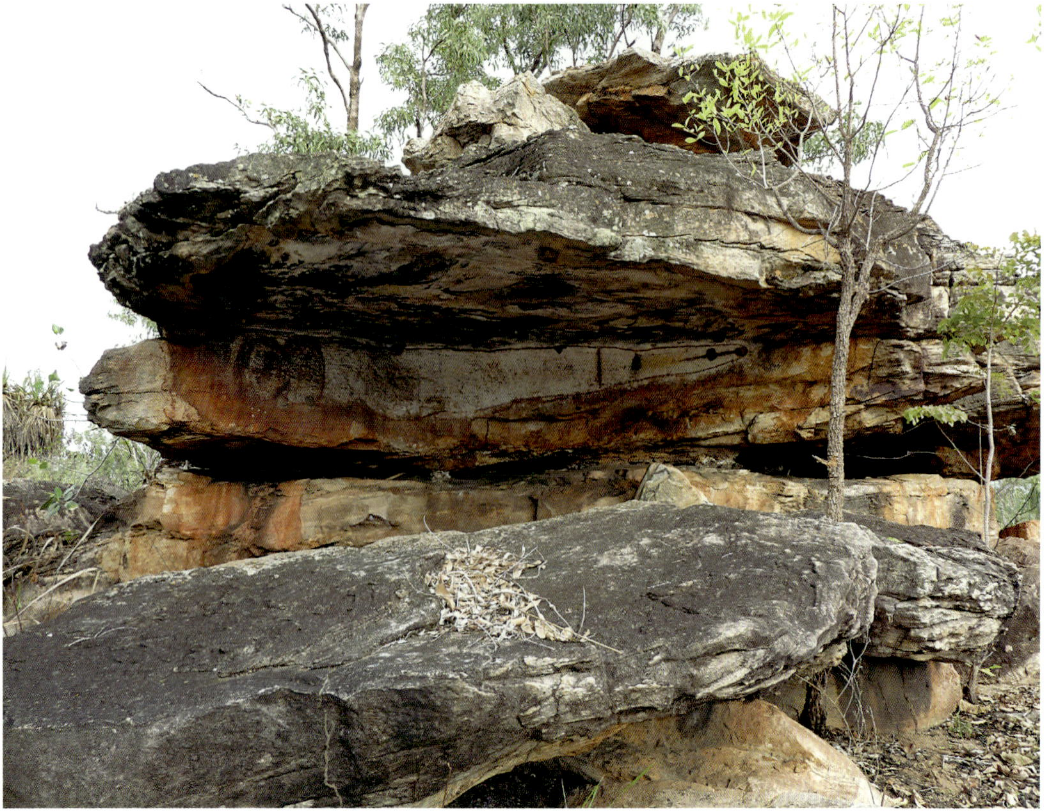

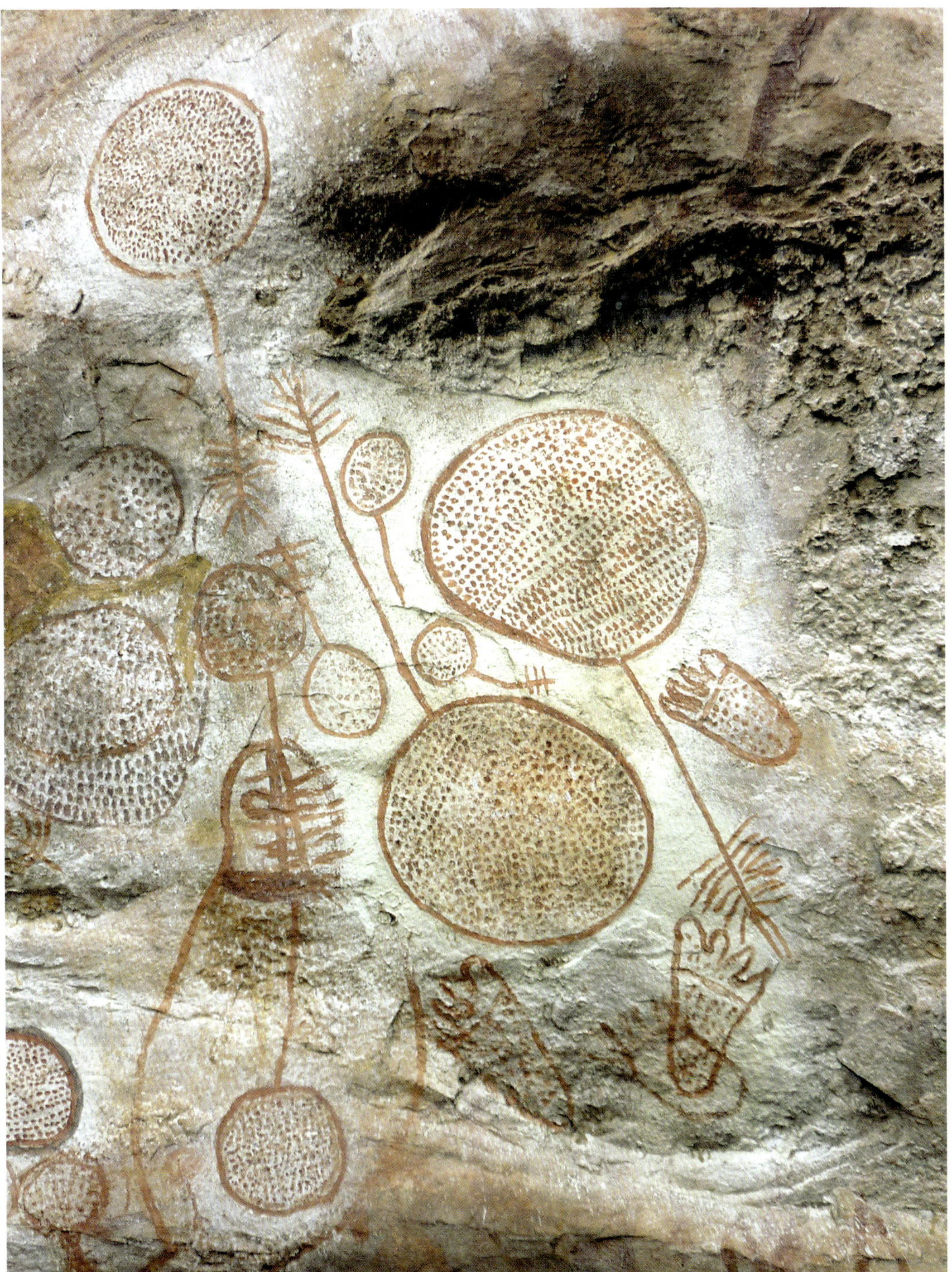

Paintings of human feet and round yams *(gunu)* with human-like properties in a large yam-Wandjina site in the central Kimberley. When the round yams are viewed lowermost, the upper lines represent their above-ground shoots. However, when viewed with the round yam uppermost, the lines below branch into arms and legs, with the round yam representing a headdress or a large head on a long thin neck.

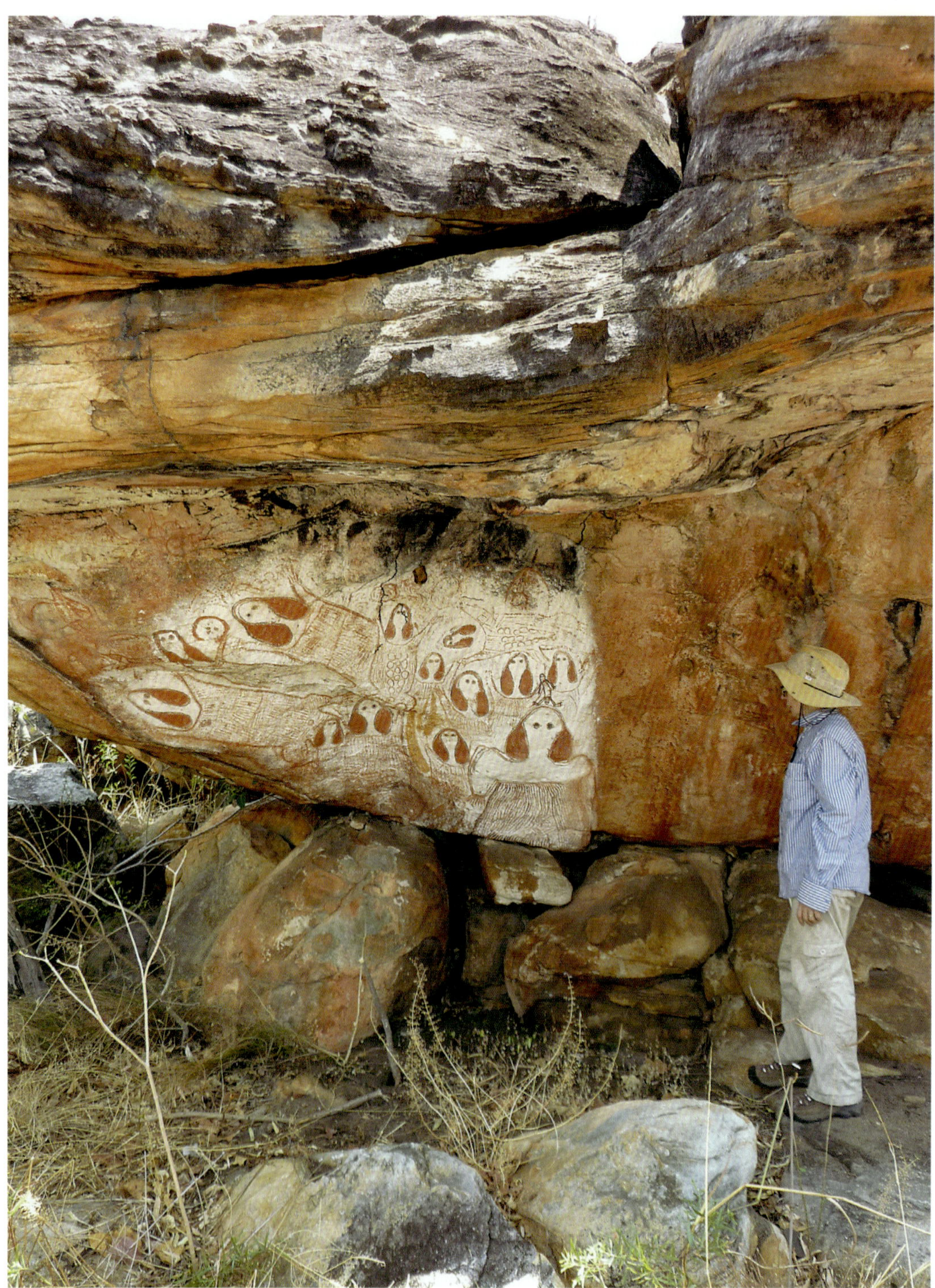

Tegulan-odin (Frill-necked lizard Dreaming), central Kimberley.

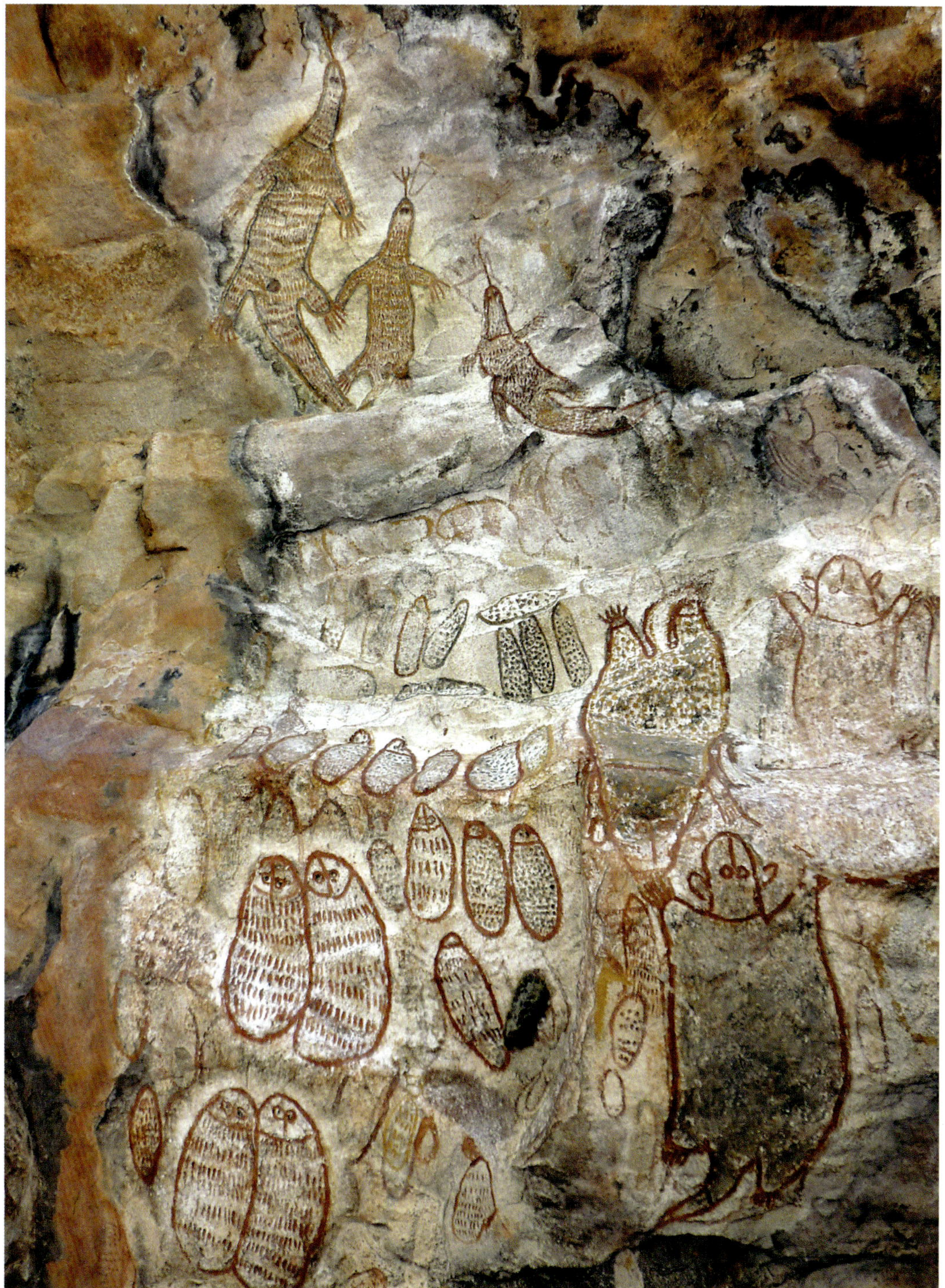

Goannas (top), a sugar glider (lower right) and numerous *lambara* (edible grubs) painted over a sloping shelter ceiling. Lambara Dreaming, Manning River, central Kimberley.

In the Kimberley, many totemic sites are rock art shelters dominated by the central theme of the totem. Examples illustrated in this chapter include totemic sites for long yams (*kanmangu* – pronounced *kun-mung-goo*), round yams (*gunu* – pronounced *goo-noo*), crocodiles, wedge-tailed eagles *(warana)*, frill-necked lizards *(tegulan)*, native bees, and edible grubs *(lambara)*.

The Wandjina painted at totemic sites are often small, and are regarded as playing a secondary role next to the totem. Sometimes the Wandjina are described as *helpers* for the totem, or they illustrate legends connecting the Wandjina with the totem. In some versions of legends, certain totems were also Wandjina in the past, and this is reflected in the art, when Wandjina features are incorporated into the totemic plant or animal. An example on page 80 shows a *sugarbag* (native bee hive) with its opening at one end and a Wandjina head at the other.

Rainbow Serpents

Totemic and Wandjina sites may include paintings and other manifestations of the Rainbow Serpent. Rainbow Serpents are large mythical snakes that produce child-spirits, and whose travels across the landscape during the Dreamtime scoured the ground, creating creeks, rivers and waterholes. They are scattered throughout the Kimberley, and manifest as paintings, upright stones, and natural landscape features such as winding rivers and creeks. They can be single or multiple, male or female. The most widespread Rainbow Serpent in the Kimberley is known as

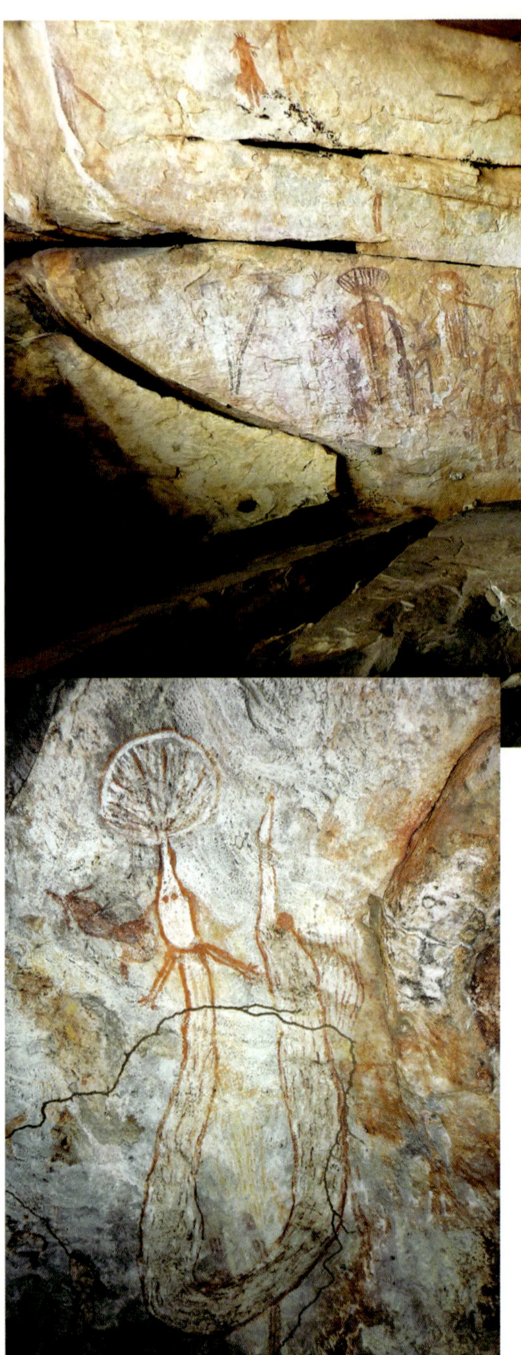

A Rainbow Serpent with circular headdress, two arms or tassels, and snake-like body. The headdress is symbolic of the round waterhole in which the Rainbow Serpent lives. The anus and tail are commonly pronounced on Aboriginal paintings of snakes. Length 143 cm. Painted across a large shelter ceiling at Lejmorro in the central Kimberley.

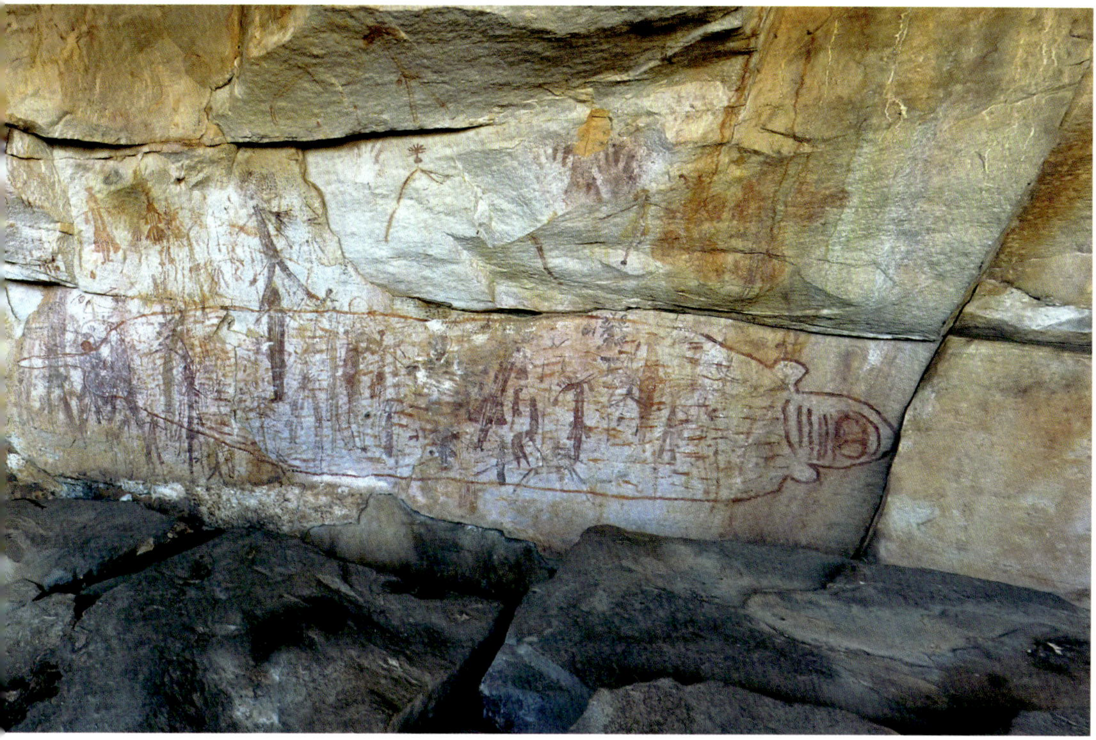

This large Rainbow Serpent, 3.4 metres long, lives in a subterranean cave in the Lawley River Valley in the northern Kimberley. It has a short tail at the left, head with two eyes at the right, and is painted over many older Straight Part Figures.

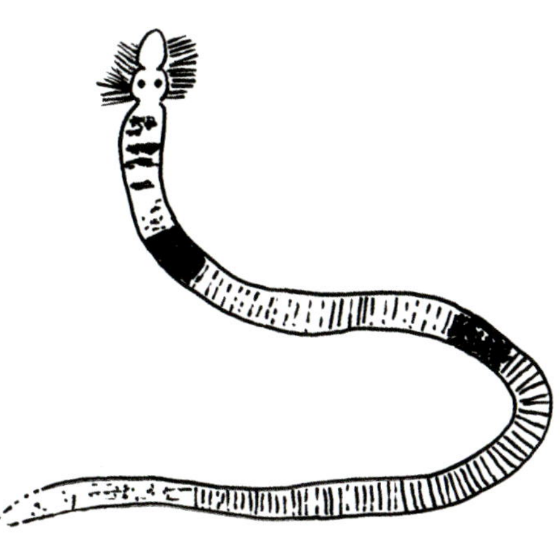

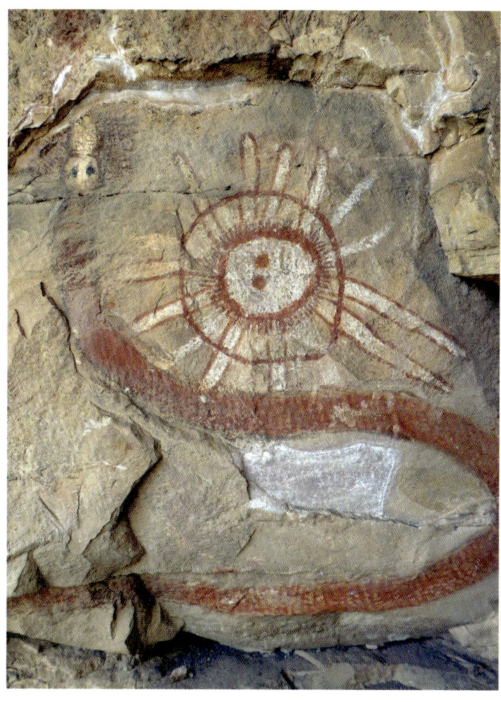

A Rainbow Serpent with two eyes and a small headdress or whiskers, painted over a sunray-human-Wandjina-like form with two eyes, and legs at the lower right. Height of serpent 80 cm. Central Kimberley.

Ungud, but the individual names and specific details of each legendary Rainbow Serpent vary from clan to clan and tribe to tribe. In the rock shelters, they appear as imaginative combined human-snake, animal-snake, and plant-snake forms.

Totemic (Dreaming) sites in the form of stone arrangements

Not all totemic sites are painted sites. Many consist of man-made stone piles, stone circles, stone lines and other

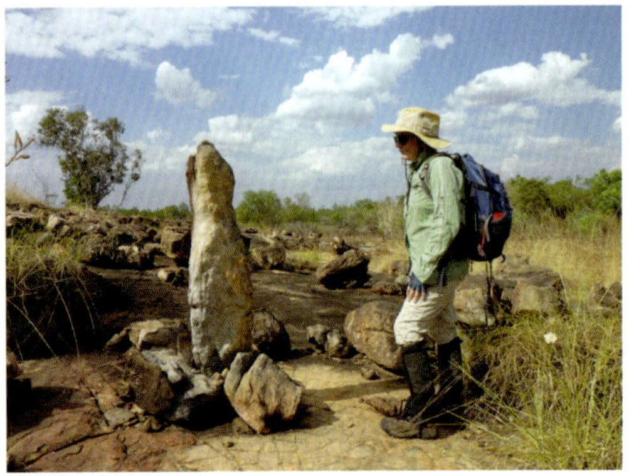

An upright stone representing Ungud the Rainbow Serpent emerging from the ground. This forms part of an extensive group of stone arrangements stretching over the raised sloping pavement. Ngarinyin territory, central Kimberley.

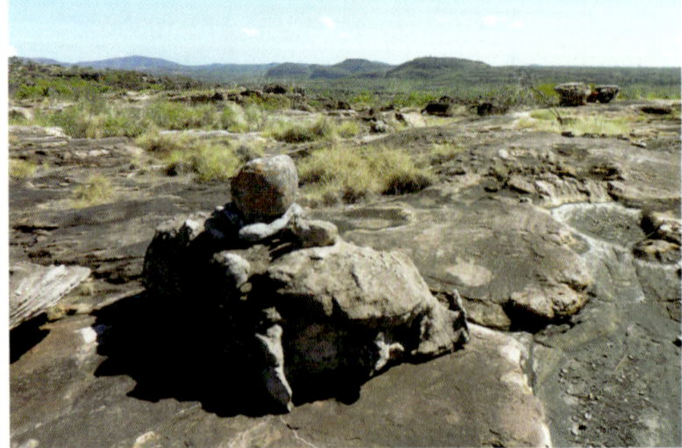

A large round stone wedged amongst smaller rocks, placed on a natural rock pedestal. The large stone has been ritually rubbed and pounded during increase ceremonies performed at the site. Western Kimberley region.

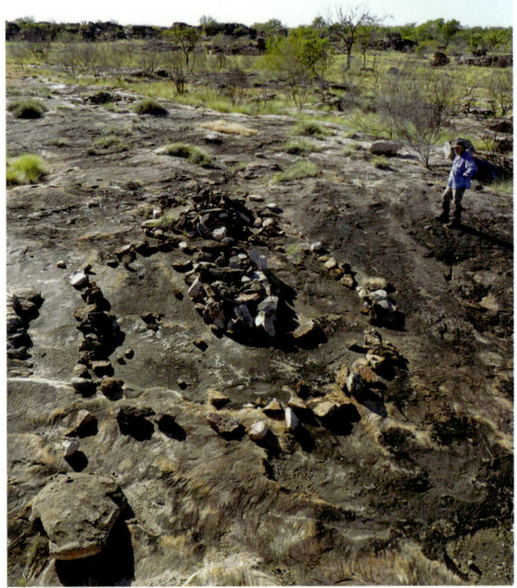

A totemic site marked by a central stone pile surrounded by a loose oval of stones, placed on a flat rocky pavement. Located beside a small creek which flows into the Lawley River, northern Kimberley.

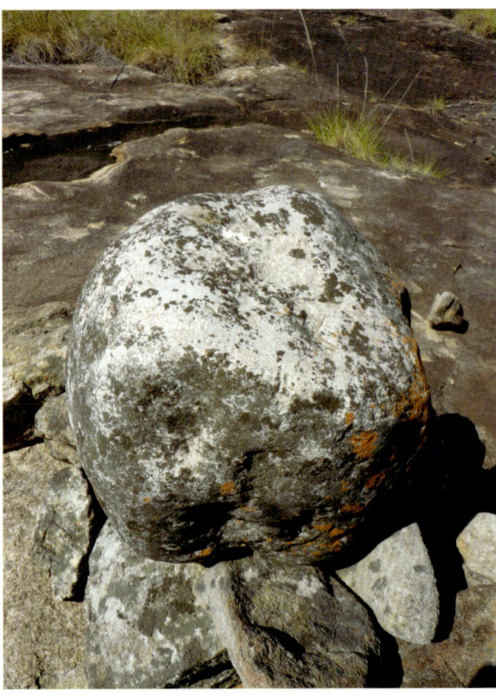

Evidence of rubbing and pounding of the stone monument.

stone arrangements. Three Kimberley sites illustrated here consist of a cluster of stones placed on a natural rock pedestal, a stone circle placed around a central stone pile, and an upright stone.

Conclusion

Belief in the power of Wandjina, the totems and the Rainbow Serpents continues amongst Kimberley people to this day. Those with artistic skills continue to produce images of Wandjina and the totems, carved on slate, boab nuts and didgeridoos, and painted on barks, canvas and paper.

Inspired by the rock paintings around Kalumburu in the Kimberley's north, Kevin Waina of the Gwini tribe has been painting *girri girri* (Bradshaw Figures) on canvas since 1992. Two of his sons (Lawrence and Uriah) and two daughters (Cassandra and Melissa) also paint *girri girri*, and the traditions of painting Wandjina and Bradshaw Figures live on amongst the people of the region.

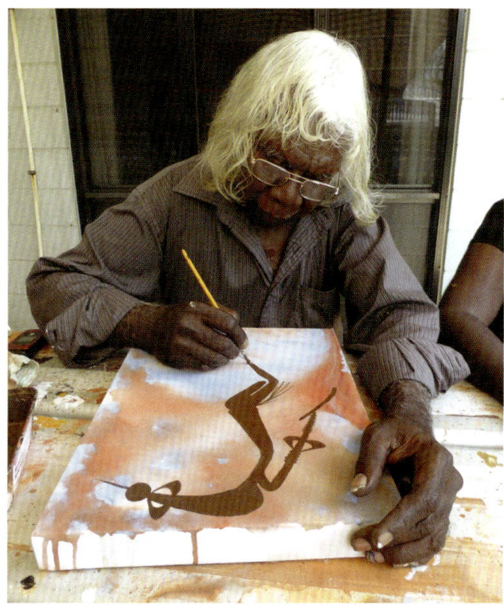

Gwini artist Kevin Waina painting *girri girri* (Bradshaw Figures) with acrylic paints on canvas in 2015.

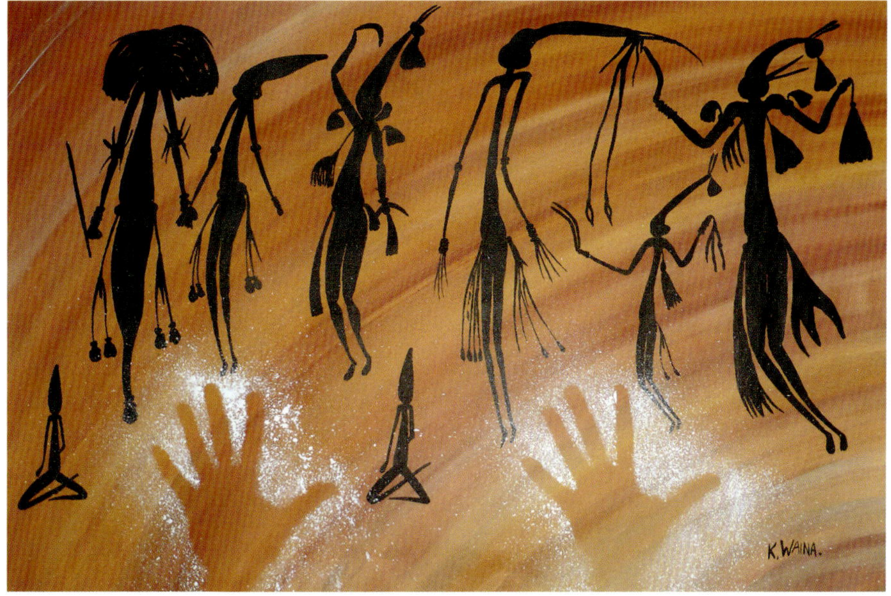

Girri girri (Bradshaw Figures) painted with acrylics on canvas by Gwini artist Kevin Waina.

Acknowledgements

Many people have assisted or been part of the author's pursuit of Kimberley Rock art over the years. Aboriginal people who have shared their cultural knowledge with the author include: Campbell Allenbrae, William Bunjuk, Paul Chapman, Dolores Cheinmora, Hector Dhungal, Jonathon Goonak, Wilfred Goonak, Jack and Lilly Karadada, Billy King, Phil Krunmurra, Sam Lovell, Scotty Martin, David Mowaljarlai, Mary Pandilo, Manuella Punan, William Tataya, Kevin Waina, Laurie Waina, Yvonne White, Alfie White and Dicky Wudmurra.

In addition to solo exploring, I have teamed up with, or discussed Kimberley rock art in the field with the following people: Dick Barkas (1979), Annie Welch (1983, 1985, 1991, 2009, 2010, 2011 and 2012), Robert Bednarik's group (1988), Charles Warner (1988), Anne and John Koeyers (1988 to the present), Grahame Walsh (1989, 1991 and 1992), Bruce McMonnies (1992), Tim Anders

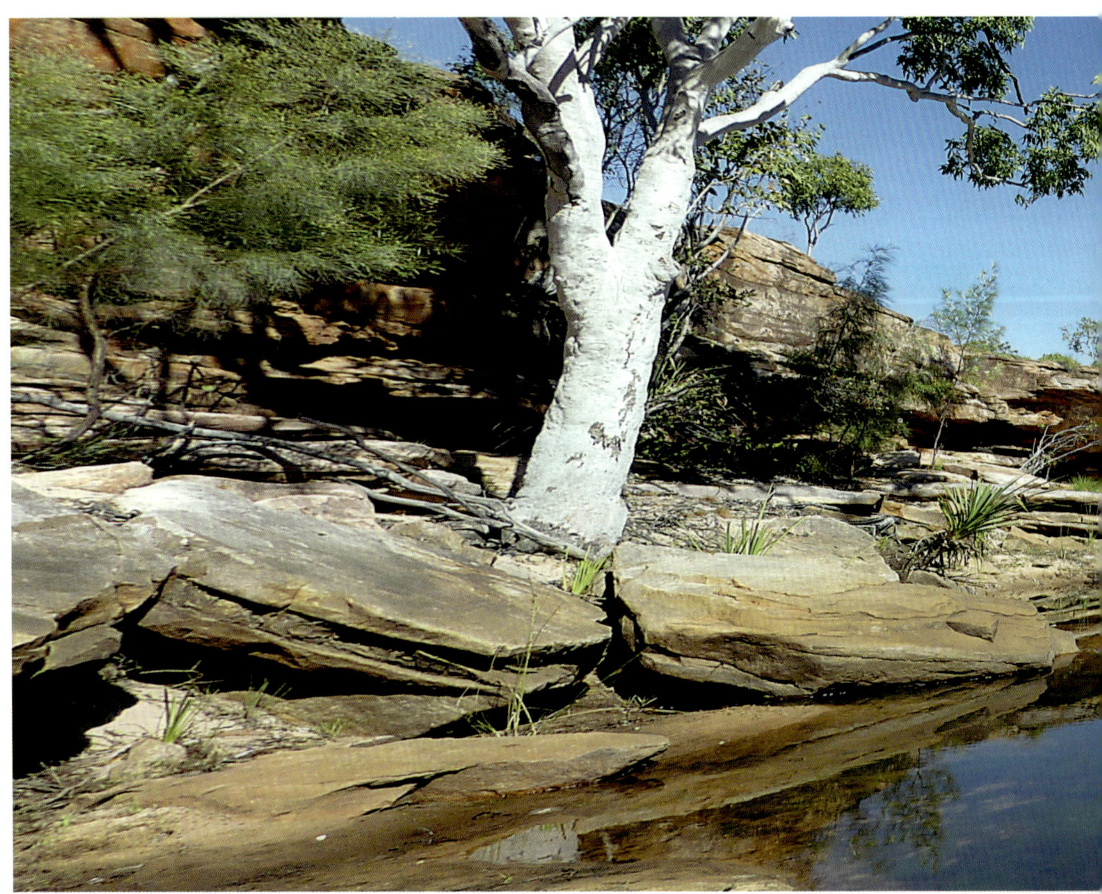

(1994), Susan Bradley (2010), Anscar McPhee (2010), Mike Donaldson's group (2011 and 2012), Joc Schmiechen (2011, 2012 and 2013), Michael Rainsbury (2012 and 2013), Jeff Gresham's group (2013), and Mike Beckingham and Stroma Lawson (2013).

Cattle Station owners and managers who have assisted in my research include Susan Bradley, Debbie and Chris Holt, Peter and Pat Lacy, and Terry and John Scott. I am particularly indebted to Anne and John Koeyers of Drysdale River Station who have provided advice, friendship, vehicle repairs and fuel for many years, making the exploration of the central and northern Kimberley easier than it would be otherwise.

Two photographs of Aranda men from Central Australia dressed in ceremonial costume were taken by Ted Strehlow circa 1949, from pages 53 and 89 of *Wüstentanz: Australien spirituell erleben*. I thank Kim Akerman for providing the photograph of Mick Rallah constructing a ceremonial headdress on page 45, and Michael Rainsbury for the photograph on the title page. Archival research has been undertaken at state and national libraries, museums and archives in the Northern Territory, Western Australia, Victoria, South Australia, New South Wales and Canberra.

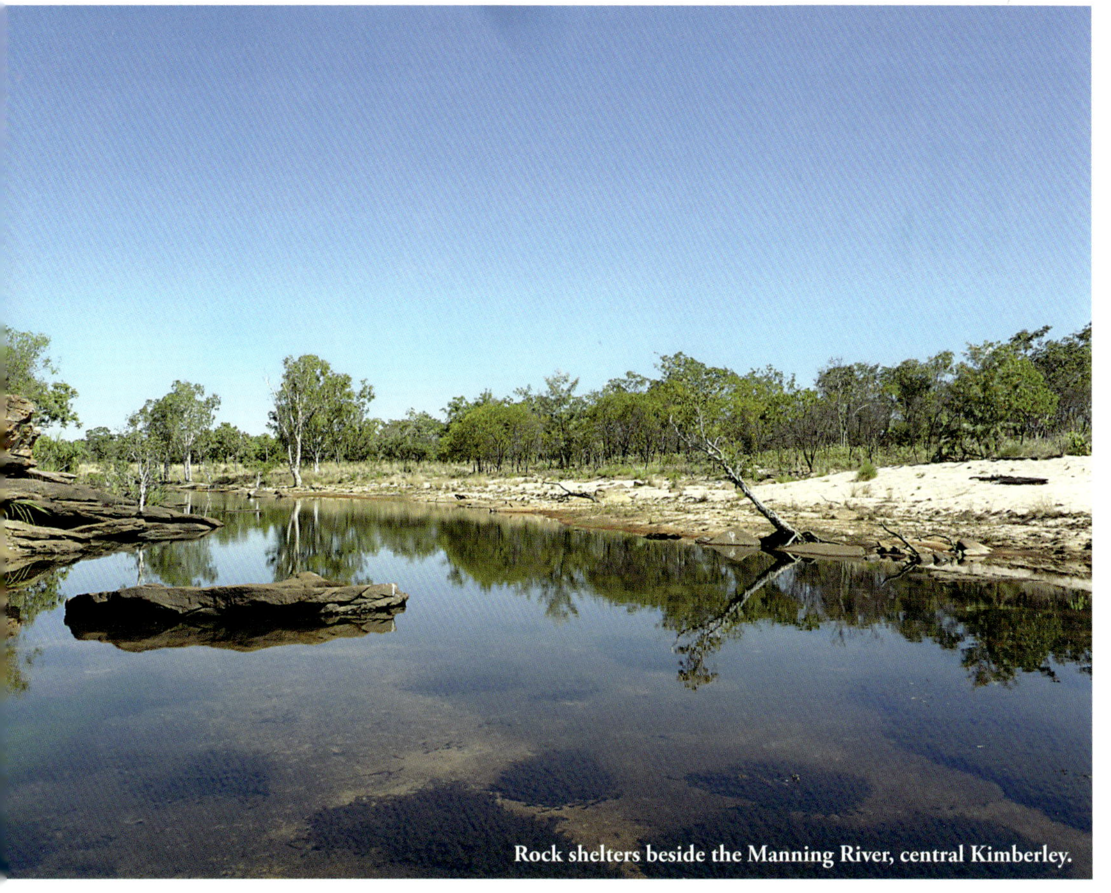

Rock shelters beside the Manning River, central Kimberley.

Books and journal articles by David M. Welch

1982. *Aboriginal Rock Art of Kakadu National Park*. Big Country Picture Company, Darwin.

1990. The Bichrome Art Period in the Kimberley, Australia. *Rock Art Research*, Vol. 7: 110-24.

1992 (a). *Proposed Chronology of Kimberley Region, Western Australia, Rock Art.* Handout for the Second AURA Congress, Cairns.

1992 (b). Kakadu Dreaming: Ancestral Beings and Mythology in the Rock Art of the Kakadu Region. In J. McDonald and I. P. Haskovec (eds) *State of the Art: Regional Rock Art Studies in Australia and Melanesia.* Occasional AURA Publication No. 6: 195-201. Australian Rock Art Research Association, Melbourne.

1993 (a). Early Naturalistic Human Figures in the Kimberley, Australia. *Rock Art Research*, Vol. 10: 24-37.

1993 (b). Stylistic change in the Kimberley rock art, Australia. In M. Lorblanchet and P. G. Bahn (editors), *Rock Art Studies: The Post-stylistic Era or Where Do We Go From Here?* Oxbow Monograph 35: 99-113, Oxford.

1993 (c). The Early Rock Art of the Kimberley, Australia: Developing a Chronology. In J. Steinbring, A. Watchman, P. Faulstich and P. S. Taçon (editors), *Time and Space: Dating and Spatial Considerations in Rock Art Research*, Occasional AURA Publication No. 8: 13-21. Australian Rock Art Research Association, Melbourne.

1995. Beeswax Rock Art in the Kimberley, Western Australia. *Rock Art Research*, Vol. 12: 23-28.

1996 (a). Material Culture in Kimberley Rock Art, Australia. *Rock Art Research*, Vol. 13: 104-123.

1996 (b). Simple Human Figures in Kimberley Rock Art, Western Australia. *The Artefact*, Vol. 19: 73:89. Archaeological and Anthropological Society of Victoria Inc. [Note: the editor of this publication placed the captions for some of the figures out of place.]

1997. Fight or Dance? Ceremony and the Spearthrower in Northern Australian Rock Art. *Rock Art Research*, Vol. 14: 88-112.

1999 (a). Cultural Change in the Kimberley Rock Art, Western Australia. In *BCSP 31-32 Grafismo E Semiotica, World*

Journal of Prehistoric and Primitive Art, pages 288-312. Centro Camuno Di Studi Preistorici, Brescia, Italy.

1999 (b). Fossilised Human Footprints on the Coast of North Western Australia. *The Artefact*, Vol. 22: 3-10. Archaeological and Anthropological Society of Victoria Inc.

2000. Hand Grip or Art: Tribal or Individual? *Rock Art Research*, Vol. 17: 128-130.

2003. Plant Motifs in Kimberley Rock-Art, Australia. *Before Farming*, 2003/4 (5): 387-398.

2004. Large Animals and Small Humans in the Rock Art of Northern Australia. *Rock Art Research*, Vol. 21, No. 1: 47-56.

2006. *Making Fire.* (Co-authored with Stephen Blake.) David M. Welch, Virginia, Northern Territory.

2007. Bradshaw Art of the Kimberley. In M. Donaldson and K. Kenneally (editors), *Rock Art of the Kimberley* (Proceedings of the Kimberley Society Rock Art Seminar held at The University of Western Australia, Perth, 2005), pages 81-100. Kimberley Society, Perth.

2011. *Darwin Gecko.* [A children's book] David M. Welch, Virginia, Northern Territory.

2012 (a). Two Kakadu Headdresses. *Rock Art Research*, Vol. 29: 115-118.

2012 (b). Oh Dear! No Deer! *Rock Art Research*, Vol. 29: 171-177.

2014. *Aboriginal Paintings at Munurru, Kimberley, Western Australia.* David M. Welch. Coolalinga, Northern Territory.

2015 (a). Palorchestes or Bunyip? *International Newsletter on Rock Art (INORA)*, No. 72: 18-24. Foix, France.

2015 (b). Thy Thylacoleo is a Thylacine. *Australian Archaeology*, No. 80: 40-47.

2015 (c). *Aboriginal Paintings of Drysdale River National Park, Kimberley, Western Australia.* David M. Welch, Coolalinga, Northern Territory.

2015 (d). *Aboriginal Paintings at Ubirr and Nourlangie, Kakadu National Park, Northern Australia.* David M. Welch, Coolalinga, Northern Territory.

Further reading

Akerman, K. 2016. *Wanjina: Notes on Some Iconic Ancestral Beings of the Northern Kimberley.* Hesperian Press, Carlisle, Western Australia.

Akerman, K. and J. Ryan. 1993. *Images of Power: Aboriginal Art of the Kimberley.* National Gallery of Victoria, Melbourne.

Blundell, V. and D. Woolagoodja. 2005. *Keeping the Wanjinas Fresh.* Fremantle Arts Centre Press, Fremantle.

Bradshaw, J. 1892. Notes on a Recent Trip to Prince Regent's River. *Transactions, Royal Geographical Society of Australia (Victorian Branch)* 9 (part 2): 90-103.

Chalarimeri, A. M. 2001. *The Man from the Sunrise Side.* Magabala Books, Broome.

Crawford, I. M. 1968. *The Art of the Wandjina.* Oxford University Press, Melbourne.

Crawford, I. M. 1977. The Relationship of Bradshaw and Wandjina Art in North-West Kimberley. In P. J. Ucko (editor), *Form in Indigenous Art: Schematisation in the Art of Aboriginal Australia and Prehistoric Europe*, pages 357-369. Australian Institute of Aboriginal Studies, Canberra.

Donaldson, M. 2012. *Kimberley Rock Art. Volume 1: Mitchell Plateau Area.* Wildrocks Publications, Mount Lawley, Western Australia.

Donaldson, M. 2012. *Kimberley Rock Art. Volume 2: North Kimberley.* Wildrocks Publications, Mount Lawley, Western Australia.

Donaldson, M. 2013. *Kimberley Rock Art. Volume 3: Rivers and Ranges.* Wildrocks Publications, Mount Lawley, Western Australia.

Doring, J. 2000. *Gwion Gwion.* Kőnemann Verlagsgesellschaft, Cologne, Germany.

Huntley, J., M. Aubert, J. Ross, H. E. A. Brand and M. J. Morwood. 2013. One Colour, (At Least) Two Minerals: A Study of Mulberry Rock Art Pigment and a Mulberry Pigment "Quarry" from the Kimberley, Northern Australia. *Archaeometry*, 57: 77-99. University of Oxford.

Lommel, A. 1997. *The Unambal: a Tribe in Northwest Australia.* Takarakka Nowan Kas Publications, Carnarvon Gorge, Queensland.

Morwood, M. J., G. L. Walsh and A. L. Watchman. 2010. AMS Radiocarbon Ages for Beeswax and Charcoal Pigments in North Kimberley Rock Art. *Rock Art Research*, Vol. 27, No. 1: 3-8.

Mowaljarlai, D. and J. Malnic. 1993.

Yorro Yorro, Spirit of the Kimberley. Magabala Books Aboriginal Corporation, Broome, Western Australia.

O'Connor, S. 1995. Carpenter's Gap Rockshelter 1: 40,000 Years of Aboriginal Occupation in the Napier Ranges, Kimberley, WA. *Australian Archaeology*, No. 40: 58-59.

Petri, H. 2011. *The Dying World in Northwest Australia.* Hesperian Press, Carlisle, Western Australia.

Playford, P. E. 1960. Aboriginal Rock Paintings of the West Kimberley Region. Western Australia, *Journal of the Royal Society of Western Australia*, Vol. 43: 112-122.

Roberts, R., G. L. Walsh, A. Murray, J. Olley, R. Jones, M. J. Morwood, C. Tuniz, E. Lawson, M. Macphall, D. Bowdery and I. Naumann. 1997. Luminescence Dating of Rock Art and Past Environments Using Mud-wasp Nests in Northern Australia. *Nature*, Vol. 387: 696-699.

Schmiechen, J. 1986. *Survey of Aboriginal Rock Art and Cultural Sites. Drysdale River, East Kimberley, Western Australia. Report of Findings: Drysdale River Expedition 1986, Operation Raleigh.* Unpublished report.

Schmiechen, J. 1994. *Shadows in Stone: A Report on Aboriginal Rock Art: Survey Expeditions 1988 and 1991, Drysdale River National Park, Kimberley, Western Australia.* Unpublished report.

Schulz, A. S. 1956. North-west Australian Rock Paintings. *Memoirs of the National Museum of Victoria*, No. 20.

Walsh, G. L. 1988. *Australia's Greatest Rock Art.* E. J. Brill – Robert Brown & Associates, Bathurst.

Walsh, G. L. 1994. *Bradshaws: Ancient Rock Paintings of North-West Australia.* Edition Limitée, Switzerland.

Walsh, G. L. 2000. *Bradshaw Art of the Kimberley.* Takarakka Nowan Kas Publications, Toowong.

Wilson, I. 2006. *Lost World of the Kimberley: Extraordinary glimpses of Australia's Ice Age ancestors.* Allen and Unwin, Crows Nest.

Wunambal-Gaambera Aboriginal Corporation, 2000. *Land of Wandjina and Wunggurr: Ngauwudu Management Plan.* Kimberley Land Council, Broome.

Index

AUSTRALIAN ABORIGINAL CULTURE SERIES

Published by David M. Welch www.aboriginalculture.com.au

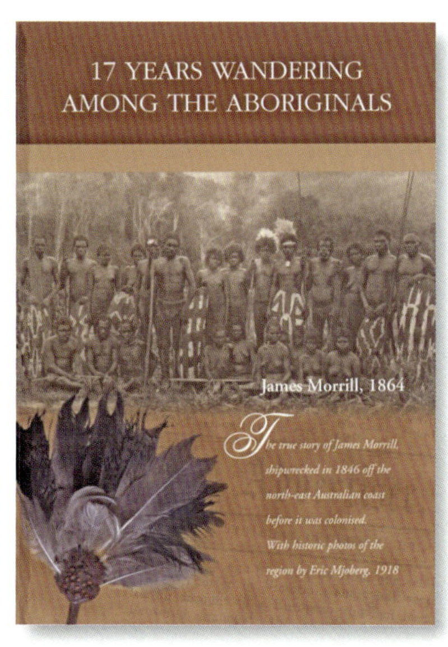

No. 1:

17 Years Wandering Among the Aboriginals.

James Morrill. 2006

ISBN 978-0-9775035-0-6

The author was shipwrecked and lived with Queensland tribes from 1846-1863. Includes many photos from the late 1800s.

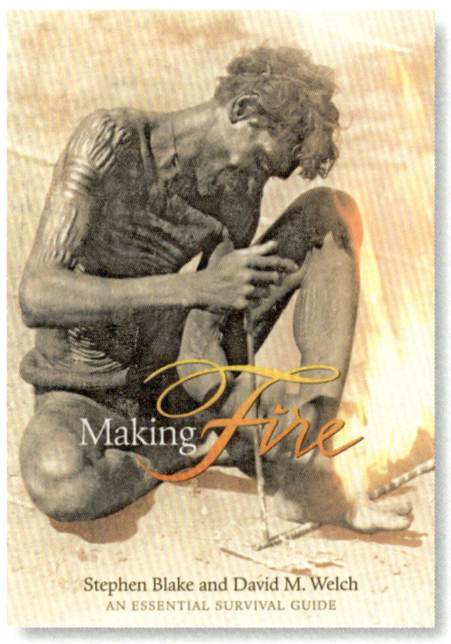

No. 2:

Making Fire.

Stephen Blake and David M. Welch. 2006

ISBN 978-0-9775035-1-3

Describes the evolution of making fire by rubbing together two sticks, as well as a practical guide to achieve this.

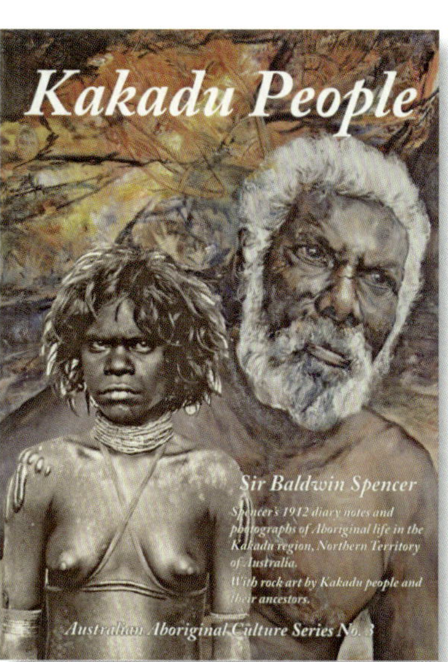

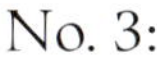

No. 3:

***Kakadu People*.**

Baldwin Spencer. 2008

ISBN 978-0-9775035-3-7

Spencer's 1912 diary notes and photographs of Kakadu people, enhanced by additional colour images of local rock art, wildlife and scenery. Includes 204 illustrations with 47 of rock art.

No. 4:

An Uncontrollable Child: The Autobiography of an Aboriginal Artist.

Reggie Sultan. 2008

ISBN 978-0-9775035-2-0

An unusual autobiography containing images of Reggie Sultan's paintings of bush foods and landscapes, and providing insights into the motifs found in Central Australian Aboriginal art.

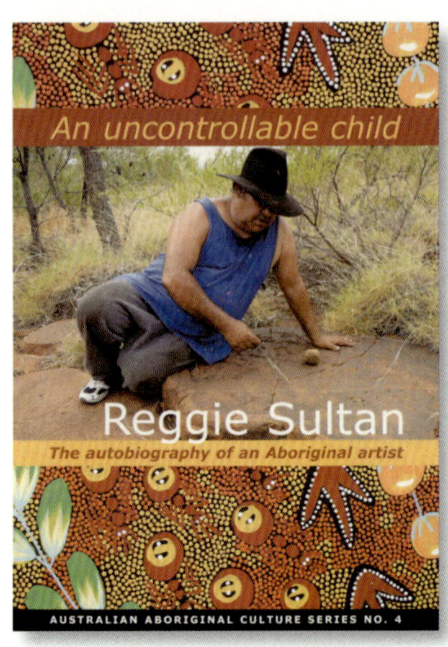

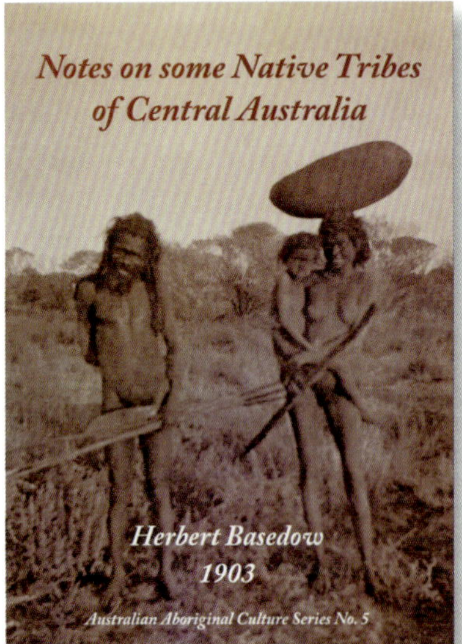

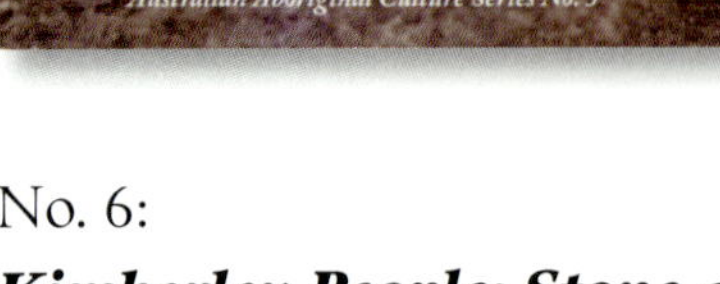

No. 5:

Notes on some Native Tribes of Central Australia.

Herbert Basedow. 2008

ISBN 978-0-9775035-4-4

Basedow's 1903 anthropological expedition to Central Australia includes his original illustrations of rock art and photographs of people living in a harsh desert environment.

No. 6:

Kimberley People: Stone age Bushmen of Today.

J. R. B. Love. 2009

ISBN 978-0-9775035-6-8

A first-hand account of life with northern Kimberley Aborigines, written in 1936, with many previously unpublished photographs from the region.

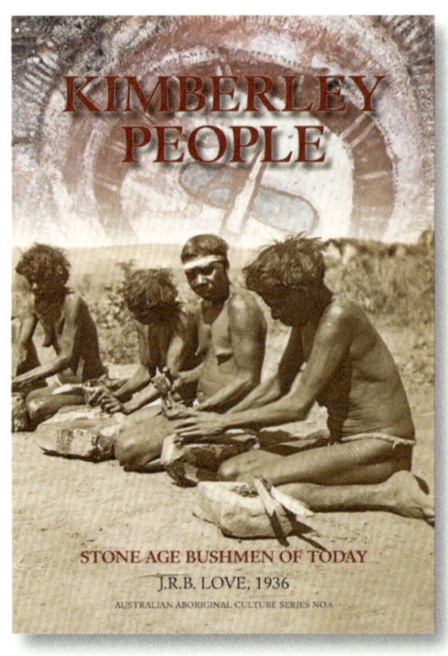

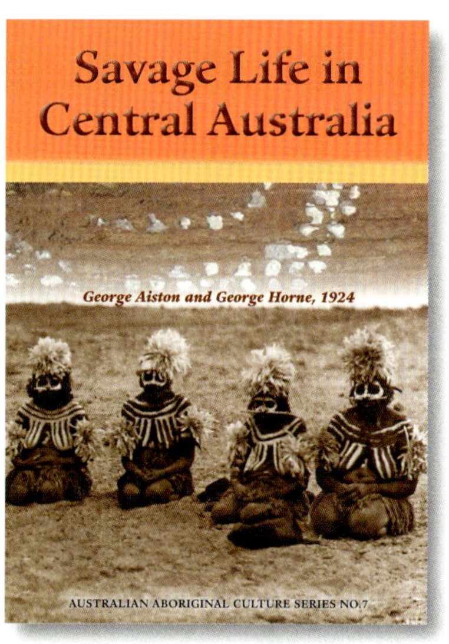

No. 7:

Savage Life in Central Australia.

George Aiston & George Horne. 2009

ISBN 978-0-9775035-7-5

A compilation of the original 1924 text with added historic and recent photographs of cultural activities, sacred sites and bush foods from the *Dieri* and *Wangkangurru* tribal lands.

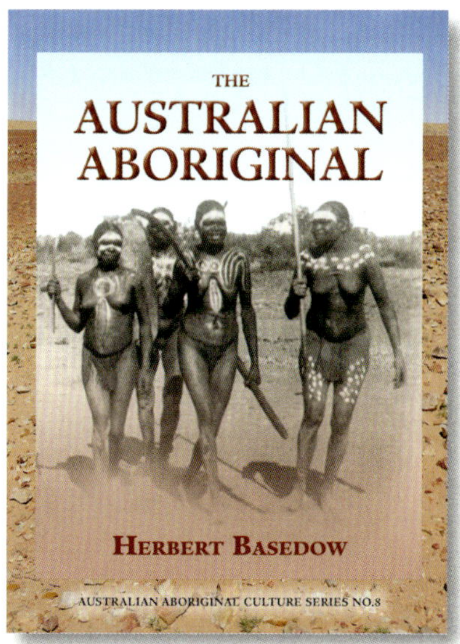

No. 8:

The Australian Aboriginal.

Herbert Basedow. 2012

ISBN 978-0-9871389-3-4

Hardcover

The culmination of the life's work of Dr. Herbert Basedow who travelled the most remote parts of Australia from 1903 to 1928. 472 pages with over 300 photographs and illustrations.

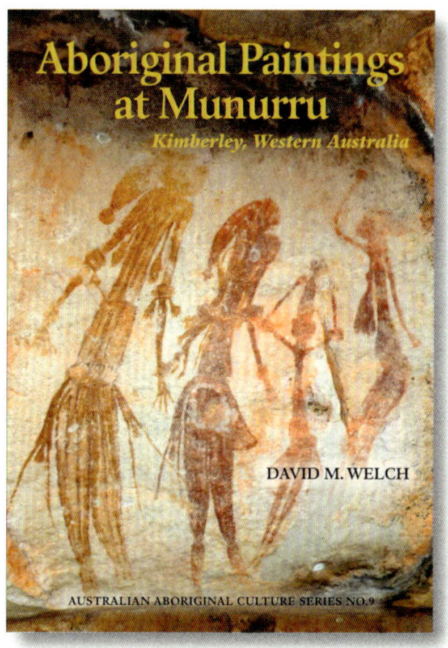

No. 9:

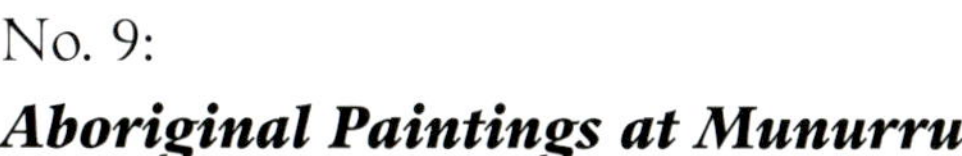

Aboriginal Paintings at Munurru.

David M. Welch. 2014

ISBN 978-0-9871389-2-7

A visitors' guide to Wandjina and early Kimberley rock art shelters at Munurru, located beside the King Edward River in the northern Kimberley.

No. 10:

Aboriginal Paintings of Drysdale River National Park.

David M. Welch. 2015

ISBN 978-0-9871389-7-2

Drysdale River National Park in far north Western Australia contains a wealth of ancient Aboriginal paintings perfectly preserved in the caves and recesses along the river gorges, valleys and side gullies.

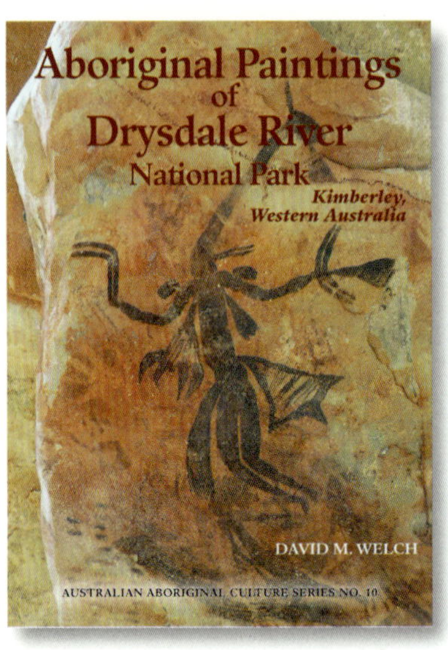

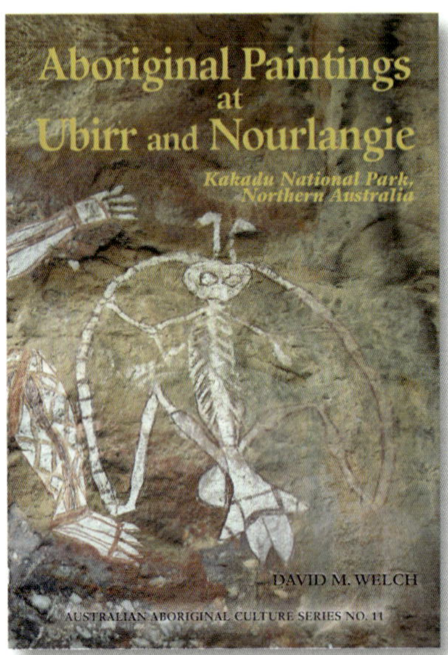

No. 11:

Aboriginal Paintings at Ubirr and Nourlangie.

David M. Welch. 2015

ISBN 978-0-9871389-8-9

Ubirr and Nourlangie, two monumental rocks in Kakadu National Park, are adorned with Aboriginal paintings of the Rainbow Serpent, Lightning Man, Cockatoo Lady, Ancestral Beings, sorcery figures and ceremonially-dressed dancing figures.

No. 12:

From Bradshaw to Wandjina: Aboriginal Paintings of the Kimberley Region, Western Australia.

David M. Welch. 2016

ISBN 978-0-9871389-9-6

The Kimberley's rock shelter paintings trace changes in Aboriginal ceremonial dress and religious beliefs from ancient times to the present.

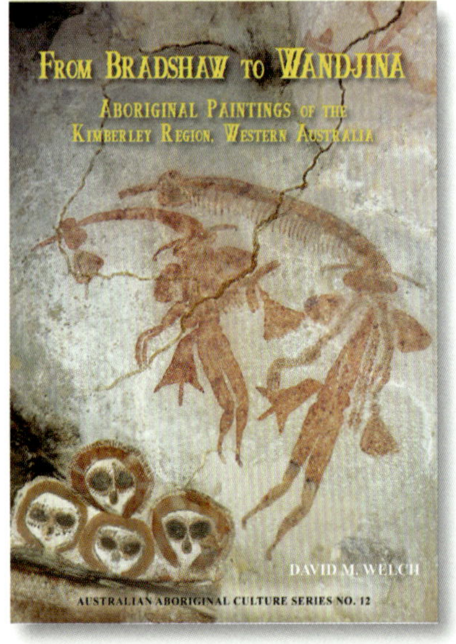

By the same publisher:

The Arunta.

Spencer and Gillen. 1927

ISBN 978-0-9871389-1-0

Facsimile edition 2011.

Hard cover, two volume set in a boxed case. Spencer and Gillen worked amongst the Arunta of Central Australia between 1894 and 1902, producing their account of the organisation, customs, beliefs and general culture of the people.

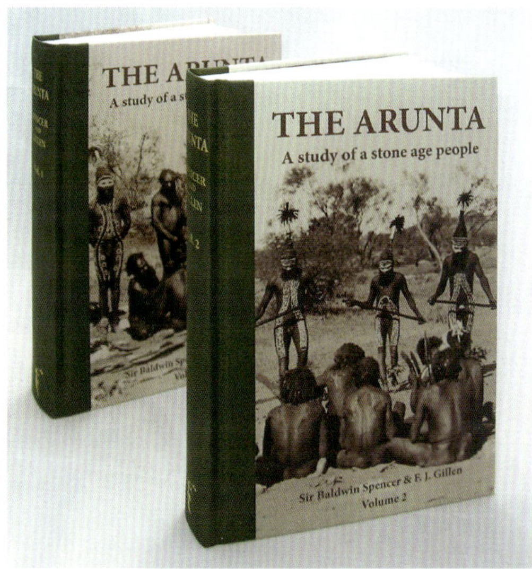

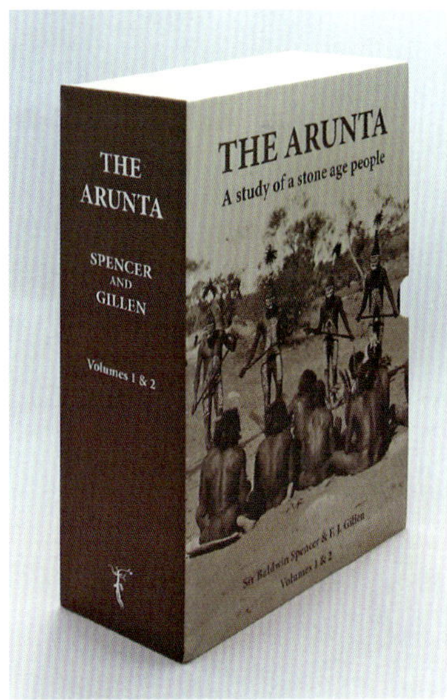

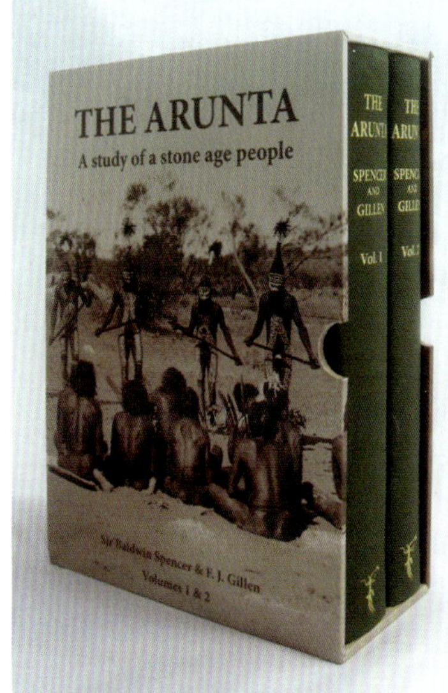

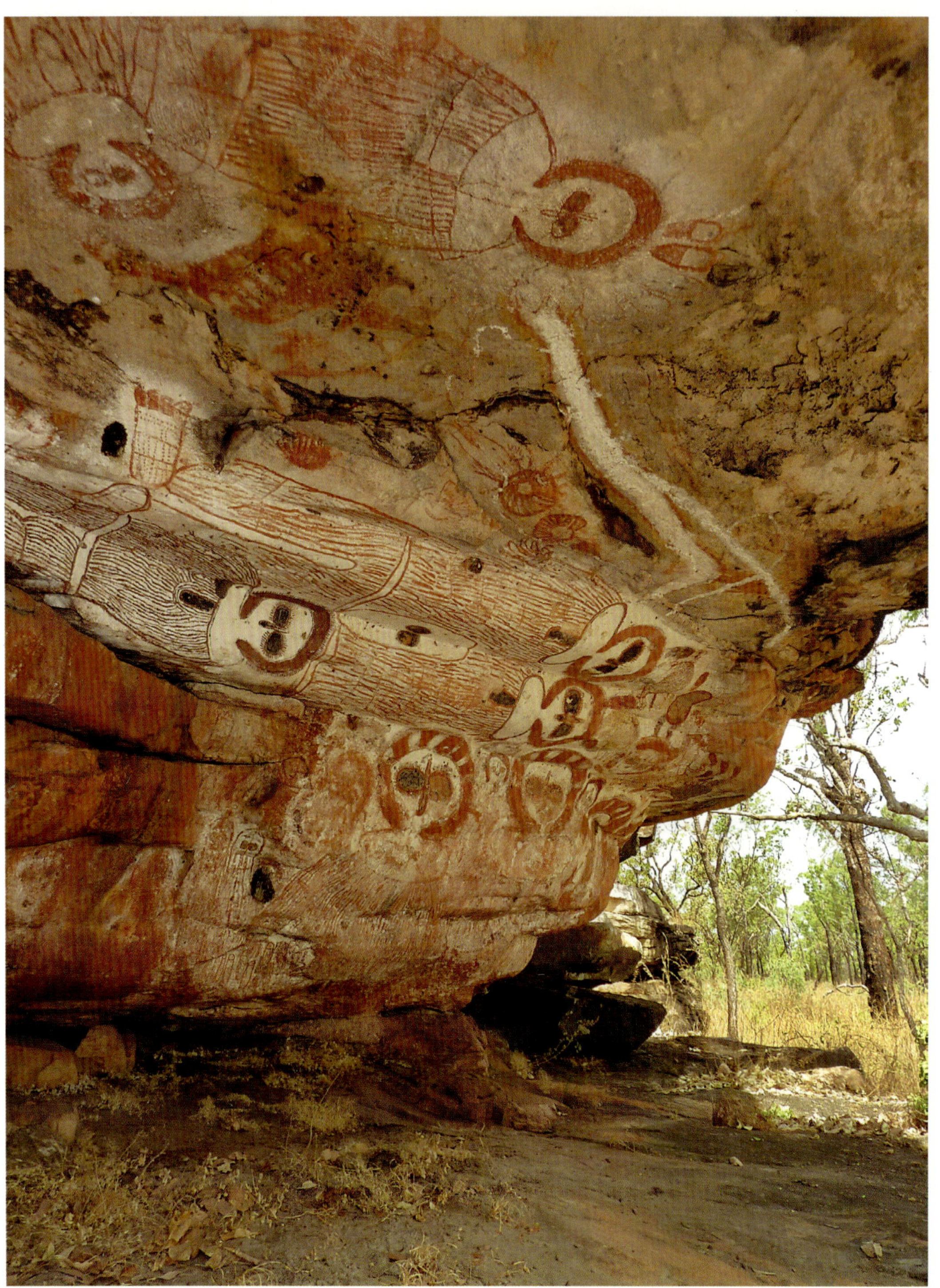

A shallow rock shelter in the central Kimberley filled with Wandjina images. Bands of white paint across the ceiling represent forked lightning associated with the Wandjina.